Bullshit and Philosophy

Popular Culture and Philosophy®

Series Editor: George A. Reisch

AD FACTS, ITS BEAUTIES, AND

Popular Culture and Philosophy®

Bullshit and Philosophy

*Guaranteed to Get Perfect
Results Every Time*

Edited by

GARY L. HARDCASTLE

and

GEORGE A. REISCH

OPEN COURT
Chicago and La Salle, Illinois

Volume 24 in the series, Popular Culture and Philosophy™

To order books from Open Court, call 1-800-815-2280, or visit our website at www.opencourtbooks.com.

Open Court Publishing Company is a division of Carus Publishing Company.

Library of Congress Cataloging-in-Publication Data

Bullshit and philosophy : guaranteed to get perfect results every time / edited by Gary L. Hardcastle and George A. Reisch.
     p. cm. — (Popular culture and philosophy)
    Summary: "Sixteen essays offer discussions, interpretations, and criticisms related to Harry G. Frankfort's essay "On Bullshit" and other philosophical work on bullshit. Topics addressed include: the definition of bullshit; the ethics and epistemology of bullshit; and the role of bullshit in contemporary culture" — Provided by publisher.
    Includes bibliographical references and index.
    ISBN-13: 978-0-8126-9611-0 (trade pbk. : alk. paper)
    ISBN-10: 0-8126-9611-5 (trade pbk. : alk. paper)
    1. Truthfullness and falsehood. I. Hardcastle, Gary L. II. Reisch, George A., 1962-
BJ1421.B85 2006
177'.3—dc22

                       2006025918

RELY BY BEING SLAVISHLY SUBDUED BY THE TERROR THAT COMES FF

Contents

I

To Shoot the Bull?

Rethinking and Responding to Bullshit 1

II

The Bull by the Horns

III

It's All Around Us

On Bullshitmania

GEORGE A. REISCH and GARY L. HARDCASTLE

It was just a book, after all—a book written by an Ivy League philosopher, Princeton's Harry G. Frankfurt, attempting to clarify a particular concept. That clarification would be achieved, moreover, in an ordinary way, at least for Ivy League philosophers. Philosophical authorities from the past would be cited, quoted, and interpreted; the flaws in their analyses pointed out; and suddenly a concept or term we *thought* we had understood would be revealed as in fact confused, vague, and murky. Then, at the work's intellectual crescendo, a new and clearer interpretation of the concept would emerge for other philosophers to consider and, eventually, tear apart once again. A day in the life of professional philosophy.

But this book was unusual. It was very small, even cute. Sitting on bookstore shelves and display tables, it could easily have been mistaken for a children's book, or a pocket-size collection of affirmations. The austere, classical style of its cover and its title might rather have suggested an ancient oration or a collection of lyric poems. But the words elegantly printed on the cover did not say "On Love," "On Poetics," or even, "On Truth (and its General Scarcity)." They said "On Bullshit," and the public loved it.[1]

No other work by a living academic philosopher has been so well received. After twenty-six weeks on *The New York Times* bestseller list, *On Bullshit* is poised to sell more copies than ar

---

[1] "On Bullshit" first appeared as an essay in *The Raritan Review* VI:2 (1986) then reprinted in Frankfurt's *The Importance of What We Care About* (C Cambridge University Press, 1988), pp. 117–133. In 2005, "On Bullshit" wa as the book, *On Bullshit* (Princeton: Princeton University Press). Throug and Philosophy, all references to *On Bullshit* are to the 2005 edition.

commercial philosophy book, ever. Yes, philosophically themed books like *Zen and the Art of Motorcycle Maintenance* and *Gödel, Escher, Bach* were hugely successful. But they were written for wide, popular audiences. *On Bullshit*, in contrast, circulated for two decades exclusively among professional academic philosophers. Such experts in logic, conceptual analysis and (Frankfurt's specialty) moral theory usually have little interest in popular philosophical writings. All the more surprising, then, that on leaving the ivory tower for main street, *On Bullshit* became such a hit.

Apropos for Today

Why did it happen? One answer, easy and obvious, was suggested by comedian Jon Stewart, host of television's *The Daily Show*. Stewart interviewed Frankfurt after the book had become a bestseller. When Frankfurt explained his idea that, unlike the liar, "the bullshitter doesn't really care whether what he says is true," the audience erupted in laughter and giggles. "I should warn you," Stewart said, leaning in to reassure his startled guest. "When they hear *that word*, it tickles them." "Especially coming from an Ivy League Professor," Frankfurt added.

True, *that word* does not often (or, really, *ever*) appear in the title of academic treatises. But this book's appeal cannot be fully explained by its cover. Like a sweet little old lady giving someone the finger, the novelty of a minor obscenity quickly gets old. *On Bullshit* is different. Even for those who may see the book as merely a joke, or a most appropriate gift for an annoying boss or co-worker, it is a joke that seems to have hit a cultural nerve.

As it turns out, Stewart also suggested a deeper, and better, answer. The book, he noted, is "very apropos for today." He did not elaborate; he just asked Frankfurt about its origin and joked about whether Frankfurt had his facts right or was just . . . never mind. Truth is, Stewart didn't *need* to explain why the book is apropos. There was, as the saying goes, an elephant in the room during that interview. It was the same elephant that haunted Stewart's other appearances on television and radio. On each it lounged next to Frankfurt and his interviewer, waiting to be named, discussed, or at least acknowledged. Yet not Stewart, who makes his living with clever, incisive parody of politics and its news coverage, mentioned explicitly *why it is* that *On Bullshit* is "very apropos for today."

The elephant was, of course, a war. Like most others in United States' history, it sharply divided popular opinion. But this war was highly unusual, too. Its supporters as well as its critics came to agree that the *official* reasons for waging it, the ones put to the public, to Congress, and to the United States' allies, turned out to be . . . well, put it this way: the claims that once seemed to make the invasion of Iraq necessary and urgent—that Iraq possessed and planned to use nuclear and chemical weapons of mass destruction, that it had high-technology devices (such as remote controlled airplanes) for deploying those weapons, and that it was complicit in the attacks of September 11th, 2001—are now understood to be best described by *that word*.

That's why Stewart's audience seemed to shift uncomfortably in their seats as he and Frankfurt discussed bullshit's indifference to truth and falsity, its hidden interest in manipulating belief and behavior, and the way one senses, as Frankfurt put it in his book, that the "bullshitter is trying to get away with something." The audience had come to see Stewart and his writers skewer current political events, after all, so few would have missed the obvious referents—the absence of weapons of mass destruction in Iraq and the admission that sources for these claims were, in retrospect, not credible—that made the book so apropos. There is and will likely remain little agreement about *who*, exactly, got away with *what*, exactly, in the run-up to the war. But there is a widespread sense that United States citizens, soldiers, and allies have been taken in.[2]

These are troubling suspicions. They are unmentionable, if not unthinkable, for some, because they threaten cherished ideals about the political and moral integrity of the United

---

[2] Among the many books critical of the second Bush administration are several by former Washington insiders and United Nations officials who offer first-hand accoun alleged manipulations of intelligence used to promote the Iraq war. There is, for ple, Richard A. Clarke's *Against All Enemies: Inside America's War on Terror* (Ne Free Press, 2004); John W. Dean's *Worse than Watergate: The Secret Presidency W. Bush* (New York: Little, Brown, 2004); Scott Ritter and Seymour He *Confidential: The Untold Story of the Intelligence Conspiracy to Undermine Overthrow Saddam Hussein* (New York: Tauris, 2005); and Hans Blix's *D* (New York: Pantheon, 2004).

States. That's why this elephant is difficult to acknowledge. One way to acknowledge it, though, is through the cushion of humor. Everyone in Stewart's audience had surely heard the joke that WMDs had finally been located: they were weapons of mass *distraction*, and they were stockpiled in Washington D.C. Others no doubt found a cushion in the small and inviting form of the book. It had just the right author—an Ivy League philosopher, expert in the kind of critical, balanced, and objective thinking that, as the invasion of Iraq drew near, seemed eclipsed by frightening memories of 9/11 and frightening talk of WMDs. And it struck a comforting tone—its classical title and book jacket portray bullshit not as something alien, massive, and menacing but rather as just one of the many human foibles that have puzzled thinkers and artists for centuries. Indeed, Frankfurt's philosophical detachment from contemporary events, necessitated in one respect by the essay's history, makes *On Bullshit* apropos in an altogether different way. Call it bullshit without tears. It allows readers to approach that elephant abstractly, generically, and as it recurs throughout the ages—without having to take up those disturbing questions that make the book so relevant in the first place.

The Year in Bullshit

When Stewart asked Frankfurt whether our culture occasionally cleans house by "truth-telling," or whether "it just keeps piling," Frankfurt thought carefully for a moment and scored another laugh with his audience—"I think it just keeps piling." Again, they knew what he meant. For in the wake of the missing WMDs, *On Bullshit* appeared amidst an explosion of various kinds of fraud and deception. Some, such as identity theft and eBay swindles, were enabled by new technologies of commerce, the Internet, and the demise of the photograph as a trustworthy document (see the neologism '*to photoshop*'). Yet other ...nds seem inexplicable without positing something like a cul-...l attitude or *climate* in which truth has become—much as ...kfurt feared—less important than the demands of political, ...ercial, artistic, and even scientific success.
...ence for this abounds in Laura Penny, *Your Call Is ...t to Us: The Truth about Bullshit*, which appeared on ... shelves shortly after *On Bullshit*. Reflecting on years

of headline scandals involving the Catholic Church, the mutual fund industry, and fallen corporate titans such as Enron and MCI, Penny observed that we live in an "era of unprecedented bullshit production" (p. 1). What's especially striking is the sudden prominence of fraud within institutions that have heretofore been very careful about what's fiction and what's not.

Like publishing. One of the more dramatic scandals surrounding truth and authenticity belonged to Oprah Winfrey and author James Frey, whose *A Million Little Pieces* Oprah recommended to her enormous, book-hungry audience as a true, inspirational story. After the book was exposed as largely fiction, Ms. Winfrey first defended the book (as nonetheless inspirational) but then dramatically retracted her support and scolded a remorseful, tearful Frey on national television for his betrayal of trust and truth. Within weeks, another celebrated novelist, J.T. Leroy, whose autobiographical writings detailed his rise from teen-age poverty and truck-stop prostitution to New York-style literary success, took his whacks—once again—for peddling fictional stories as nonfiction memoirs. Unlike Frey, however, J.T. Leroy felt little remorse, or pain. In fact, he didn't exist. This fiction included the author himself, who turned out to be constructed by an aspiring female writer who for years posed successfully as the celebrated author's friend, confidant, and business agent. (When cameras were present, J.T. Leroy himself was impersonated by a boyish female friend wearing men's clothes and dark glasses.)

The distinction between fiction and non-fiction has never been terribly popular in advertising circles. But professional advertising has at least always recognized the distinction between what is an advertisement and what is not an advertisement. Until recently, advertisements announce themselves on signs or billboards, and they remain confined between programming segments on radio or television—all of which helps us recognize them *as advertisements*. Two emerging trends, however, seem designed to blur this distinction and create advertisements that appear to be something else entirely. "Product placement" injects recognizable products or brands into movies or television shows, while "word of mouth advertising" takes the additional step of blurring the distinction between professional advertisers and ordinary citizens. On this model, individuals are compensated to "talk-up" specific products with others whom they may encounter in the course of ordinary life—at work, in the supermarket, at soccer practice, and so on. Here, advertising begins to seamlessly join ordinary life in ways that make it increasingly difficult to determine not only whether claims are true or false, but additionally whether a friend, colleague or family member is recommending a product because they honestly like it or because they are rewarded for recommending it.

Perhaps the most striking and surprising of bullshit's successes are the inroads it has made into the worlds of science and scientific research. The philosopher Karl Popper held that science deserves respect precisely because it seeks to falsify its own claims—actively eliminating, so to speak, its own bullshit. Yet that ideal seems to be fading behind headlines about scientific fraud and misconduct. Some of the more familiar examples:

- Investigative panels determine that research purported to have established some result, taken as gospel by other labs, was fabricated.

- Pharmaceutical corporations generously fund scientific studies and publish only those that appear to document the safety of their products.

- Tenured university professors promote their religious convictions in the guise of scientific expertise.

- Political appointees at federal science agencies insert special wording in agency-publications designed to promote religious criticisms of established scientific knowledge.

There's nothing new in the appeal to science by individuals, corporations, or governments seeking to legitimate and advance their specific interests and plans. What is new is the notion that this is very easy to do—that legitimate scientific knowledge consists merely in whatever claims may be hyped through an effective public relations campaign, or published without controversy in a magazine or journal.

And then there's "that word." Though it has become as ordinary and common as these kinds of fraud and misrepresentation to which it usually refers, there remain some frontiers it has not yet conquered. While most academics (not those writing here, of course) shun its vulgarity, that politeness has not stopped the establishment of a new academic journal—

Plagiary: Cross-Disciplinary Studies in Plagiarism, Fabrication and Falsification—dedicated to analyzing and better understanding all such varieties of fraud and misrepresentation throughout modern culture. Others, if less polite, are more direct. The popular writer and radio commentator Al Franken has lately augmented the rules of his call-in quiz show "Spot the Weasel" with a new, fourth choice. Callers attempting to match wits with Franken and his guests can now identify recorded statements by politicians as either true, a lie, a weasel, or "BS." While Comedy Central's *The Daily Show* goes all the way with mentioning "bullshit," the other major networks, as of this writing at least, continue to censor the word. Still, it's hard to miss. When Bright Eyes (aka Conor Oberst) sang "When the President Talks to God" on Jay Leno's *Tonight Show*, he asked,

> When the President talks to God
> Does he ever think that maybe he's not?
> That that voice is just inside his head
> When he kneels next to the presidential bed
> Does he ever smell his own *[bleep]*
> When the President talks to God?

One could also ask whether these censors were effective. Did this audience, unlike Jon Stewart's, remain unaware that Oberst had again used "that word" to point to that elephant? The answer was at the end of Oberst's song, as he sang, "I doubt it. I doubt it."

It's this sense of despair and cynicism, finally, surrounding our era of bullshit that most fundamentally explains the appeal of Frankfurt's book. No doubt, some of those who picked up *On Bullshit* did so only for the novelty of reading an Ivy League philosophy professor expound on the topic. But for many that curiosity was connected to deeper worries about what lay ahead for a culture so knee-deep. As *New York Times* columnist Frank Rich put it when commenting on Ms. Winfrey's theatrical defense of truth, the scandal surrounding *A Million Little Pieces* was larger than the question of "whether Mr. Frey's autobiography is true or not, or whether it sits on a fiction or nonfiction shelf at Barnes and Noble." The genuine scandal is that "such distinctions have long since washed away in much of our public life." In an age of bullshit, we all become politicians or white-collar criminals, able neither to confirm nor deny the veracity of what we see, or know, or think we know. "It's as if the country is living in a permanent state of suspension of disbelief," Rich suggested as he put his finger on the potentially enormous social and cultural costs of bullshit's dominance (*New York Times*, 22nd January, 2006). For constant, nagging suspicions— that political leaders are consciously deceiving the public, that your favorite teacher is bent on partisan indoctrination, or that your family doctor, your senator, stockbroker, or product-recommending neighbor is in some corporation's pocket—would seem to be socially corrosive and destabilizing. The fear that simple, direct communication, free of hidden agendas and interests, is becoming impossible may have led many (including those television and radio producers who made Frankfurt a sudden celebrity) to seize Frankfurt as a popular guru with a prescient, prophetic warning—a Marshall McLuhan or Timothy Leary for the post-Enron, post-Iraq era. After all, the opening line of *On Bullshit*, that "one of the most salient features of our culture is that there is so much bullshit," was written in 1985. Twenty years later, there's so much more.

The Dream of a Bullshit-Free Culture

If ours is a culture of bullshit, then why was it that a *philosopher* took center stage as America's main bullshit-analyzer? Why not a novelist or sociologist? We don't pretend to understand the vagaries of fashion and popular taste better than anyone else. But part of the answer, we think, is that Frankfurt is reviving a *philosophical* tradition. Philosophers have long sought to understand exactly how it is that certain statements or beliefs seem to deceive us, take us in, or make us not care very much whether they are true or false. Long before Frankfurt, that is, philosophers have been trying to determine exactly what bullshit is and how it works its magic.

   This may be a surprising claim. Philosophy itself, after all, is often regarded as part and parcel with the bullshit of popular culture. The person who survives a personal tragedy by reflecting on the mysteries of the universe, someone might say, is "taking things philosophically." That's more polite and respectful, after all, than pointing out that she's distracting herself from unbearable loss or disappointment by almost absent-mindedly contemplating abstractions or pondering paradoxes—bullshit-ting herself. A walk through the "philosophy" section at your local bookstore may confirm the impression that philosophers' interests are in that otherworldly arcana of the supernatural, the occult, and the "metaphysical."

Not so. Some of the most influential and enduring philoso-phy, dating back centuries, is devoted to identifying and under-standing bullshit. This is not so that it may be indulged in further, but so that we may liberate ourselves from its delusions and deceptions. The archetypal sage-in-a-toga Socrates, for example, is justly revered for dedicating his life to the search for persons who were truly wise, rather than interested merely in passing on opinion, or hearsay, or beliefs of any sort bereft of evidence or simply good sense.

Twenty centuries later, the French polymath René Descartes started off the first of his six *Meditations on First Philosophy* with the rather brave recognition that so much of what he learned in the best French schools of the time was just plain false. "Some years ago I was struck," he wrote, "by the large number of false-hoods that I had accepted as true in my childhood, and by the highly doubtful nature of the whole edifice that I had subse-quently based on them."[3] Descartes's remedy was a program of self-discipline that began with the rejection of those beliefs that fell short of certainty and, that completed, proceeded with the construction of a system of beliefs that was "stable and likely to last." It was a lonely, individualistic enterprise, but the very fact that Descartes recorded his progress in his *Meditations* reveals that it was something he believed others could, and ought, to do as well. It was, indeed, a common Enlightenment fantasy that *everyone* would follow along. The result would be a world with a lot less bullshit, maybe none at all.

That vision was shared by the next century's David Hume (who otherwise shared precious little with Descartes, but it was enough). Hume held that all real knowledge took the form either of mathematics and similar "formal" sciences (which he termed "relations of ideas") or of natural science (for Hume, "matters of fact"), and he ended his *An Enquiry Concerning*

---

[3] René Descartes, *Meditations on First Philosophy: With Selections from the Objections and Replies* (Cambridge: Cambridge University Press, 1996), p. 12. Emphasis in original.

Human Understanding (a popularization, relatively speaking, of his two-volume *A Treatise of Human Nature*) with clear instructions for how to treat bits of speech that pretended to, but in fact did not, belong in either category:

> When we run over libraries, persuaded of these principles, what havoc must we make? If we take in our hand any volume; of divinity or school metaphysics, for instance; let us ask, *Does it contain any abstract reasoning concerning quantity or number?* No. *Does it contain any experimental reasoning concerning matter of fact and existence?* No. Commit it then to the flames: For it can contain nothing but sophistry and illusion.[4]

An Enlightenment call *for book burning?* Not quite. The books Hume would have us cast into the flames are books only in the most literal sense—they have pages, bindings, covers and words strung together into sentences and paragraphs. But they *say* nothing. Their offense, moreover, is that they are presented as though they *do* say something. That's the illusion, and it's perpetrated by the sophistry of printed words, pages, bindings, covers, blurbs, reviews, and the rest. Better to burn such sham books, such bullshit, says Hume. Burn it all.

The Enlightenment passion that carried Hume to the end of his *Treatise* continued to inspire in philosophers visions of a bullshit-free world. You find them in the writings of Immanuel Kant, John Stuart Mill, and Ludwig Wittgenstein, for example, though again you'd be hard-pressed to find much more in common among these philosophers or, for that matter, all the philosophers who have railed against bullshit. The twentieth-century apotheosis of the anti-bullshit crusade, however, is certainly the Vienna Circle, a collective of science and math-minded Germans and Austrians that shook a communal fist at the culture of their time and place, the intellectual free-for-all of Germany and Austria in the 1920s and 1930s (*that* culture, sadly, shook its much more powerful fist back, sending nearly all of the Circle flying to England and the United States by 1939). The Vienna Circle's preferred term for bullshit was 'metaphysics', and so their 1929 manifesto, the *Wissenschaftliche Weltauffassung* ("Scientific

---

[4] David Hume, *An Enquiry Concerning Human Understanding* (Indianapolis: Hackett, 1993), p. 114.

World-Conception"), led off with the worry that "metaphysical and theologizing thought is again on the increase today, not only in life but in science."[5] The "Scientific World-Conception" would be the antidote. It was an embrace of modern science and a scientific attitude toward things, as well as the "new objectivity" (or *neue Sachlichkeit*) pursued by many artists, designers and architects in European culture.

The Vienna Circle's target was not the intellectual diversity that surrounded them but the putative parts of it that were presented (even accepted) as meaningful—indeed, profoundly meaningful—but in fact amounted to nothing. In 1932 the Circle's Rudolf Carnap criticized Martin Heidegger, perhaps the most prominent German-speaking philosopher of the time, on precisely these grounds.[6] In his 1929 book *What Is Metaphysics?*, Heidegger ruminated on the nature of *Das Nichts* (literally, "the nothing"), and inspired Carnap to figure out exactly what was wrong with such supposedly deep and insightful metaphysical inquiries. In statements like Heidegger's '*Das Nichts selbst nichtet*' ("The nothing nothings"), Carnap concluded, there was only the appearance of a meaningful statement. Behind that appearance, there was *Nichts*, leading Carnap to suggest that metaphysicians were like "musicians without musical ability." Much as a tone deaf musician would likely misuse an instrument, metaphysicians misused language and presented things that could not be conveyed in words as though they could be. Carnap and others of the Circle argued and debated about just how dangerous this passing off, this bullshitting, was. But it was bullshit all the same, and it met with a similar response: if one wanted to express an attitude towards life, that's fine, but don't pass it off as science or something similar. Better to take up poetry, as Friedrich Nietzsche does, for example, in his *Thus Spake Zarathustra* (which Carnap cites, incidentally, with approval).

---

[5] *Wissenschaftliche Weltauffassung. Der Wiener Kreis*. Translated as *The Scientific Conception of the World: The Vienna Circle*, and reprinted in S. Sarkar, ed. *Emergence of Logical Empiricism from 1900 to the Vienna Circle* (New York: G 1996), p. 321.

[6] Rudolf Carnap, "Überwindung der Metaphysik durch Logische Analyse der *Erkenntnis* 2 (1932): 219–241, translated as "The Elimination of Metaphys... Logical Analysis of Language" in A.J. Ayer, ed., *Logical Positivism* (New Yo... Press, 1959), pp. ...

It's almost an intellectual tragedy that the Vienna Circle and its philosophical legacies, logical positivism and logical empiricism, came to be associated with stodgy, dispassionate, irrelevant logic-chopping. That characterization occludes the Circle's *raison d'être*, which was nothing less than the cultivation of a critical attitude to concentrations of bullshit in pseudoscience and philosophy that would, when taken up generally, reduce bullshit in government, religion, the market, and everyday life. The Vienna Circle's members thought of themselves not simply as professional philosophers who happened to live and work in Vienna, but as the keepers of a tradition of liberal, Enlightenment thinking that had made Vienna the cradle of progressive housing programs, adult education, architecture, art and design. Oh, and progressive philosophy.

Which brings us back to Frankfurt's *On Bullshit*. Perhaps by now it's clear that we see Frankfurt as the latest carrier of the anti-bullshit torch in the Enlightenment Olympics, now several centuries running. In this light, the real significance of this bullshitmania is that an age-old impulse within philosophy to establish itself as a cultural, and not just an academic, enterprise may finally have found the right formula and the right language. If so, the best explanation for the popular interest in *On Bullshit* may have been that first one, about the novelty of the word itself. Indeed it may all come down to *that word*—understood not as a joke, but as a welcome point of connection between what goes on in philosophy seminar rooms and what goes on when the lights go out and philosophers join their fellow citizens in the marketplace, coffee shop, town hall, and voting booth.

How This Book Came to Be

These are the considerations that led us to put together the collection of chapters that is *Bullshit and Philosophy*. If it's true, as we suspect, that the popularity of Frankfurt's book signals a willingness among the public to see what philosophers have to about bullshit, then we ought, we thought, to assemble who were up to the task and tell them to let it rip. What means, of course, will vary among our authors. That said, there are some things this book *is not*.

For example, the chapters that follow are not a guided tour through various varieties of bullshit in modern culture. Nor does this book intend to equip you with a "bullshit detector" that you might use to *finally* shut Uncle Ned up about the wisdom of tax cuts or the alien bodies the government is storing at Area 51. Nor do we offer a collection of indignant would-be radio commentators angling for a guest spot on Rush Limbaugh. What this book does, instead, is offer discussions, interpretations, and criticisms related to Frankfurt's essay and other philosophical work on bullshit. Since *On Bullshit* was originally written for academic philosophers, and our book is written for people intrigued by *On Bullshit* but otherwise only tourists in the halls of philosophy, some chapters will help explain what philosophical essays like Frankfurt's aim to do and how they work. What does it mean, for example, to propose a "theory" of bullshit, given that theories of this or that usually come from laboratories filled with test tubes and expensive instruments? What does it mean to articulate "the structure of a concept"—as Frankfurt intends to do for bullshit?

In this regard, we could have called our book *A Complete Idiot's Guide to Bullshit*. But we didn't. We're not complete idiots, and we have no desire to go to court for copyright infringement. More importantly, the success of *On Bullshit* makes it plain that neither idiots nor Ivy League professors have a special claim to insights about bullshit. If bullshit is one of the defining marks of modern culture, then everyone has a stake in it, and everyone can benefit from thinking about it and understanding it. With this in mind, and recognizing that thought and understanding are the province of philosophers, we bring you *Bullshit and Philosophy*.

Part I of *Bullshit and Philosophy*, "To Shoot the Bull? Re-thinking and Responding to Bullshit," contains papers that say something about bullshit itself—its causes, say, or its effects, or the reactions we have to it. One natural reaction to most forms of bullshit, for example, accuses the bullshitmania of our time (and books like this) of over-reaction. What's so bad about bullshit?, one might ask.

Scott Kimbrough's "On Letting It Slide" takes up this question, noting that in many situations we gladly sacrifice our usual regard for truth for the sake of (among other things) the feelings of others, keeping the peace, or simply entertaining ourselves. Kimbrough reminds us that we let much (though not all) bullshit slide, and perhaps we ought to.

For Conseulo Preti, avoiding bullshit (a "menace," she argues, for which audience as much as manufacturer is to blame) might be a matter of emulating a life notably bullshit-free; her "A Defense of Common Sense" offers the early twentieth-century analytic philosopher G.E. Moore as one such exemplary life.

George Reisch's "The Pragmatics of Bullshit, Intelligently Designed" looks at bullshit and pseudoscience to argue that bullshit is not an indifference to truth, or meaning, as Frankfurt and Cohen suggest, but rather an attempt by the bullshitter to run two conversations at once, one, as Reisch puts it, "concealed within or downplayed alongside the other." Reisch's approach, he claims, explains why we are often so tolerant of bullshit.

But for Kenneth Taylor and Sara Bernal the interesting questions about bullshit pertain less to its definition or our reaction to it than to the reasons for its ubiquity. Taylor's "Bullshit and the Foibles of the Human Mind," for example, suggests that the institutional bullshit that surrounds us is abetted by mechanisms of reasoning deeply embedded in our shared cognitive architecture. Taylor's chapter illustrates these well-established "foibles" of the human mind, but it also points the way to a culture less steeped in the bullshit these foibles enable. We must, Taylor implores, marshal education to guard ourselves and our children against our own cognitive foibles, and we must deliver "the very means of public representation and persuasion" to a far wider and more diverse array of people. Sara Bernal, in contrast, is struck by a parallel between bullshit and various pathologies of personality. In "Bullshit and Personality" she argues that the extraordinary bullshit of the disordered personality arises from an impaired social cognition and results, naturally, in hobbled social relations.

In "Performing Bullshit and the Post-Sincere Condition," Alan Richardson unveils a variety of bullshit yet unnoted in the chapters so far—"performative bullshit," exemplified in Customer Service Pledges and Mission Statements. Responding to *this* bullshit, Richardson suggests, is a matter either of producing "self-evident bullshit that outperforms its covert competitors" (in the manner of Jon Stewart's *The Daily Show*) or of rethinking our inherited Enlightenment values.

Cornelis de Waal, on the other hand, sees bullshit as a violation of a pragmatism-inspired "general epistemic imperative" to always "proceed upon the hope that there is a true answer to the questions we ask and act from a desire to find that answer." De Waal's "The Importance of Being Earnest: A Pragmatic Approach to Bullshitting," thus argues that satisfying the imperative—avoiding bullshit—is largely a matter of sharing the burden of inquiry with our community rather than shouldering it ourselves in the fashion of Descartes.

Part II, "The Bull by the Horns: Defining Bullshit," contains four papers that, in one way or another, try to fix our target— that is, to define exactly what bullshit is, so that we can more easily spot it, at least, and get rid of it, at best. Leading off this section is G.A. Cohen's classic essay, "Deeper Into Bullshit,"[7] a direct response to Frankfurt's "On Bullshit" (and the only chapter in this book not written especially for it). In "Deeper Into Bullshit," Cohen suggests that Frankfurt's definition has missed the mark, or at least failed to attend to a kind of bullshit characterizable not in terms of the *intention* of the person who produces it (per Frankfurt's approach) but in terms of its "unclarifiable unclarity." Many of this book's other chapters respond to Cohen's essay.[8]

The next three chapters shed light on this debate by bringing various other intellectual resources to the table. For Gary Hardcastle, the dinner guest is the anti-metaphysical thought of the Vienna Circle's Rudolf Carnap. Hardcastle's "The Unity of Bullshit" argues that the anti-metaphysical program of Carnap and his fellow scientific philosophers of the 1920s and 1930s gives us a perspective that unites the sort of bullshit identified by Frankfurt and Cohen.

Andrew Aberdein, by contrast, in his "Raising the Tone: Definition, Bullshit, and the Definition of Bullshit," calls upon Charles Stevenson's notion of a "persuasive definition" to help

---

[7] Originally published in S. Buss and L. Overton, eds., *Contours of Agency: Essays on Themes from Harry Frankfurt* (Cambridge, Massachusetts: MIT Press), pp. 321–339. Reproduced as Chapter 8 of *Bullshit and Philosophy*. Throughout *Bullshit and Philosophy*, all references to "Deeper Into Bullshit" are to the work as it appears in this volume.

[8] Frankfurt himself has also replied briefly to Cohen: "Reply to G.A. Cohen," in *Contours of Agency*, pp. 340–44. Here Frankfurt arguably cedes ground to Cohen's critique, but maintains the significance of the intention-oriented bullshit he defined. Truth-indifferent bullshit, Frankfurt insists, much more than the kind of academic obscurity Cohen targets, threatens our "respect for the distinction between the true and the false" on which the very "conduct of civilized life" depends (p. 343).

us place Frankfurt's definition of bullshit in a wider context. Per his title, Aberdein reaches back to the nineteenth century's Gottlob Frege to re-introduce the concept of tone into the debate about bullshit.

And then, Hans Maes's and Katrien Schaubroeck's "Different Kinds and Aspects of Bullshit" raises fundamental and critical questions for Frankfurt's definition of bullshit (including questions about the moral status of bullshit, but more on that below), considers Cohen's thoughts on bullshit on this score, and raises the question of where pseudoscience belongs in the ever-lusher garden of bullshit.

Though it has been enjoying its recent foray through literary and philosophical treatises under its own name, bullshit lives and breaths in the world off the page. Our final section, then, is "It's All Around Us: Bullshit in Politics, Science, Education, and the Law." In *On Bullshit*, Frankfurt suggested that democracy, in demanding of everyone an opinion on everything, inadvertently promotes bullshit. Mark Evans's chapter, "The Republic of Bullshit, Or: Were Plato, Strauss and Those Guys Right All Along?" examines this suggestion among historically significant criticisms of democracy.

Similarly, Vanessa Neumann's "Political Bullshit and the Stoic Story of the Self" provides a detailed account of the sort of bullshit one is apt to find in international politics. She suggests that we can better understand and manage such bullshit if we attend to Stoic theories of self and the role narrative plays in persons' lives.

In "Bullshit at the Interface of Science and Policy: Global Warming, Toxic Substances, and Other Pesky Problems," Heather Douglas treats us to examples of bullshit drawn from the skeptical side of the debate over global warming. She shows how incomplete information and, perhaps more significantly, mistaken understandings of scientific objectivity can serve the ends of bullshit.

David Tietge is concerned to defend rhetoric, understood as the study of language and the role it plays in our lives, from its all-too-frequent association with bullshit. His "Rhetoric Is Not Bullshit" makes the case that a resuscitation of rhetoric in the college and even the high-school classroom may be precisely the antidote to bullshit. Finally, *Bullshit and Philosophy* closes with an chapter from Steve Fuller, fresh from his role as an expert witness in Kitzmiller v. Dover Area School District, *et al.*, concerning the place of Intelligent Design in the ninth-grade public school classroom. Fuller's wide-ranging chapter, "Just Bullshit," draws upon a wealth of examples from popular culture, the history of science, and jurisprudence to call attention to the threat of bullshit in anti-bullshit programs themselves.

As we noted, Frankfurt's *On Bullshit* did not *initiate* an interest among philosophers in bullshit; that interest had been there for centuries, if not millennia. But the book's popularity did manage to remind philosophers and non-philosophers alike of academic philosophy's special relation to bullshit. Our hope, of course, is not just that these chapters help others learn and think about bullshit, but that they also remind philosophy itself that its links to popular culture are much closer and mutually rewarding that most of us realize. To borrow from a tale told here by Scott Kimbrough, there is something right in the common reaction—"that's bullshit"—many have to academic philosophy. But that's not because philosophy produces it, it's because philosophy is one of our best defenses against it.

THOSE WHO HAVE SO PERVERTED THOUGHT TO THE PURPOSES OF PLEA

I

To Shoot the Bull?

Rethinking and Responding
to Bullshit

1
On Letting It Slide

SCOTT KIMBROUGH

I have a very frank six-year-old daughter. Recently, upon seeing our house painter puffing away his break, she shouted that smoking is unhealthy—loudly enough to be heard through the closed window. Mortified, my wife and I immediately shushed her. She doesn't yet understand why anyone should be offended by an accurate point of information. But there are many offensive truths. William Ian Miller notes the danger of indiscreet truth-telling in his remarkable book, *Faking It* (Cambridge: Cambridge University Press, 2003):

> Truth is not accepted as a defense in such cases; in fact, one of the chief themes of this book is that truth is an offense, seldom, if ever, a defense. (p.142)

Miller's reminder that truth isn't always welcomed can help solve a puzzle posed by Harry Frankfurt in *On Bullshit*:

> The problem of understanding why our attitude toward bullshit is generally more benign than our attitude toward lying is an important one, which I shall leave as an exercise for the reader. (p. 50)

Frankfurt raises this issue because he worries about the damaging consequences of a declining respect for truth. Bullshitting, in his view, constitutes a greater threat to truth than lying. For unlike bullshitters, liars at least care what the truth is. Frankfurt defines bullshit as a lack of concern for truth, writing that "indifference to how things really are . . . [is] the essence of bullshit"

3

(p.34). Consequently, if we really care about truth, Frankfurt reasons that we should condemn bullshitters even more than liars. But of course that's not what happens: more often than not, we let bullshit slide. Frankfurt wonders why this is the case, though he doesn't try to explain it himself. This essay takes up Frankfurt's unanswered question.

Tolerable Bullshit

Assume Frankfurt's definition of bullshit is correct: bullshit results from a lack of concern for truth. Now put that definition together with Miller's insight that truth is not always our primary goal in conversation. It follows that much of what we say on a daily basis is bullshit. But does it also follow that we should change our ways? Not always. Far from merely tolerating bullshit, we often value it as an indispensable resource.

For example, Miller offers a trenchant analysis of the social point of apology. We teach our children to apologize by forcing them to say things they don't really mean. Truth, in this context, is the last thing we want. A true description of my son's state of mind after hitting his sister would go something like this: "I hurt her because I wanted to." In place of this accurate account, we teach him to say that he's sorry. Perhaps someday he'll mean it. In the meantime, he at least learns that hitting will not be tolerated. Plus, his sister gets to see him humbled for his wrongdoing. Miller explains the dynamic:

> Q: What is the substance of the satisfaction to the wronged person in an unfelt apology? A: The pain it costs the apologizer to give it. . . . Apology is a ritual, pure and simple, of humiliation. (*Faking It*, p. 88)

In characterizing apology as a humiliation ritual, Miller by no means rejects or discourages it. Quite the contrary, he sees that injurers must pay for their wrongs or they will never learn to stop committing them. Like many other cases of moral instruction, the teaching of the art of apology sacrifices truth for more immediately worthy goals, including peace and character building.

Miller doesn't mention what coerced recitations he visits upon the child who receives the apology, but in my house the victim is forced to say she accepts the apology. She doesn't mean it, either. But the message of the exchange is clear: hostilities are at an end, and further escalation will not be tolerated. Hopefully someday they will learn to settle their differences civilly, even sincerely. As Miller notes, however, it's foolish to hold out for sincerity in the short term. If you have any doubts about that, consider the mother who told me that she does not make her son apologize unless he means it. I think it's fair to anticipate that he will not learn to mean it on his own whenever proper manners dictate. Nor will he learn the importance of faking it when necessary, as remains indispensable well into adulthood. Marital spats would more frequently escalate to divorce if it weren't for faked apologies. Public figures who make "offensive" remarks must master the form of apology as a way of acknowledging, if not fully embracing, the legitimacy of the offended parties' perspective.

Learning when and how to apologize is one chapter in the book of good manners. Like apology, politeness in general sacrifices truth for peace and comfort. Miller again astutely points out both the fakeness and the virtue of politeness:

> Politeness doesn't need an excuse; fakery is openly admitted to lie at the structural core of the virtue. Politeness is immune to many forms of hypocrisy because a certain benign form of hypocrisy is precisely its virtue . . . at relatively little cost, it saves people from unnecessary pain in social encounters. (*Faking It*, p. 35)

Saving people pain often deserves more importance than a concern for truth. If we strictly apply Frankfurt's definition of bullshit, according to which bullshit manifests an indifference to truth, it follows that bullshit constitutes the greater part of civility.

Not all bullshit is motivated by delicate manners, however. Take advertising. We tend to tolerate bullshit advertising, and it isn't out of politeness. One reason for our acceptance is entertainment value. For example, the advertisements during the Super Bowl famously receive as much attention as the game itself. And it's not just bullshit advertising that pleases. The student newspaper at my university ran an editorial decrying communist professors on campus. The piece could hardly have been more silly, despite the serious intentions of the author. As

I discovered in class discussions, many of the students were delighted by the piece *because* it was bullshit. They thought it was funny, and accordingly preferred it to a soberly argued treatment of a relevant topic.

Like politeness, however, entertainment cannot be the full explanation of our tolerance of bullshit. Public relations draws on many of the same tricks as advertising, but frequently without the entertainment value. A deeper explanation of our tolerance for bullshit in advertising and public relations is our respect for the ends they serve. We understand the importance of making a buck, and don't begrudge the professional the most effective means to do so. When a public relations consultant presents Exxon as a leader in protecting the environment, or a political hack spins a legislative failure as a successful compromise, they're just doing their jobs. Were we in their place, we would want the same dispensation.

And it turns out many of us are in their place. A huge proportion of the professions involve selling or representing something. It's not always about greed and power, either. Even those whose efforts serve loftier goals than bare profit—like teachers, fund-raisers for charity, and military recruiters—would be hobbled if they eschewed bullshitting in favor of unembellished truth-telling. Furthermore, when faced with competition, to insist on truth when it doesn't sell is not just naïve, it's a losing strategy. To forego the use of bullshit is thus to settle for being a loser. We prefer winners to losers. And we don't want to be losers ourselves by forbidding ourselves a winning gameplan.

However much we respect effectiveness, we don't allow any and all means to an end, even when the end is agreed on all sides to be a valuable one. We outlaw outright lying, even in advertising. How do we draw the line? Why do we sympathize with the liar's victim, but not the bullshitter's? Look at it this way: we can either sympathize with bullshitters or their victims. The bullshitters have a job to do and skillfully apply the most effective means to do so. The victims, in contrast, allow themselves to be mentally lazy and blinded by desire. They're suckers. We may pity suckers, but we certainly don't respect them. Our contempt for suckers reflects the judgment that anyone taken in by a line of bullshit deserves their fate.

Intolerable Bullshit

Bullshit doesn't always get a warm reception. That's because indifference to truth frequently causes trouble. Think of the last time you "called bullshit." It probably wasn't about something you were prepared to tolerate. In ordinary use, the charge of bullshit most commonly comes up when we can't be bothered to take something seriously, or when we're treated unfairly.

We often call bullshit when faced with something we regard as ridiculous, irrelevant, or misguided. We thereby declare an intention to ignore the speaker—to refuse to take his efforts at justification seriously. I can sadly provide an example in which I was the target of such an accusation. I presented a talk entitled "The Structure and Function of Bullshit" at a "philosophy slam," which is an open discussion guided by a speaker who defends a controversial position against the crowd. These events take place in the back room of a coffeehouse and bar popular with the counter-cultural set. One of the attendees told me afterwards of a brief conversation he had with a few of the regulars who were outside for a smoke. They asked him what was going on inside. Without mentioning the topic, he told them it was a philosophy slam. Their response: "That's bullshit." Such uses of the term indicate an unwillingness to listen based on a disdainful expectation that nothing is to be gained from doing so.

Disdain gives way to indignation when bad reasons affect more than just our patience. Because of its tenuous connection to truth, bullshit makes a poor justification for important decisions. Bullshit reasons are bad reasons, and we feel indignant when mistreated for bad reasons. Consider the song "Shut up" by The Black Eyed Peas. After a verse describing a typical happy courtship, the male singer recounts the decline of the relationship while the female singer provides the commentary:

> But then something got out of hand.
> You started yelling when I was with friends,
> Even though I had legitimate reasons.
> > Bullshit!
> You know I have to make them dividends.
> > Bullshit!

The girlfriend has a point. Her man is full of shit and she knows it. (Incidentally, the terms "bullshit" and "full of shit" correlate: to say that someone is full of shit is an informal (albeit circular) way to explain why what they say is bullshit, and a warning to expect more of the same.) The problem, from her perspective, is that he's hiding his true motivations. If he truly loves her, she feels, he should want her to be with him. Even if there is some truth to his "legitimate reasons," he's ditching her when he could include her. She feels indignant because her boyfriend's effort to "explain" adds insult—the contemptuous judgment that he can manipulate her—to the injury of leaving her behind. She calls bullshit to express her indignation, and to warn him that she won't stick around if such treatment continues.

Now imagine you get passed over for a promotion at work. The boss tells you that your candidacy was given careful consideration, but they were looking for more of a proactive teambuilder—someone to bring fresh ideas into the organization. But you can't help noticing that the less qualified person hired for the job came over from the company where the boss used to work. The boss's rationalization of the decision is bullshit. The reasons she provided are not completely irrelevant to the task of justifying her decision, but they miss the mark badly both because they are not the real reasons for the decision and because, even if they were, you judge that they shouldn't be given as much weight as your more extensive experience and qualifications. Her reasoning has the *form* of rational argument, but it falls badly short of genuine justification. The case fits Frankfurt's definition because the boss's rationalization shows a lack of concern for the truth, in that the boss fails to communicate the true reasons for the decision. But the deeper problem here is that, even if the boss has sincerely convinced herself of the truth of her argument, the reasons given don't justify the decision. Maddeningly, however, there is nothing you can do about it. Except to say that it's bullshit.

Political speech deals with issues that affect our lives in ways we have even less control over than our own promotion at work. George Orwell's work makes this problem a central theme. His novel *Nineteen Eighty-Four* imaginatively illustrates the danger of unchecked bullshit from government authority. He also addressed the problem in a non-fiction essay, "Politics and the English Language."[1] In that essay, Orwell decries the

---

[1] The essay is in *The Collected Essays, Journalism, and Letters of George Orwell*, Volume 4 (Harcourt, Brace, 1968), pp. 127–140.

decline of the English language, and blames politics for it. Political writing must be bad writing, he argues, because only bad writing could "justify" the actions of government:

> In our time, political speech and writing are largely the defense of the indefensible. Things like the continuance of British rule in India, the Russian purges and deportations, the dropping of the atom bombs on Japan, can indeed be defended, but only by arguments which are too brutal for most people to face, and which do not square with the professed aims of the political parties. Thus political language has to consist largely of euphemism, question-begging and sheer cloudy vagueness. (p. 136)

Orwell was referring to mid-twentieth-century times, but the situation has not improved. Our taste for euphemism continues to be fed with terms like "smart bomb," "collateral damage," "surgical strike," and "friendly fire," which are all euphemistic ways to talk about killing. A recent cable news segment entitled "Fighting Terror" showed an American fighter jet pulverizing an Iraqi hut. It struck me that "terror" was an odd description of a hut, and that nothing could be more terrifying than a dive-bombing fighter jet.

Why do we tolerate this kind of bullshit? The reasons scouted in the previous section continue to have their weight: politeness makes us hesitant to puncture the poses of authority, inflated rhetoric makes for more entertaining news programming, and effective waging of war requires rhetorical posturing. History shows that these reasons often fall short of justifying our toleration. There are also less respectable reasons at work. Orwell offers one of them:

> [Modern writing] consists in gumming together long strips of words which have already been set in order by someone else, and making the results presentable by sheer humbug. The attraction of this way of writing is that it is easy. (p. 134)

The same attraction underlies widespread acceptance of such writing. Absorbing and repeating what we hear is much easier than thinking about it. It's easier for media outlets to repeat government spin than to seek a more direct description of the kind Orwell favors. Plus, in a media market, consumers would probably not sustain a news program following Orwell's principles.

WHATEVER DOES NOT REFER TO BELIEF IS NO PART OF THE THOUGHT IT

Finally, if bullshit is the language of power, as Orwell's analysis suggests, then to go along with bullshit is to go along with power. Power can be very persuasive.

The problem is that the powerful do not always use their force of persuasion in ways that serve one's own values and interests. Thus the need for vigilance against bullshit: to be effective in pursuing your own goals, you have to avoid being taken in by a line of bull that, upon examination, works against those goals. The danger here is the same whether you fall for the bullshit of others or start believing your own. Consider the advertising case. An effective advertiser rigorously gathers demographic and psychographic data about potential customers, as well as studying competitors' products and tactics. If bullshit works in a given ad, it's because of its effect on the customer, not on the advertiser. The advertiser should know why and how the ad works rather than buying the pitch himself or herself. The most effective bullshitters know the truth, including the truth about when to bullshit and when to give the straight shit. The instrumental effectiveness of bullshit thus presupposes and exploits the instrumental effectiveness of truth: to enjoy the benefits of bullshitting without succumbing to the dangers of being bullshitted, a lively concern for the truth must be constantly maintained.

Indeed, one of the biggest dangers of bullshit in politics is that politicians will come to believe their own bullshit. When they do, their policies often fail because public support alone does not make a policy work when implemented. The same is true at the individual level. Convincing yourself of the excellence of your plans does not suffice for success (notwithstanding the advice of motivational speakers). At this point, however, it's necessary to consider how it's even possible to believe one's own bullshit. For bullshit, as Frankfurt understands it, requires both a bullshitter, who intentionally disregards the truth, and a potential dupe. How can a single person play both roles?

Bullshit and Self-Deception

The paradox of believing your own bullshit parallels the paradox of self-deception. If a deceiver by definition knows that the belief he induces is false, it's hard to see how he can convince himself that the selfsame belief is true. Reflection on the parallel between self-deception and believing your own bullshit sheds light on the debate between Cohen and Frankfurt about the nature of bullshit. Indeed, one man's self-deception is another man's bullshit.

In his book *Self Deception Unmasked* (Princeton: Princeton University Press, 2001), Alfred Mele argues that self deception should not be understood on the model of interpersonal deception. In interpersonal deception, the deceiver does not believe the claim that he hopes his victim will accept as true. If self deception were to fit the interpersonal model, then the self-deceived person would have to play both roles, both affirming and denying the same belief. Mele takes this consequence to show that the interpersonal model fails. For self deception happens quite frequently, and belief in outright logical contradictions rarely seems involved.

A husband may self-deceptively maintain the belief that his wife is faithful, despite contrary evidence that would cause an unbiased person to be suspicious (p. 57ff). It makes little sense to suggest that his self-deception consists in his first believing that his wife is unfaithful, followed by an unconscious effort to suppress this belief in favor of the (simultaneously held?) belief that she is faithful. No: his problem is that he masks the evidence of her infidelity from himself, not that he manipulates himself after having accepted it. Mele maintains that psychological processes such as motivated misinterpretation of evidence and selective evidence gathering explain self-deception much more plausibly than the interpersonal model.

One of the most common forms of self-deception is an inflated self-image. Mele opens his book by citing the statistic that ninety-four percent of university professors believe that they are better at their jobs than their average colleague (p. 3). In the face of a statistic like this, I think it's fair to guess that most people also overestimate how thoroughly justified their beliefs are. Our cuckolded husband may sincerely believe he has reviewed the data objectively. Similarly, half-baked prejudices often come along with the demonstrably false conviction that the evidence has been duly considered. For example, I was recently informed that smart boys are smarter than smart girls. Although Frankfurt tends to suggest that bullshitting is the sort of thing that must be done on purpose, examples like these show that a lack of concern for truth can be present unintentionally because we deceive

ourselves about the adequacy of our reasons. Particularly when
it comes to entrenched prejudices, it can be difficult for a person to see that what he believes bears little if any connection to
the truth.

G.A. Cohen actually notices that self-deception can cause
acceptance of bullshit, but doesn't make it central to his definition. In attempting to explain why people like his younger self
put up with unclarifiable texts by Althusserian Marxists, Cohen
postulates "a blend, perhaps, of 'cognitive dissonance reduction'
and 'adaptive preference formation' . . . [that is] at work quite
widely."[2] Because these psychological processes make it possible to produce bullshit unintentionally, Cohen criticizes
Frankfurt for focusing too much on the state of mind of the bullshitter:

> [It] is neither necessary nor sufficient for every kind of bullshit that
> it be produced by one who is informed by indifference to the truth,
> or indeed, by any other distinctive intentional state. (p. 130)

Cohen concludes that Frankfurt's "process-centered" definition
of bullshit, which focuses attention on the state of mind of the
bullshitter, must be replaced by an "out-put centered" definition
that attends to features of the bullshit itself. Cohen fastens upon
unclarifiability as the distinctive trait of bullshit.

While Cohen is right that it's a mistake to require that bullshit be produced by a person who is aware of her own lack of
concern for truth, his attempt to focus on the product rather
than the process cannot work. For example, consider the case
of an avid fan of conservative talk radio. He "learns" many
things on his program, including that the French are an irrational
and ungrateful people, and that liberals have an anti-Christmas
agenda. There is nothing unclarifiable about these claims, but
they are most assuredly bullshit.

To avoid admitting that bullshit can be produced unintentionally, Frankfurt reasons that repeating second-hand bullshit
can't make you a bullshitter any more than repeating second
hand lies makes you a liar.[3] So in Frankfurt's view the radio fan's
pronouncements are only warmed over bullshit, deriving their

---

[2] G.A. Cohen, "Deeper into Bullshit," Chapter 8 in this volume, p. 118.
[3] See Frankfurt's "Reply to G.A. Cohen," in *Contours of Agency*, pp. 340–44.

status from the radio host's intentional indifference to truth. However, the typical student of talk radio does not restrict himself to repeating what he hears. He will go beyond the conclusions of his on-air mentors, arguing for conclusions of his own. Perhaps he favors nuking the French, or punishing by law anyone who refers to Christmas trees as Holiday trees. If anyone were to challenge his commitment to truth, he would (as his mentors have trained him to do) take offense and write off the challenger as a dupe of the liberal media. He's not in the same league as the radio host, who knowingly dissembles. But his intellectual sloppiness can't shield him from the accusation of bullshit. Rather, as a result of self-deception, he believes his own bullshit.

Blameless Bullshit

Frankfurt probably doesn't care to defend self-deceived talk radio fans. But he has a deeper reason to object to the idea of unintentional bullshit. Even in the absence of self-deception, some people fail badly to get at the truth. We now reject whole conceptual systems, like alchemy, that no one at the time suspected of incoherence. For example, Isaac Newton studied alchemy, and he was no intellectual slouch. Frankfurt refuses to classify hopeless theories like alchemy as bullshit to protect serious theorists like Newton from being called bullshitters:

> It seems inappropriate to insist that those statements were always bullshit. Characterizing something as bullshit is naturally construed as seriously pejorative, and in the kind of case I have imagined, the opprobrium is not warranted. ("Reply to G.A. Cohen," p. 343)

Frankfurt is right that we shouldn't condemn Newton as a bullshitter, but we now know that alchemy is bullshit. The point of calling alchemy bullshit is not to slam men like Newton, but to excuse us from taking it seriously. In fact, that's the same reason we dismiss the rants of both the talk radio fan and his on-air mentor as bullshit—so we don't have to pay attention to them. The charge, to be justified, requires that the methods involved are so unpromising they can be safely ignored. Otherwise, the person who calls bullshit is unjustified in adopting an attitude of disdain and, ultimately, disinterest. To call something bullshit in the pejorative sense is thus to marginalize it, to exclude it from the status of serious discussion.

Cohen's attack on the Althusserians illustrates this marginalizing function. He recognizes that they do not intentionally disregard the truth in the way Frankfurt condemns, and he doesn't want to base his objection on the contentious and insulting claim that all Althusserians are self-deceived. But he regards their methods as hopelessly obscure. So he shifts the focus from their moral character to their theories:

> . . . these moral faults should not be our primary focus. For reasons of courtesy, strategy, and good evidence, we should criticize the product, which is visible, and not the process, which is not. (p. 336)

Pace Cohen, it's just not possible to call bullshit courteously. In rejecting the product, one necessarily rejects the process that led to it and the persons using the process. The process in question at this point, however, is not psychological, but methodological. Adopting a hopeless method justifies marginalization whether one's adoption results from self-deception or, as in the case of Newton, blameless ignorance of future science.

Return now to the talk radio fan. Exposing his self-deception is one good way to back up the accusation of bullshit. Another way to justify dismissing his claims is to criticize his methods directly. Taking views on testimony is a method. It's a respectable method to the extent that one's sources are respectable. When those sources adopt poor methods, such as the "method" of cherry-picking facts to support a political agenda, the result is bullshit. And it's bullshit to repeat the results not only because what is repeated is bullshit, but because the method of arriving at the opinion in question is not to be trusted. Warmed over bullshit is not merely a stale imitation of the original, but a fresh deposit that compounds the methodological faults of the original.

Shifting the focus from psychological processes to methodology allows us to recognize Cohen's insight that bullshit can be produced unintentionally, without giving up on Frankfurt's point that the way bullshit is produced matters most. Adopting this shift has its costs, however: the concept of bullshit becomes more contentious to apply because evaluating a methodology is a difficult matter, even in principle. For example, the Althusserians can be counted on to respond to Cohen by arguing that their methods clarify rather than obscure the study of politics. Calling names cannot settle this dispute. For one thing, sometimes the inadequacy of a method can only be revealed by providing a new and better alternative, like modern chemistry stands to alchemy. Even in more immediately tractable cases, the method as a whole, rather than a discrete variable like intentional indifference to truth, must be evaluated. Sometimes this is easy to do, as with the talk radio fan. In other cases, however, the jury is likely to remain out indefinitely. Consider the status of philosophy.

Given the difficulty of settling on reliable methods, we must admit that avoiding self-deception does not suffice for avoiding bullshit. Sometimes, through no fault of our own, we unintentionally end up with bullshit beliefs. Frankfurt's ear cannot tolerate this conclusion because he finds the accusation of bullshit necessarily pejorative. However, his reservations can be met by considering a parallel example: the term "killer." It verges on oxymoron to talk of blameless killers. We typically reserve the term "killer" for murderers because terms like "killer" connote intention. Indeed, the suffix "-er" is the staple device for forming the name of occupations, like "lawyer," "gambler," "dancer," and so forth. Similarly, we use the same suffix and its cognates to classify sinners by their sins, as in "liar," "cheater," and "adulterer." However, even if it's true to say that only murderers count as killers, plenty of people kill without murdering.

Consider the difference between two drivers who each kill a pedestrian: the first driver runs up on the sidewalk while reading a book; the second driver drives safely but the doomed pedestrian darts out between parked cars. The first driver's negligence makes him criminally liable despite the fact that we find it awkward to call him a killer. Calling the second driver a killer is worse than awkward: it would be positively cruel under the circumstances because he is completely blameless and, indeed, to be pitied. However, the impropriety of calling either driver a killer sadly does not change the fact that the pedestrians were killed. The term "bullshitter" is similar. Frankfurt's intentional bullshitter is paradigmatic because of his conscious disregard for truth. The self-deceived talk radio fan is similar to the neglige driver. He doesn't mean to spread bullshit, but he neglige adopts the method of embellishing radio propaganda. Finally, people like Newton are similar to the blameless driver: their theories may have proven over time to be bullshit, but they cannot be accused of self-deception or any other serious intellectual fault. The term "bullshit" remains pejorative, but the opprobrium rests with the theory, not the people who propound it.

Bullshit and Truth

If I'm right, bullshit results from the adoption of lame methods of justification, whether intentionally, blamelessly or as a result of self-deception. The function of the term is to emphatically express that a given claim lacks any serious justification, whether or not the speaker realizes it. By calling bullshit, we express our disdain for the speaker's lack of justification, and indignation for any harm we suffer as a result.

Although everyone who calls bullshit is concerned with justification, they aren't always concerned with truth. A person's values inevitably inform his perception of what counts as a lame justification. Thus, because he values truth so deeply, Frankfurt calls bullshit whenever he sees truth disregarded. But many people call bullshit when other values than truth are threatened. For example, a bottom-line oriented businessman will reject discussions of business ethics as bullshit. If the government investigates his dodgy accounting practices, he'll indignantly condemn the investigation as bureaucratic bullshit. Truth is not the issue for him. Rather, he directs his disdain and indignation toward obstacles impeding his cash flow.

The same dynamic explains why so many people think philosophy is bullshit: they may only be interested in money, or in entertainment. *Bullshit and Philosophy* excluded, philosophy rarely entertains. Even those who do care about truth may be interested in more narrowly technical questions, like how to develop medical therapies using stem cells. For such people, philosophical and ethical questions constitute an annoying distraction from the truths that interest them. And the endless cycle of debate within philosophy frustrates people who just want to know the answer and get on with their lives. Finally, it must be admitted that a lot of philosophy obscures the truth rather than capturing it. At the very least, proponents of different methodologies within philosophy will direct that accusation at each other. I'm guessing the Althusserians think Cohen's brand of Marxism is bullshit, too. Likewise, a linguist might reject this essay (and Frankfurt's) as bullshit on the grounds that any serious investigation of words must be based on empirical methods rather than the philosophers' armchair method of reflecting on a few examples.

Given all this disagreement about what's bullshit and what's not, should we adopt a subjective definition of bullshit, according to which bullshit is whatever elicits the emotional reactions of disdain and indignation? I don't think so. In the end, although Frankfurt is wrong to neglect unintentional examples of bullshit, he is right that bullshit results from a lack of connection with truth. Methodological disagreements may be difficult to resolve, but they are among the most important disagreements. Likewise, there are few more serious arguments than arguments over what goals we should be seeking. Frankfurt rightly notes that skepticism about justification in these areas is one reason there is so much bullshit (*On Bullshit*, p. 64). He goes on to deftly show that retreating to subjectivism can't work, ending his essay with the memorable line, "sincerity itself is bullshit" (*On Bullshit*, p. 67). We can also put the point this way: the idea that truth does n't matter is bullshit. However, it doesn't follow, as Frankfurt assumes, that the proper response is to eradicate every instance of bullshit. Rather, bullshit must be recognized for what it is, and restricted to truly justifiable uses.

How do we do that? Not by just bullshitting our way through. Justifying the preference for bullshit over truth in a given situation requires an ability to tell the difference between the two. Likewise, we've already seen that effective use of bullshit for instrumental purposes, as in advertising, presupposes a lively respect for truths about the attitudes of one's target audience and suchlike. Thus, there can be no justification for wholesale indifference to truth, even if one's primary goals are instrumental. Furthermore, to pretend that no justification need be offered for adopting purely instrumental goals, like the bottom-line oriented businessman considered above, is itself unjustifiable. If we conceal the lameness of our reasons from ourselves, we end up self-deceptively believing our own bullshit, or manipulated by the bullshit of others. In both cases, it's our own goals and interests that are endangered. Orwell recognized as much: his quest to reverse the decline of the English language stemmed not from a grammatical puritanism, but from deep concerns about abuse of power and exploitation. His crusade against bad writing is a contribution to ethics more than literary criticism. I'll close my chapter by endorsing Orwell's advice:

> If you simplify your English, you are freed from the worst follies of orthodoxy. You cannot speak any of the necessary dialects, and when you make a stupid remark, its stupidity will be obvious, even to yourself. (p. 139)[4]

---

[4] Thanks to my colleague Erich Freiberger, who got me started on this topic, and my wife Tonia Cook Kimbrough, who improved an earlier draft and, in general, calls bullshit whenever I have it coming.

2
A Defense of Common Sense

CONSUELO PRETI

When it comes to bullshit, we know it when we hear it. But that's not good enough for philosophers. Philosophers don't roll eyes- -shrug—move on when it comes to getting to the bottom of something.

When confronted with something both as familiar and widespread as bullshit—when something looks as if there isn't much more to be said about it—*that's* when philosophers kick into gear. When it comes to bullshit, it's not that we don't get it; we get it alright, every day and from all corners. But the way in which we are acquainted with it falls short of being the whole story. We know bullshit when we hear it, but that doesn't mean we are pro-bullshit. There is certainly something about bullshit we could do without. So the trick is to give a clear set of distinctive characteristics for something to be bullshit, and, at the same time, reveal what it is about bullshit that we could lose, and, maybe, what we can do about it.

In his seminal essay *On Bullshit*, Harry Frankfurt—who reminds us that an analytic philosopher, in particular, has a special concern for the clarification of concepts—says that he aims, as a philosopher in that tradition, to clarify the concept of bullshit. Frankfurt argues that the difference between bullshit and lying is that bullshit doesn't care about *distorting* the truth. Distorting the truth is, after all, a way of respecting and keeping a relation to the truth, so as to steer us away from it. Instead, according to Frankfurt, it is all the same to bullshit whether or not what it asserts is true. Bullshit's lack of concern for truth and falsity is at the heart of its nature and represents its threat to core

19

values of civilization; its insidiousness comes from the way it depends on scorning the difference between what is, or is not, the case.

G.A. Cohen, in his analysis of Frankfurt's essay (Chapter 8 in this volume), adds to Frankfurt's conception the category of specifically academic bullshit, which, he claims, differs from lay bullshit in its disregard for *meaning* rather than in its disregard for *truth*. Cohen resists the view that there is one criterion for bullshit, and argues that the difficulty in giving a consistent criterion across all the cases of what we can and do call bullshit rests on the difference between what constitutes bullshit in itself and what constitutes the production of it. Bullshit in itself, Cohen argues, is characterized by semantic obscurity. The bullshitter, on the other hand, disregards or disdains the truth. The former type of bullshit is independent of the intentions of a speaker; the latter is characterized essentially by the speaker's intentions.

Both Frankfurt's and Cohen's analyses, I believe, leave out a third element, essential to bullshit: its audience. Bullshit needs our compliance, and there is something about bullshit that succeeds in getting that compliance; bullshit, I think we all know, has a sneaky appeal. After all, bullshit, as Frankfurt points out, is in it for something—and so, it needs us to go along. I think that academic bullshit, by Cohen's criterion, is also in it for something, and it also needs us to play along. So: what is bullshit in it for, and how do we end up playing along? It seems pretty clear that bullshit tries to sell us something: but not, I think, just the *things* it is used to promote (Prada shoes, a date, an A, a reputation, the buzz). Bullshit, rather, employs indirect but powerful means: what it tries to do, I would suggest, is sell us on our own estimation or judgment of what matters.

Getting the Dior handbag or the invite to Mar-a-Lago matters. The guy who bullshits us into going to bed with him, or worse, giving him tenure, has made himself matter. Our own estimation of things matters to us, of course, for many reasons. When bullshit succeeds, it succeeds, mainly, by making our own estimation of what matters matter more than anything else.

We can see how this would cover bullshit in the academy as well. Academic bullshit also tries to sell us on significance: the intellectual import and status of its pronouncements. Anyone who slogged through graduate school is familiar with the psychological tension Cohen describes: the hours spent poring over some obscure text, justifying the hours of work by believing—even arguing—that the work in question is deeply important and terribly profound; the more so, because of its obscurity.

There is another type of bullshit in the academy, by the way, that Cohen doesn't discuss: the type that characterizes the decision-making process. This isn't unique to the academy, of course, but there does seem to be something particularly fetid about the atmosphere there, which tends to characterize the kinds of justification that academics give for their decisions, particularly with respect to the merit of the work of others. A disdain or disregard for the truth would seem to be precisely the right way to describe it, consistent with Frankfurt's analysis.

Bullshit is definitely a drag. It's even more of a drag now that it looks as if it involves, for its success, our own shameful desires to be flattered, feel important, and be made much of as arbiters of significance. But does bullshit really undermine the 'core values of civilization'? Is this a call to arms? I'm going to argue that (1) bullshit is a menace, in the street and in the seminar room; (2) it does undermine one of the core planks of civilized society; but that (3) that we can identify it and oppose it; and, moreover, that we should. Neither meaning nor truth may matter to bullshit, on the face of it, but what I would like to investigate here is the possibility that *something* does: what matters to bullshit is that it should make something matter to us.

For the incentive to resist bullshit we can reach back to one of the pioneers of early twentieth-century philosophy, G.E. Moore, and the philosophical common sense he has come to represent. Moore, in person and in deed, shows us in unexpected ways what it is about bullshit that is the most dangerous, and how we might resist it. Much of the history of Anglo-American philosophy through the twentieth century has built on aspects of Moore's method; here, I will single out one element of it: his commonsense and uncompromising commitment to *caring* about truth and meaning. This concern, we will argue, is probably the best tool that we can deploy today against the various forms of bullshit that importune us, both in the culture and in the seminar room.

The Truth Matters

But wait. Isn't all this just a little *quaint*? Nobody ever thought that academics were exactly plugged into the real world, after all; and the irony of a group of card-carrying eggheads holding forth on *bullshit*, of all things, is unmistakable. Easy does it, everybody. Surely bullshit is just one of the costs of doing business; we get it, we're not that threatened by it; it's not such a big deal. Isn't it a bit much to call it a threat to civilized society?

Well, no, as a matter of fact. It is just *that* kind of attitude that seems to illustrate the kind of menace we join with Frankfurt and Cohen to plant a flag against. If we have gotten to the point—and there are many ways in which it seems we might have—where we think that it's silly or quixotic (at best) even to *think* in terms of truth, respect for truth, credibility, or even related concepts like character and integrity, the disease has taken hold. So, if this is so, and this is bad, is there anything we can do about it? And where, exactly, should we start?

We can start with an example. Consider the case of James Frey, a pitiful (and frankly boring) substance abuser, who wrote up an account of his addiction and recovery. The account was shopped around as fiction, found no takers, and was reconsidered—and marketed—as a memoir. Frey's book, *A Million Little Pieces*, did a respectable business, but then, when Oprah Winfrey—perhaps the closest thing to the *Zeitgeist* in human form—chose it for her Book Club in October, 2005, sales went into the stratosphere. Everybody felt good about supporting and being a part of a story arc that in American culture, particularly, has legs: surrender, degradation, realization, recovery; and, of course, *inspiration*.

Except not much of it was true. But if what Frey wrote was sold as a memoir, then the issue of its truth is important, since—philosophical aside—if it didn't happen, you can't *remember* it, though you can pretend to, or think you can. So far, so good. But isn't this just lying? Fraud? Stupidity? Greed? Where's the bullshit, specifically, in this? Recall that Frankfurt claims that bullshit lies (so to speak), mainly, in *intention*. If *x* just doesn't care whether what he says is true, then *x* is bullshitting. A liar *cares* about the truth, honors it, so to speak, by intending to steer us away from it. So if Frey and his publishers' intent was to palm off a series of made up events as truth, he lied and they committed fraud; but if it didn't matter to them one way or another, then they were bullshitting (and, as Cohen makes clear, you can both bullshit *and* lie).

But we don't know, beyond question, what their intentions were. We do know, however, what Oprah's were—when she said, memorably, that *it was irrelevant* whether Frey's story was true. What mattered was that it stood as an inspiration, that it affected people, that it was an important story.[1]

Whether the story was true was irrelevant? It didn't matter? It didn't matter that the things that were meant to be an inspiration didn't actually happen? Or, if they did, they didn't happen quite the way they were inspiring us? Pause for philosophical reflection. Maybe something doesn't have to be true to be inspiring. We could find strength and example from all sorts of sources, and the fact that the examples stand as sources of inspiration is distinct from whether they have to be true (the Bible, say). So Frey gave us an inspiring account of dragging himself back from the brink of addiction, and just because it wasn't true doesn't mean it wasn't inspiring.

But that doesn't seem *entirely* right. The key question in a case like this is: *what* inspires us? If the inspiration I cull from your story is tied to the assumed truth of the account, then to discover that the account was made up means that the organ of inspiration is corrupted. I can be inspired by a tale of woe to be a better person, say, but if what inspires me in your tale of degradation and recovery is that you *were* degraded and *did* recover, then to discover that you *weren't* degraded or *didn't* recover sabotages the inspirational effect of your story on me. In other words, if I know that Prince Charming didn't really awaken Sleeping Beauty with a kiss, but am inspired by the story to continue to believe in true love, I have, by my own lights, adapted the story to something about which I am motivated independently to believe anyway. But if I think that your specific story *S* is true, and I am inspired by *it*, then to discover it isn't true, is to discover that there is nothing in it *by which* to be inspired.

The issue here, therefore, isn't that Frey made his story up; it was Oprah's own avowal that it didn't matter whether or not he

---

[1] Oprah Winfrey, January 11th, 2006, during a CNN broadcast of the *Larry King Show*.

had been lying. The *volte-face* that occurred when she went head to head on her turf with Frey, holding him to account, and chastising him for his deception, was as good an example as any of the menace of bullshit.[2] When Oprah said "I made a mistake and I left the impression that the truth does not matter. And I am deeply sorry about that, because that is not is what I believe," she summed up the core of the problem with bullshit: the truth matters, and it should matter. If bullshit threatens to turn Oprah's head, after all, we *are* in deep shit. Apparently, it *did* matter: his deception made *her* look like a bullshitter. Her own credibility suddenly became the story, as she belatedly seemed to realize. And loss of credibility should matter.

There is a philosophical question running under this discussion, which, a little uncharacteristically for a philosophical subject, made a national splash, thanks to Oprah: is *disdain* for truth worse than *distorting* it? Frankfurt and Cohen, who both argue that it is, seem vindicated by the train-wreck that Oprah narrowly avoided with her eleventh-hour grab at moral high-mindedness in the face of the growing scandal. If both Frankfurt and Cohen are right, the menace wrought by bullshit takes place on the inside, where any kind of respect for what's true and what's false starts to look downright expendable. Accepting, or being complacent to (or worse, colluding with) a disdain for a distinction between truth and falsity is not so innocuous— becoming inured to it is to stop caring about what's true and what's not, or even worse, to stop caring that it's not OK to stop caring about what's true and what's not. So the danger of bullshit is that it will grow increasingly resistant to treatment, so much so that we won't even notice that we stopped caring about truth and falsity. And this starts to look more and more like something we should be worried about.

In order to *counter* bullshit effectively—beyond just recognizing it—we need to turn it against itself. Bullshit, after all, has one significant weakness: it needs to be believed or accepted. Its *assertion,* though annoying, may not be a problem we can solve head on. To be believed or accepted, however, it does need us to co-operate. Bullshit doesn't care about the truth, but bullshit has to care about whether we care about the fact that it

---

[2] *The Oprah Winfrey Show,* January 26th, 2006.

doesn't. Truth doesn't matter to bullshit, but it matters to bullshit that bullshit can be made to matter to us. If we care more about the truth, then *a fortiori* we care less about bullshit. The less we care, the less hold it has over us—and bullshit, according to Frankfurt, is instrumental. It needs to find a way to be convincing and to make us care. If we care more about truth, bullshit will not succeed by not caring about truth. So if we resist caring about the assertions of bullshit—and being immune to its temptations—we might be able to undermine it, to no small degree.

What we could use now—perhaps one lesson of *l'affaire* Frey—is a genuine inspiration. The history of philosophy has delivered plenty of examples of the intellectually rigorous, and the detachedly rational, but perhaps fewer examples of the kind of thing we're looking for: a resolute *carer* about the truth and meaning. Luckily, both Frankfurt's and Cohen's discussions suggest some illuminating links to the early twentieth-century philosopher George Edward Moore (1873–1958). Moore, it turns out, is the philosopher specifically known for having introduced to philosophy precisely the "special concern" for the clarification of concepts that Frankfurt explicitly tells us he takes as his mission, and that Cohen could regard as a foil, in the right hands, to academic bullshit.

G.E. Moore might never have felt that it was entirely appropriate to respond to a muddled formulation of some philosophical concept or argument by actually snorting the word "bullshit," but Moore would be thoroughly opposed to anything so *dishonorable* as bullshit. Add to this Moore's character and his passion for truth, and he emerges as a potent force against bullshit, one we can find ways to emulate.[3]

"What Exactly Do You Mean?"

Moore was an undergraduate at Trinity College, Cambridge, from 1892 to 1896; in 1898 he was awarded a six-year fellowship, which he held at Trinity until 1904. He left Cambridge until 1911, when he returned to Trinity College as a lecturer, retiring as Professor in 1939. Along with his contemporary as an undergraduate, Bertrand Russell, and with his colleague at Trinity

---

[3] The difference between what Frankfurt cites as Wittgenstein's reaction to suspected bullshit, with what I will claim is Moore's, is instructive.

from 1929 to 1939, Ludwig Wittgenstein, Moore is credited with establishing what is now colloquially (if not entirely accurately) known as analytic philosophy. Analytic philosophy is known, very roughly, for its approach to the problems of philosophy as problems of meaning. Clarification and analysis of meanings, or concepts, was held to be the key to solving philosophical problems, some of which, it was surmised, would even dissolve upon clearer formulation.

Moore's most important and long-reaching achievement in the history of twentieth-century philosophy, however, was his seemingly casual and *sui generis* demolition of the philosophical tradition frequently dismissed, if sometimes in caricature, as Hall-of-Fame-worthy bullshit: Absolute Idealism, the view that one way or another, the ultimate nature of reality is mental. Both Moore and Russell produced early work that demonstrates a leaning toward Idealism. But in 1899 Moore published a paper entitled "The Nature of Judgment," in the journal *Mind,* which decisively repudiated any idealist metaphysics (particularly with respect to the nature of thought and its objects), and which opened up a new front against the problems of philosophy. Russell himself credited Moore with having initiated what he calls the 'revolt' against Idealism of their youth, and the approach introduced by Moore and Russell after 1899 in their work established a methodology still very much dominant today in analytic philosophy.

In 1903 Moore published perhaps his most well-known work, titled *Principia Ethica,* a book whose effect was so profound on the young men who arrived as undergraduates at Cambridge in 1902, and who later formed the core of the Bloomsbury group, that they referred to it as their religion. Moore did not share Russell's occasionally malicious flamboyance; and Wittgenstein early on wounded Moore so deeply with his impatience and prickliness that they did not speak for nearly twenty years. Moore has been described by Russell, Leonard Woolf, and John Maynard Keynes as having a purity of character without comparison, a smile described as "lovable," and a simplicity, ingenuousness, and directness that impressed itself completely and lastingly on those who knew him. Russell, in his autobiography, writes:[4]

---

[4] *The Autobiography of Bertrand Russell* (London: Allen and Unwin, Volume 1, 1967), p. 61.

In my third year . . . I met G.E. Moore, who was then a freshman, and for some years he fulfilled my ideal of genius. He was in those days beautiful and slim, with a look almost of inspiration, and with an intellect as deeply passionate as Spinoza's. He had a kind of exquisite purity. I have never but once succeeded in making him tell a lie, that was by a subterfuge, 'Moore', I said, 'do you *always* speak the truth?' 'No,' he replied. I believe this to be the only lie he ever told.

Woolf, for his part, is fulsome about the aspects of Moore's personality that resonate significantly here:[5]

> . . . Moore was a great man, the only great man whom I have ever met or known in the world of ordinary, real life. There was in him an element which can, I think, be accurately called greatness, a combination of mind and character and behavior, of thought and feeling which made him qualitatively different from anyone else I have ever known. . . . he had a passion for truth . . . Moore could never tolerate anything but truth, common sense, and reality . . . he had an extra-ordinary profundity and clarity of thought, and he pursued truth with the tenacity of a bulldog and the integrity of a saint.

These personal qualities appeared to have been instrumental to the evolution of the method most associated with Moore, usually known as the method of common sense. Much of the evaluation of the effect of Moore, in the words of his friends, at least, makes reference to it. John Maynard Keynes,[6] for example, writes:

> It was all under the influence of Moore's method, according to which you could hope to make essentially vague notions clear by using precise language about them and asking exact questions. It was a method of discovery by the instrument of impeccable grammar and an unambiguous dictionary. 'What *exactly* do you mean?' was the phrase most frequently on our lips. If it appeared under cross-examination that you did not mean *exactly* anything, you lay under a strong suspicion of meaning nothing whatever . . .
>   In practice, victory was with those who could speak with the greatest appearance of clear, undoubting conviction, and could

---

[5] *Sowing: An Autobiography of the Years 1880–1904* (London: Hogarth, 1960), pp. 110–131.
[6] Keynes, *Two Memoirs* (New York: Hart-Davis, 1949), p. 85

best use the accents of infallibility. Moore at this time was a master of this method—greeting one's remarks with a gasp of incredulity—*Do* you *really* think *that*, an expression of face as if to hear such a thing reduced him to a state of wonder verging on imbecility, with his mouth wide open and wagging his head in the negative no violently that his hair shook. *Oh!* He would say, goggling at you as if either you or he must be mad; and no reply was possible.

Now, Moore occasionally went, at least in his own estimation, a little too far. At the beginning of the third of a set of lectures that Moore delivered in 1898,[7] he says:

> I believe I owe you a public apology for my behavior during part of the discussion last Thursday. To one gentleman, in particular, I do owe such an apology. In the heat of the moment I certainly entertained, and implied by my words, the belief that one question which he addressed to me was not due to any serious difficulty felt by him, with regard to the matter in question . . . My feeling was that the question was merely a vexatious one, was indeed only momentary, but that does not excuse it.

Apparently, if anything could send Moore to immoderate lengths (for him), it was bullshit; here in the case of a question he believed was not intended as *genuine*. It was difficult for Moore, as we see here, to tolerate with too much equanimity even the possibility that someone would bother to raise a question without being seriously interested in its formulation or outcome. This, I think, is a key to adapting Moorean attitudes as resistance to bullshit. So let us analyze what form this immunity could take today and strengthen it against our susceptibility to bullshit.

Let's Stop Bullshitting Ourselves

Moore's friends and acquaintances were entirely unanimous on his goodness—the essence, after all, of one we look to for inspiration. But the descriptions of Moore's character as 'saintly' and 'pure', though no doubt charming, may tempt the reader into

---

[7] "Hedonism," in Tom Regan, ed., *The Elements of Ethics* (Philadelphia: Temple University Press, 1991), p. 41

suspecting they lack a certain practicality. Surely a Moorean attitude is impossible, today, to resurrect. After all, Moore and his cohorts were products of an era so entirely bygone that it might appear fruitless even to attempt to harness a Moorean attitude to anything, let alone something as seemingly steeped in the modern as bullshit, as least as far as its current pervasiveness goes. Keynes notes something of this in his memoir:[8]

> I have said that we were amongst the first to escape from Benthamism. But of another eighteenth-century heresy we were the unrepentant heirs and last upholders. We were among the last of the Utopians, or meliorists as they are sometimes called, who believe in a continuing moral progress by virtue of which the human race already consists of reliable, rational, decent people, influenced by truth and objective standards, who can be safely released from the outward restraints of convention and traditional standards and inflexible rules of conduct, and left, from now onwards, to their own sensible devices, pure motives and reliable intuitions of the good . . . It did not occur to us to respect the extraordinary accomplishment of our predecessors in the ordering of life . . . It was not only that intellectually we were pre-Freudian . . . I still suffer incurably from attributing an unreal rationality to other people's feelings and behavior . . . There is one small but extraordinarily silly manifestation of this absurd idea of what is 'normal', namely the impulse to *protest* . . . I behave as if there really existed some authority or standard to which I can successfully appeal if I shout loud enough . . . But this is why I say that there may have been just a grain of truth when Lawrence said in 1914 that we were 'done for'.

A sharp eye on the essence of the Moorean *attitude* directly connect us to Frankfurt's charge that bullshit is a threat to civilization—note the melancholy 'done for' at the end of Keynes's remarks, above. What the Moorean attitude has, and what we might think about deploying more explicitly, is his dispassionate respect for the truth such that it considers any attitude that falls short—such as disdain for truth—as a disgrace. Moore himself is

---

[8] "My Early Beliefs," in *Two Memoirs* (pp. 88–100). But Woolf takes exception to some aspects of Keynes's recollections. D.H. Lawrence, mentioned in the passage, had met the young men at Cambridge at the turn of the century and was violently disgusted by what he thought was their lack of reverence, an interesting connection, conceptually, to the topic here.

the ideal, to be sure; someone in whom philosophical insight, character, and action were seamlessly blended; an emissary, perhaps, from that possible world where bullshit has withered for lack of collaborators. But I think there are elements of the Moorean attitude that are accessible and realistic and that now is as good a time as any to man up and face bullshit down. I suggested above that bullshit has an uncanny way of selling us on ourselves, so to speak. I will close by spelling this out more clearly, adding a sense of the Moorean attitude of common sense to counter it, as the title of this essay suggests.[9]

People have been bullshitting one another since the dawn of time, to be sure, but something that both Frankfurt's and Cohen's analyses suggest, and that we could be more aware of, is that bullshit can be deflated. Bullshit, as we have seen, doesn't care one way or another whether what it expresses is true, or even strictly meaningful. It does care, however, about getting us to fall in with it. Bullshit has to care about something: it has to care about us and what we care about. If we care more about the difference between truth and falsity, bullshit will find it easier to take hold. So, to resist it, all we need to do is make a resolute stand on the difference between what is true and what isn't.

Easier said than done, perhaps—which of us really thinks that our estimation of truth is shabby or questionable?. But it may come as no surprise here that the practical solution to this will be to adopt a philosophical attitude—in particular, a Moorean attitude. Consider this passage from Moore's "A Defence of Common Sense," where his asperity firmly conveys that when it comes to bullshit, even in philosophy, enough is enough:

> In what I have just said, I have assumed that there is some meaning which is *the* ordinary or popular meaning of such expressions as 'The earth has existed for many years past.' And this, I am afraid, is an assumption which some philosophers are capable of disputing. They seem to think that the question 'Do you believe that the earth has existed for many years past?' is not a plain question, such as should be met either by a plain 'Yes' or 'No' or by a plain 'I can't make up my mind,' but is the sort of question which can be prop-

---

[9] Moore's "A Defence of Common Sense" was originally published in 1925 in J.H. Muirhead, ed., *Contemporary British Philosophy* (London: Allen and Unwin).

erly met by 'It all depends on what you mean by "the earth" and "exists" and "years": if you mean so and so, and so and so, and so and so, then I do; but if you mean so and so, and so and so, and so and so, or so and so, and so and so, and so and so, or so and so, and so and so and so and so, then I don't, or at least I think it is profoundly doubtful'. It seems to me that such a view is as profoundly mistaken as any view can be.

Moore didn't suffer bullshit gladly, and we can do the same. An ounce of prevention is worth a pound of cure, as the platitude goes. What Moore's resistance against forms of what we'd call bullshit takes as a priority is clarity. Moore shows us that a doggedness about getting clear about the content of an utterance or statement to get to the bottom of what it could really mean can really pay off—say, in the indisputable effect of revealing the characteristic scorn for the difference between truth and falsity that bullshit purveys. The scorn for truth that characterizes bullshit, after all, must be masked in various ways, or bullshit itself would run the risk of imploding. So, on top of disingenuous vagueness, equivocation, downright incoherence, and a whole host of other tactics for skirting the truth, what bullshit really needs is for us to be less inquisitive, less analytical, less determined to follow along and scrutinize its claims. Bullshit needs us, but we don't need bullshit. So to thwart it, we must instead adopt the 'tenacity of a bulldog', that Woolf describes as the characteristic of a Moorean pursuit of clarity and truth; especially, it goes without saying, with respect to ourselves.

So my suggestion for resisting bullshit is the adoption of the critical stance, characteristic of philosophy, toward any claims on our mental lives; our beliefs and certainties, including the ones that characterize our deepest convictions about ourselves and our ability to tell truth from falsity. G.E. Moore is an example of a philosopher who *lived* the method that he is best known for in his work and who connected a philosophical method to everyday life. Moore may have been iconic in this regard, to be sure, but his method is adaptable to us, and to now. It's common sense that bullshit has to care about something. But it's also just common sense to realize that caring about the distinction between what's true and what's false matters a lot to us. If we care more about the truth, then bullshit has to find another way. But now bullshit has to care whether we care about the truth, and so it more or less undermines its own position, withering away from the inside out, so to speak. This is the paradox of bullshit; both street and academic. Truth and meaning don't matter to bullshit; but bullshit has to make itself matter to us. So what matters to us is going to have to matter to bullshit. If it matters to us not to scorn the difference between truth and falsity, and if it matters to us to take the search for clarity in our concepts and statements seriously, bullshit ends up on a short leash. And, thanks to Moore, we now have a strategy to keep it there. Enough, indeed, is enough. What *exactly* do you mean?

3
The Pragmatics of Bullshit, Intelligently Designed

GEORGE A. REISCH

Harry Frankfurt admits that his definition of bullshit leaves us with a puzzle. It has to do with the difference between bullshitters and liars. Liars, Frankfurt says, must pay attention to truth, if only to avoid speaking it. Bullshitters don't. They are essentially indifferent to whether or not what they say is true. They just don't care and their indifference may be infectious. That is why Frankfurt takes bullshit to be especially dangerous and socially corrosive. It looms above modern culture as "a greater enemy of the truth than lies are."[1]

If that's so, then bullshitters, more than liars, should be feared and punished in our culture. But that's not the way it is. In fact, it's the reverse. We are generally *more tolerant* of bullshit than lies. When he first wrote *On Bullshit*, Frankfurt posed this fact as a puzzle, an "exercise," for his readers to figure out (p. 50). Today, some twenty years later, the puzzle remains unsolved. During a radio interview about *On Bullshit*, Frankfurt said:

> One of the questions I'm still puzzled by is that we seem to have a much more benign attitude toward BS than we have toward lying. . . . The liar is regarded . . . as a bad person; what he does is almost criminal. . . . Whereas BS we accept; we're tolerant of it. We may turn away from it with an irritated shrug, but we don't react to it with the same kind of vehemence and anger that lies frequently invoke and I really don't understand just why that is.[2]

---

[1] *On Bullshit*, pp. 60–61.
[2] Frankfurt was interviewed on WBUR's "On Point" (17th February, 2005).

In philosophy, an unsolved puzzle can be a good sign. It can mean that our understanding of things is rightly moving forward into new, unfamiliar territory. But it can also indicate that we've fallen into a trap, possibly one of our own making. That's what has happened with Frankfurt's definition of bullshit. He took a wrong turn in formulating his definition and the result has saddled him (and us) with this persistent, misleading puzzle.

What we need is a different definition of bullshit. I will offer one here that is quite different from Frankfurt's, partly because it rests on a distinction between the semantic and the pragmatic analysis of language. Making that distinction clear will be worth the effort, however, because the definition of bullshit that results accounts for those examples of bullshit that Frankfurt points to *and* solves this puzzle. It provides some good reasons, that is, for why we are more tolerant of bullshit and bullshitters, properly understood, than we are of lies and liars.

The Example of Intelligent Design

Another reason my definition of bullshit is different from Frankfurt's is that it is inspired by the Intelligent Design (ID) movement—an example of bullshit that Frankfurt could not have used when he wrote *On Bullshit* in the mid-1980s. ID was then merely a gleam in the eyes of its founders and leaders. By now, however, ID is well known for its criticisms of evolutionary theory and its claim that organisms are too complex to have evolved solely under the influence of natural evolutionary processes. Instead, ID's supporters insist, science itself indicates that the history of life on earth involved intervention by some supernatural "intelligent designer." When scientists finally accept this fact, they say, biology will be transformed and our understanding of life on earth will be greatly advanced.[3]

Why should these claims be taken as a typical illustration of bullshit? On the face of it, they are similar to other species of well-recognized bullshit in politics, public relations, and advertising—what Frankfurt calls "the most indisputable and classic paradigms of the concept" p. 22). Like these, ID speaks to us

---

[3] A useful introduction to the ID movement and its critics is Robert T. Pennock, ed., *Intelligent Design Creationism and Its Critics* (Cambridge, Massachusetts: MIT Press, 2001).

insistently and urgently. Just as the advertiser needs us to buy her product, the politician needs our vote, and the public relations specialist needs us to accept his view of things, the ID movement needs us to support and approve its proposals for biology and high-school science teaching. Like politicians and advertisers, moreover, ID claims that it is *in our interest* to do so. Just as your laundry will be cleaner with the right detergent, your child's education will benefit from bringing ID into the public school classroom and "teaching the controversy."

Another reason we should take ID to be a typical instance of bullshit is that bullshitters, as Frankfurt puts it, are usually "trying to get away with something" (p. 23). The recent history of the ID movement suggests what it might be trying to get away with. It descended from the explicitly religious program known as "creation science," which claims that the Bible presents accurate scientific information about the world. But, in the 1980s, efforts to introduce creation science into public school classrooms were defeated in the courts on constitutional grounds. So, in the 1990s, largely inspired by Philip Johnson's book *Darwin on Trial*, the ID movement arrived to rescue the creationist cause by presenting a new, strictly scientific and philosophical criticism of evolutionary theory. Accordingly, the literature of ID is filled with references to technical concepts from philosophy of science, theoretical debates in biology, and ID's own, favorite concepts like "specified complexity," "irreducible complexity," and "black boxes."[4]

There is reason to suspect, however, that ID's efforts to be scientific and theoretically sophisticated are primarily efforts to appear *non-religious*. There is no doubt that ID's leaders have religious and evangelical beliefs and motivations, but they typically distinguish these from their claimed roles as scientists or philosophers of science. Philip Johnson, for instance, appears to put on and take off his vestments according to his audience. To scientists and philosophers, he speaks of technical matters involving evidence, logic, and theories of scientific progress. He argues that science has not actually *discovered* that the history of life is guided solely by naturalistic, evolutionary processes.

---

[4] Philip Johnson, *Darwin on Trial* (Washington, D.C.: Regnery, 1991). For writings on "complexity" and related concepts in ID theory, see those by either Michael Behe or William Dembski (readily accessible on the internet).

Instead, Johnson insists, science has merely *assumed* the truth of naturalism and is now mentally straight-jacketed.

When speaking to religious or evangelical audiences, however, this complaint about the controlling naturalistic "assumptions" of evolutionary theory sometimes appears alongside other, very different claims about the customs and values of modern culture:

> Our nation is undergoing an epidemic of illegitimate births, with rates of illegitimacy among whites now soaring to 28 percent while rates among inner city blacks in some areas are over 80 percent. The majority of these illegitimate births are to teenagers.
>
> The American version of modernism does not aspire to obliterate theism, as Soviet Marxism did, but to marginalize it and thus render it harmless. Modernism is established in the sense that the intellectual community, usually invoking the power of the federal judiciary and the mystique of the Constitution, vigorously and almost always successfully insists that law and public education must be based upon naturalistic assumptions.[5]

In this article, titled "Is God Unconstitutional: The Established Religious Philosophy of America," Johnson's criticisms of "naturalistic assumptions" become part of a much larger campaign against cultural "modernism" and its tolerance of sexual promiscuity, materialism, atheism and other things—including Darwinian evolution—that evangelical Christian audiences tend to find repugnant.

It appears, then, that the ID movement is trying to get away with promoting specific, Christian cultural beliefs and values in secular, public schools—just as the creation science movement attempted. Hoping to succeed where creation science failed, however, Johnson and others have created a disguise, a cover, for this promotion in the form of an elaborate intellectual critique of biological theory. Beneath its outward packaging, that is, ID is a kind of creationism, the promotion of which in public school classrooms is forbidden by the United States Constitution. Thus went the opinion of Judge John E. Jones, who wrote in his decision in the case of Dover, Pennsylvania vs.

---

[5] Philip Johnson, "Is God Unconstitutional? The Established Religious Philosophy of America," 1996 (www.arn.org/authors/johnson_articles.html).

Kitzmiller, that "ID is a religious view, a mere re-labeling of creationism, and not a scientific theory."[6] Since the Kitzmiller case was the first major legal hurdle that the ID movement faced, it would appear that, as the saying goes, this here bullshit won't fly.

A Definition of Bullshit—*New and Improved!*

If the ID movement counts as bullshit, then Frankfurt's definition is in error. For advocates of ID are plainly *not* indifferent to truth, as Frankfurt's definition requires. We can leave open the question of whether and to what extent Johnson and his followers are sincerely concerned about the truths of biological science and natural history. But there is little doubt that they take themselves to be deeply concerned with other truths—rotten truths, they believe—about modern culture and "modernism." Johnson, in fact, is concerned not only to address these particular truths but to elevate regard for truth *itself* in popular culture. One of the problems with "modernism," Johnson says, is this:

> What modernism may lead to is a growing doubt that there is any such thing as objective truth, with a consequent fragmenting of the body politic into separate groups with no common frame of reference . . . The great need of the 21st century may turn out to be a unifying vision, and I do not think that science will be able to provide it.

Frankfurt and Johnson, it turns out, *both* care about the status of truth in our culture and share the view that we are becoming dangerously indifferent to it.

Now, this comparison may seem idiotic. What a Christian, evangelical reformer like Johnson and an Ivy League philosopher like Frankfurt *mean* by "truth" may be quite different. Precisely so—and this tells us what is wrong with Frankfurt's definition of bullshit. Frankfurt himself failed to take into account the fact that our collective beliefs about what is true—about the world, about how it works, about our place in it—are

---

[6] Memorandum Opinion, December 20th, 2005, District Court for the Middle District of Pennsylvania, Document number 342, p. 43.

extremely diverse and often contradictory. Instead, he writes of the truth to which bullshitters are allegedly indifferent as if it were a single, comprehensive, or unitary truth. Throughout *On Bullshit* he mentions "the truth" (pp. 30, 33, 40, 47, 51, 56), "the true" (p. 56), and the idea of an "accurate representation of reality" (p. 32) as if everyone—bullshitters excepted—not only *cares about* truth but further *agrees about* what "the truth" is, about "how things really are" (pp. 30, 34).

In fact, we often disagree about how things really are, and this can make it difficult to determine whether this or that example of bullshit that we may encounter comes from someone who does not care about truth (as Frankfurt claims is the case) or from someone who does indeed care about truth, albeit truths that we simply do not recognize. In fact, as the example of ID illustrates prominently, bullshitters conceal not some indifference to truth but instead a commitment to *other* truths and, usually, an agenda or enterprise that they take to be inspired or justified by those *other* truths. For many possible reasons, however, they do not want us to see these truths to which they are committed. Our knowledge of these other truths, the bullshitter may fear, will prove embarrassing or damaging to them or their cause. Or it may render their claims less persuasive and less effective. In some cases, revealing these truths would show that their project is in fact illegal or, as in ID's case, unconstitutional.

This pluralism about truth is crucial for understanding bullshit. An effective bullshitter will make use of the diverse beliefs and convictions that populate our world. She will be quite aware that a person or group does not share the truths that undergird her agenda, so she will configure her program within or alongside an altogether different kind of program that, she believes, her audience will applaud and embrace— just as the ID movement places its specific evangelical goals inside what appears to be a crusade to improve science education. If all goes well, her targets will find that outer, visible project *so* appealing, they will agree to it and unwittingly go along with what has been cloaked inside, as well. Only later— after, for example, the new textbooks have come in and talk in the biology lab increasingly turns to topics in the Bible— will some of these targets recognize that they have been duped.

The Truth in Bullshit

Even stock examples of bullshit show that bullshitters are not indifferent to truth. Consider Frankfurt's example of college "bull sessions." Here, he says, "the participants try out various thoughts and attitudes . . . without it being assumed that they are committed to what they say" (p. 36). The statements made "are like bullshit by virtue of the fact that they are in some degree unconstrained by a concern with truth" (p. 38). Language's grip on truth may be relaxed here, but that relaxation actually serves other truths and ideals that are very important to the average undergrad. These include truths about one's self image, one's social reputation, and to what degree the apple of one's eye is actually impressed by the very real possibility (as immortalized in the film *Animal House*) that a complete, self-contained universe exists within a single atom of someone *else's* fingernail. What makes such conversations bullshit-like is not their casual regard for "the truth" but rather the use of casual, hyperbolic, or inconsequential claims to unobtrusively probe or promote other truths or concerns.

The same holds for advertisers and politicians who draw our attention ostensibly to one set of truths and purposes while in fact quietly engaging us about different matters. The person who writes the slogan used to advertise a laundry detergent, or who designs the packaging to display that slogan, probably does not care about how well that detergent cleans your clothes, even though that is what the words on the package would appear to be about. But that does not mean that those words and phrases are truth-indifferent bullshit. Effective advertising and product packaging rests on truths embraced within the advertising industry about how graphic design, word associations, celebrity endorsement and other devices speak to consumers' thoughts about themselves—their self-image, social aspirations, and feelings of belonging and group identity. Politicians are also adept at conducting two (or more) conversations at once with their constituencies. One involves policy and issues, but another, as any professional campaign manager will tell you, involves clothes, postures, hairstyles, rolled-up sleeves and gestures, all of which are carefully orchestrated in an attempt to make voting groups find a candidate *personally* likeable.

Bullshit, then, consists in the orchestration of at least two different concerns and corresponding types of engagement between bullshitter and bullshitee, one concealed within or downplayed alongside the other. The two may appear to be unrelated and unconnected—as different as Philip Johnson's claims about evolutionary theory and his hoped-for dismantling of cultural "modernism." But the bullshitter has co-ordinated them in an effort to maximize his or her chances of accomplishing certain practical goals. The politician who hopes to gain your vote may reason that even if you don't agree with what he says about the issues, you may nonetheless vote for him because his clothes and mannerisms appeal to you. The auto advertiser hopes that even if you don't understand the engineering innovations spelled out in her advertising copy, you will want to appear successful, attractive, and happy, just like the models driving the car in the ad.

Whatever configuration these two engagements take, however, the phenomenon that Frankfurt takes to be essential to identifying bullshit—its indifference to truth—is either absent or only partly in play. In some cases, bullshit's overt message may be some kind of nonsensical smokescreen or a display of bluster and bluff that, indeed, even the bullshitter would regard as unconnected to truth. But even in those cases, such smokescreens typically serve to hide the motivations and truths that the bullshitter genuinely cares about. In other cases, the bullshitter's overt message may be a small, selected piece of the larger project he is trying to get away with, much as ID's attempts to criticize Darwinian evolutionary theory on strictly intellectual, scientific grounds can be understood (as Philip Johnson's comments suggest) as one small part of a more general effort to promote a supernatural, religious world view in public culture.

The Truth about Semantics

Why does Frankfurt propose a definition of bullshit which focuses on the properties of the bullshitter's speech and stops short of inquiring into these larger, ulterior goals that bullshit usually serves? Part of the answer, I suspect, involves the difference between semantic and pragmatic analyses of language. Semantics concerns properties of language such as meaning, truth or falsity—relations, that is, between words and sentences, on the one hand, and the things or states of affairs they describe or refer to, on the other. Much of modern analytic philosophy is dedicated to the semantic analysis of language and difficult questions about meaning, reference, and truth.

Frankfurt's definition of bullshit crucially involves semantics insofar as bullshitters, as he defines them, don't care whether or not their utterances are true. But some of his examples of bullshit also point to the *pragmatic* aspects of language. To see these, we must expand our picture of language to include not just meaning and truth but also the *uses* and *purposes* to which language may be put. Frankfurt's example of a politician extolling the virtues of a nation on some national holiday, for instance, takes specifically into account the politician's hope to use lofty, feel-good words and phrases for a specific purpose that has nothing to do with those things he's speaking about, such as liberty and the founding of a great nation. Rather, he hopes to *use* this language to make his audience like him (pp. 16–18).

Decades ago, pragmatics was taken to be just as important as semantics for a philosophical understanding of language. Even philosophers who specialized in semantic analysis of language, such as Rudolf Carnap, took it for granted that any "complete theory of language" must take into account pragmatic studies of how language can be used by persons in specific contexts.[7] Though few philosophers would object to Carnap's remark, philosophy itself evolved to favor semantic studies of language to the exclusion of pragmatics. There are many plausible causes for this—ranging from the sheer complexity of how language can be used, for example, to the vogue for academic specialization throughout intellectual life in the twentieth century. Whatever the causes, this neglect of philosophical pragmatics is obvious. Thumb through *The Cambridge Dictionary of Philosophy*, edited by Robert Audi, for example, and you will find twenty-six entries beginning with the word 'semantics', but only seven beginning with 'pragmatic' or 'pragmatism'.

---

[7] Rudolf Carnap, "Foundations of Logic and Mathematics," *International Encyclopedia of Unified Science* 1: 3 (Chicago: University of Chicago Press, 1939), p. 4.

If any complete theory of language must take pragmatics into account, so too must any viable theory of bullshit. The distinctive mark of bullshit that I have been describing is an essentially pragmatic, and not semantic, feature of language. It lay in the use of language to achieve certain goals or create certain effects which remain hidden from the person or persons to which the bullshit in question is directed. This is not to say that semantic aspects of language are not involved in producing or understanding bullshit. We can easily imagine our patriotic orator caring very much about the truth of certain things—like whether or not his audience is eating up his declarations as much as he hopes they will. But if we seek to understand the heart of bullshit we need to turn to pragmatics and not semantics.

Once we do, the definition of bullshit that results is quite different from both Frankfurt's and Cohen's.[8] And it shows that the difference between their definitions of bullshit—Frankfurt's concerning truth and Cohen's concerning meaning—is narrow. Both seek the defining characteristics of bullshit in semantics. But we learn more about bullshit by defining it as an essentially pragmatic phenomenon.

From the bullshitter's point of view, it springs from a pragmatic aim to co-ordinate two (or more) distinct concerns or conversations and to *use one* as a cover or container for the other. From the recipient's point of view, it is pragmatic insofar as its chances for success depend upon its being received and recognized as a pragmatic, goal-seeking enterprise. Bullshit will be more effective to the extent that the two concerns it joins together would otherwise be regarded by the target audience as independent, unconnected, and having very different aims and purposes. The more different those two concerns seem to be, the less likely it will seem that, for example, a science-education advocate could turn out to be a soul-saving evangelical in disguise, a news report on television could turn out to be a government-produced segment distributed to promote some initiative, or your neighbor the dentist who recommends some particular brand of lawn fertilizer could turn out to be a "word-of-mouth" advertising agent for the fertilizer company in question.

---

[8] Cohen's is "Deeper into Bullshit," Chapter 8 in this volume.

Solving Frankfurt's Puzzle, or, Baseball, Hot Dogs, Apple Pie, and Bullshit

Construing bullshit as an essentially pragmatic phenomenon, finally, allows us to solve Frankfurt's puzzle. Overlooking this difference between semantics and pragmatics, in fact, *creates* Frankfurt's puzzle. On his view, recall, the liar states something that he knows to be false and the bullshitter states something without caring whether it is true or false. Both the liar and the bullshitter, that is, *sin against the semantics of truth*. Yet, there appears no good reason for why we let one, but not the other, off the hook so easily.

Once we recognize that the bullshitter does not sin against semantics, however, the puzzle disappears. For the liar and the bullshitter are now understood to be doing different things. The liar attempts to mislead us about truth, about how things really are, but the bullshitter attempts to manipulate us *by cloaking the kinds of effects that he wants his speech and his enterprise to have*. He sins, rather, against the pragmatics of language by making it appear that his speech is designed to have one kind of effect (such as advancing science education, or making your laundry cleaner) while his conscious aim is to bring about a different kind of effect (such as promoting evangelical Christianity, or making money for his client).

Taking bullshit to be an essentially pragmatic, and not semantic, affair, we can see right away that we have many reasons for treating liars and lies differently from bullshitters and bullshit. For starters, lies can be dangerous in ways that bullshit usually is not because they can thwart our needs, sometimes our vital needs. When you have a bad cold, for example, and you cannot tell whether the coffee-milk at work has soured, you need to ask someone about it and you need them to tell you the truth. If they lie it will ruin your coffee, if not your morning.

Bullshit, on the other hand, engages us differently. Instead of responding to our own needs and concerns, it seeks to *create* needs or perceptions with which it can manipulate us. The difference is important, for it explains why we can ignore bullshit safely but lies only at our peril. Without a gullible, believing audience, after all, bullshit can have no effect. So, when that guy in the office comes round to chat about Darwin being completely wrong and biology being due for a scientific revolution that will finally admit *supernatural* forces in science, you are likely to respond with all the indifference his appeal deserves: "Sure, Darwin. Whatever. *Hey,* do you happen to know if the milk in the refrigerator is still good today?"

This is not to say, however, that we can be indifferent about bullshit because bullshit is indifferent to truth. Rather, we can be indifferent to it precisely because we are aware of its attempt to pragmatically manipulate truth (or truths) and make one kind of appeal or engagement appear to be a very different kind of engagement. So understood, the question this bullshit presents to us is not whether this bullshit is true, false or respectful of the distinction, but whether or not it will succeed in its pragmatic attempt to disguise one kind of engagement as another. Will it continue to enlist bullshit-believing supporters and advocates?

This leads to a second, *moral* reason for why we go easier on bullshit and bullshitters. Unlike the liar, who deliberately obscures what he takes to be true, bullshitters may often be honest and sincere. The common expression that a person "believes his own bullshit" is of some use here, the believing bullshitter having no appreciation for the manner in which bull- shit's component parts have been fashioned to fit together. Philip Johnson, for example, is probably *not* a sincere bullshit- ter in so far as he speaks about the different parts of his agenda for the ID movement in isolation from each other, using differ- ent language and different rhetorical styles for the appropriate audiences. But those who are lured to ID by its talking-points (such as the claim that biology is wracked by "controversy" over the adequacy of evolutionary theory) may have no idea that their impressions rest on strategizing, wordsmithing, issue-fram- ing, and public relations. So, when your annoying co-worker comes by with his daily update about the immanent collapse of Darwinism, you may even begin to feel sorry for him. He's been duped, taken-in. He is not even an active bullshitter, for he is merely passing along the bullshit that he himself fell for. There, but for the grace of some critical thinking, go I.

In some circumstances, we may even sympathize with active, deliberate bullshitters. Shortly after Judge Jones's ruling that ID is concealed creationism, for example, ID organizer Stephen Meyer publicly defied this ruling by asserting the opposite: "Contrary to media reports," he wrote, "intelligent design is not a religious-based idea, but instead an evidence-based scientific

theory about life's origins—one that challenges strictly material-
istic views of evolution."[9] Artists and playwrights know that this
kind of supreme confidence fascinates us. Here, we are not far
from the boundless, American optimism shared by Arthur
Miller's Willy Loman, Al Pacino's bank robber in *Dog Day
Afternoon*, and the positive-thinking salesmen in David Mamet's
Glengary Glen Ross, ever-sure that things are looking up for
them, that their *big deal* is just a phone call away—but, of
course, only if they play it *just right*. In ID's case, this optimism
would seem to lie behind its knack for successive reinvention,
with "Intelligent Design" rescuing the failed creation-science
movement, and now (it appears) a new program, "Critical
Analysis of Evolution," waiting in the wings to rescue the falter-
ing ID campaign.[10] With just the right language, and just the
right kind of public relations campaign, creationists seem to
think, they will eventually take the world by storm. Until they
do, however, failures will always be viewed as minor setbacks
and attributed to misunderstandings, inaccurate "media reports,"
and anything but the fundamental incoherence of the plan or
the dubious quality of the product in question. Here, the bullshitter is concerned about truth in a slightly different way: he
clings to the bullshit he originally created to deceive others in a
bid to *avoid* the bitter truth of his own failure or defeat.

Finally, we tolerate bullshit because it indirectly expresses
basic cultural values that we admire and uphold. That tolerance
does not extend to bullshit's insincerity, of course, but it does
extend to the myriad beliefs, practices, and discourses that serve
as bullshit's raw materials. Were it not for the relentless efforts
of ID's devotees to commandeer high school biology classes, for
example, most scientists, educators, and philosophers would not
even take pains to criticize the movement or its claims. Like the
many cultures and subcultures that dot the modern landscape,
ID-advocates are free to cultivate their own understandings
about "how things really are," and, in the United States, at least,
they enjoy constitutional and civil protections to speak their
minds. We may regret that they promote their own agendas

---

[9] "Not by Chance," *National Post of Canada* (1st December 2005).
[10] Lesson plans for teaching "Critical Analysis of Evolution" in high schools can be
at the creationist Discovery Institute's website, discovery.

duplicitously and at the expense of other people's concerns and practices, but we can hardly regret this pluralism and variety itself.

The Case for Purism about Bullshit

So, if bullshit taps into our sympathies for others who have been taken in, and reflects the myriad beliefs and agendas that make modern life go, you might think that our culture is knee-deep in it. You'd get the same impression from the common use of the word 'bullshit'. Yet that impression would be wrong. One implication of this pragmatic definition of bullshit is that there's really *not* quite that much of it about. It has a specific pragmatic structure, does not come into being by accident, and is certainly not very effective unless it is crafted with good measures of creativity and pragmatic intelligence in the use of language. All that is obscured, however, by our casual use of "Bullshit!" or "That's just bullshit" to express disagreement, disapproval, or disappointment about, more or less, anything at all.

But if you look at things from any bullshitter's point of view, all this vagueness and misidentification of bullshit is a good thing. The less discerning we are about bullshit, the less able we are to identify the real thing when it comes along. So, when your significant other announces that your relationship is over, for instance, you should not say "that's bullshit!" It's not. Yes, saying "Gee, that's very bad news for me. I'm sorry to learn of it" doesn't seem appropriate to the occasion. But bad news is not bullshit. Nor is a White House official's claim that the citizens of some oil-rich nation, but for its controlling dictator, are eager to embrace Western-style democracy and economic markets. These are just announcements which—semantics, again— may be true or false, credible or incredible, clear or unclear. They are not bullshit.

Bullshit, instead, is your significant other's effort to part ways through very different means—such as conversations about feeling misunderstood, or smothered, or something feeling "not right"—that just might lead to a mutual, blame-free breakup. Bullshit, instead, is being informed that this dictator possesses nuclear weapons and soon plans to use them on ~~ies~~ and neighboring nations. Indeed, I suspect it will only be ~~sible~~ to understand the seemingly magical power of language to persuade and manipulate individual and popular opinion when we begin to appreciate bullshit as a specific and precise creation, like a poem or symphony with multiple, inter-connected layers of meaning that are intelligently designed and artfully orchestrated.[11]

---

[11] Special thanks to Gary Hardcastle for reading several drafts of this essay and bullshitting me about the problems he found.

ALITY *OF* THE OBJECT WHICH IS ESSE

4

Bullshit and the Foibles of the Human Mind, or: What the Masters of the Dark Arts Know

KENNETH A. TAYLOR

Public discourse in our times is in many ways debased. It contains a depressing stew of bullshit, propaganda, spin, and outright lies. The sources of these debasements are many. Those who seek to distract, manipulate, scam or mislead have full and easy access to the instruments of mass representation, communication and persuasion, while those who aim merely to speak the truth, no matter how discomforting or inconvenient, or to advocate for hard, but necessary choices struggle to be heard.

Political discourse is the outstanding example. Politicians and their handlers typically subject us to an unrelenting stream of manipulative, mendacious misinformation, designed to mobilize the angry and dishearten the sober. We are seldom treated as democracy's primary and essential stakeholders, hardly ever treated to an honest, systematic and fair-minded exploration of the issues that face us, the cost and benefits of the available alternatives, or the real potential winners and losers of our policy choices. And politics is by no means the only contributor to the debasement of the public sphere. We are enticed by the hypnotic techniques of contemporary marketing into ever more buying and consumption, with hardly a concern for the downside costs of that consumption. Night after night on the so-called news, we are numbed by stories that momentarily titillate or shock, but seldom offer meat for sober reflection or lasting enlightenment.

It would be easy to lay blame for the debased state of public discourse in our times squarely and solely on the shoulders of those who purvey this endless stream of propaganda, bullshit,

49

spin and outright lies. Certainly, in these times, the production of bullshit, propaganda, and spin have been exquisitely honed into high, if dark, arts.[1] Nor is it altogether surprising that the bullshitting arts, as I will call the whole lot, should have reached such exalted heights. Given a putatively open public square, in which competing interests must freely contend for control of the means of shared representation and persuasion, the bullshitting arts could not dominate without being highly developed, insidious and infectious.

In a totalitarian state, by contrast, these arts can afford to remain crude and underdeveloped. Such a state exercises exclusive control over the means of public representation and persuasion. And it reserves onto itself the right to bludgeon citizens into at least the pretense of belief when official bullshit and its cousins fail to persuade of their own powers. Where the bullshitting arts are not backed by the power to bludgeon, they must stand entirely on their own and win dominance over the means of public representation and persuasion through their own art and artifice. Though one might antecedently have hoped that in an open marketplace of ideas, good discourse would spontaneously drive out bad, the purveyors of bullshit have proven themselves more than adequate to the seemingly daunting task of dominating large swaths of the marketplace. Over the air, on the printed page, in public debate, even in the lecture halls of the academy, bullshit confronts us at every turn.[2]

But the purveyors of bullshit, propaganda, spin and the outright lie cannot sell what we do not buy. So the fault for the pervasiveness of bullshit must lie partly within ourselves. The human mind is a powerful instrument, one of natural selection's most amazing products. It's the creator of art, science, and philosophy. It has spawned complex forms of social life and a

---

[1] I use the term 'bullshit' for a broader range of phenomena than Harry Frankfurt does. My focus here is less on one-on-one bullshit, and more on what we might call official, institutional bullshit.

[2] There is by now a vast and varied literature, written from a variety of scientific or political perspectives, on techniques of mass persuasion and propaganda and on how and why it works on the human mind. For a few recent and classical examples see Anthony Pratkanis and Elliot Aronson, *Age of Propaganda: The Everyday Use and Abuse of Persuasion* (New York: Freeman, 1992); Edward S. Herman and Noam Chomsky, *Manufacturing Consent: The Political Economy of the Mass Media* (New York: Pantheon, 2002); Edward Bernays, *Propaganda* (New York: Ig, 2004 [1928]), and Philip M. Taylor, *Munitions of the Mind: A History of Propaganda* (Manchester: Manchester University Press, 2003).

dizzying variety of cultural formations. Yet, for all its astounding cognitive and cultural achievements, that very same mind not only produces, but is regularly taken in by bullshit, propaganda, spin, and the outright lie. Our susceptibility to these is, I shall argue, deeply rooted in the very architecture of the human mind. The human mind is afflicted with certain built-in architectural foibles and limits that render it permanently susceptible to a host of manipulations. Wherever there are humans cognizing, there is bound to be a niche for the bullshit artist, for purveyors of easy and comforting falsehoods or half-truths.

To be sure, no one self-consciously and explicitly says to herself, "That is pure bullshit, but I will take it at face value, nonetheless." Like its cousins, the outright lie or the self-serving spin, bullshit works best when we don't recognize it or acknowledge it for what it is. It's most effective when we are blind to its effects. This is not to deny that we sometimes do willingly, if not quite knowingly or consciously, *co-operate* with the bullshit artist, the spinner, or even the liar. Allowing oneself to be taken in by a misrepresentation, but not quite consciously so, is, perhaps, an effective means of self-deception, one requiring less torturous mental gymnastics than the wholly self-driven variety. But even granting our propensity to believe the comforting falsehood over the discomforting truth, it is not altogether easy to explain why there is so very much bullshit and other forms of misrepresentation around, why we are so often taken in by it, and why we find it so hard to distinguish bullshit from its contraries. I address the bulk of this essay to these questions and focus on just a few of the many foibles of the human mind that render it liable to be taken in by bullshit and other forms of misrepresentation.

Some Cognitive Foibles of the Human Mind

In recent decades, cognitive and evolutionary psychologists have logged a depressing catalog of the foibles of the human mind. For all our amazing cognitive achievements as a species, human cognition turns out to be a bewitching stew of the good and the bad. We are subject to confirmation bias, prone to self-deception, and bad at many and diverse forms of reasoning—including statistical reasoning, reasoning about conditionals, and the assessment of risks and rewards.

Consider the run-up to the war in Iraq. Many putatively authoritative voices in the administration and the media told us repeatedly that we would be welcomed as liberators, that stockpiles of WMD were present in Iraq, that Iraq bore some vague connection to 9/11, that the war would be quick, cheap, and largely financed by Iraqi oil. Far off center stage, a few dissenting voices could be heard whispering that none of it was so. By and large, the public ignored those voices and bought the tale they were told by the putatively more authoritative voices shouting from center stage. I am not at present concerned with what led to widespread acceptance of the initial tale in the first place, but rather with the persistence of belief in that tale long after an ever-increasing body of evidence spoke decisively against it. Though belief in the wisdom of the war is at this writing far less widespread than it once was, there is no doubt that for a long while certain falsehoods held a vice-grip on the minds of many in ways that rendered those beliefs at least temporarily impervious to any subsequent disconfirming evidence.

This vice-grip reflects what social psychologists call confirmation bias—the tendency to notice and seek out things that confirm one's beliefs, and to ignore, avoid, or undervalue the relevance of things that would disconfirm one's beliefs.[3] Confirmation bias is not a merely occasional affliction of the human mind. It's deeply ingrained and endemic to it. Confirmation bias helps to explain the imperviousness of already adopted beliefs to contravening evidence and it also helps to explain our tendency to overestimate our own epistemic reliability. If one believes some proposition, then one typically will also believe that one has good reason for believing that very proposition. We tend, that is, not to believe that our beliefs are ungrounded or ill-formed. And we tend to reject not just evidence inconsistent with already adopted beliefs, but also evidence that would tend to challenge our own epistemic reliability or authority. So if one believes Bush's rationale for the Iraq

---

[3] The psychological literature on confirmation bias is vast. For early studies documenting this phenomenon, see P.C. Wason, "On the Failure to Eliminate Hypotheses in a Conceptual Task," *Quarterly Journal of Experimental Psychology* 12 (1960); P.C. Wason, "Reasoning," in B.M. Foss, ed., *New Horizons in Psychology I* (Harmondsworth: Penguin, 1966). Among more recent studies see R.S. Nickerson, "Confirmation Bias: A Ubiquitous Phenomenon in Many Guises," *Review of General Psychology* 2 (1998).

BARRIER IN THE WAY OF PERSPICUOUS THINKING; SO THAT IT EQUALLY I

war, then one will tend also to believe that it is perfectly reasonable to believe Bush's rationale, that one was not being duped or deceived into believing that rationale, and that any reasonable person would share one's belief. Such confidence, even when undeserved, will lead one to reject not just evidence suggesting that what Bush said was false, but any evidence suggesting that one was foolhardy or in some ways irrational in accepting that rationale. By the lights of the true believer, the person who rejects Bush's rationale for the war is not just mistaken but irrational, or in some way self-deceived. It is not the believer who is a dupe or a fool, but the unbeliever. But the deeper point is that any evidence that the skeptic might muster to try to convince the true believer otherwise is, in effect, antecedently discounted before the argument ever begins.

Confirmation bias helps to explain our dogged resistance to changing our beliefs.[4] But it may appear that confirmation bias must play only a negligible role in the *initial* formation of new beliefs. As such, it may appear to be of little aid to the propagandist or the bullshit artist in gaining initial leverage over our beliefs. Though there is a certain truth to this, we should not underestimate the extent to which confirmation bias aids the spread of bull. One has only to consider the rise of information cocoons like Fox News, right wing talk radio, Air America, and the fragmented and unruly blogosphere. Information cocoons systematically promote a certain narrow range of views and outlooks and systematically misrepresent or exclude alternative points of view and competing sources of evidence. That more and more Americans self-consciously seek their news and information from information cocoons is the direct result of confirmation bias run rampant. Though the creators of such cocoons are merely responding to our own self-generated demand, they are nonetheless able to exert great influence over public discourse through their highly skilled management of such cocoons. Once an information consumer's confirmation bias has led her to give herself over to the managers of an information cocoon, she has, I suggest, made herself easy pickings for the propagandist, the spinner, and the bullshit artist.

---

[4] Explaining why exactly we should be liable to confirmation bias at all is, of course, an entirely different matter. I will not try to give an answer here.

There are, to be sure, a host of foibles of the mind that more directly and immediately affect the initial formation of our beliefs—and preferences—rather than just the dogged maintenance of them. I have in mind our susceptibility to framing effects on the formation of beliefs and preferences.[5] Imagine that the US government is preparing for an outbreak of the Avian flu. Suppose that without intervention the disease is expected to kill, say, six thousand people. Two alternative programs to combat the disease have been proposed. The exact scientific estimates of the consequences of each program are as follows:

> If Program A is adopted, two thousand people will be saved.

> If program B is adopted, there is one-third chance that six thousand people will be saved and a two-thirds chance that no one will be saved.

When experimental subjects are asked to choose between these programs, seventy-two percent choose program A, while twenty-eight percent choose program B.

Notice that the "expected return" in lives saved of the two programs is identical. So why are subjects not indifferent between the two programs? Because we tend to be *risk averse* when we choose between outcomes all of which have a positive expected return. That is, people tend to prefer a sure thing to a risky thing of equal or greater expected return when both expected returns are positive. This means that people tend to prefer the certainty of saving two thousand lives over an alternative that risks losing more lives, even if that alternative involves the possibility that more lives will be saved. In preferring A to B, people assign disproportionately greater weight to the two thousand additional lives that might be lost than to the additional four thousand lives that might be saved by pursuing program B.

---

[5] This example is adapted from a discussion in D. Kahneman and A. Tversky, "Prospect Theory: An Analysis of Decision under Risk," *Econometrica* (1979). Reprinted in Kahneman and Tversky, *Choices, Values, and Frames* (Cambridge: Cambridge University Press, 2000).

Now consider an alternative scenario that is typically presented to a different set of experimental subjects. As before, the government is preparing for an outbreak of the Avian flu. Two programs are being contemplated in response to the outbreak. The exact scientific estimates of the effectiveness of the programs look like this:

If program C is adopted, four thousand people will die.

If program D is adopted, there is a one-third chance that no one will die and a two-thirds chance that six thousand people will die.

Presented with a choice between programs C and D, seventy-eight percent of experimental subjects will choose program D, while twenty-two percent choose program C. Again, the expected return, this time in lives lost, is identical on the two programs. And again, we might wonder why subjects should prefer plan D to plan C. The answer is that people tend to be *risk seeking* with respect to losses. This means that people tend to prefer pursuing the chance that no one will die—even if it pursuing that chance means running the risk of more deaths— to the certainty that fewer will die. In preferring D to C, people are, in effect, assigning disproportionately less weight to the two thousand additional lives that might be lost than to the four thousand additional lives that might be saved by pursuing plan D over plan C.

What is striking about these results is the fact that program C and program A are *identical programs*. They are merely described differently—one in terms of lives lost, the other in terms of lives saved. If we pursue program A, two thousand people will be saved. But that just means that four thousand will die who otherwise might not have. *Exactly* this set of outcomes is envisioned by program C. Similarly, programs B and D also envision the same exact outcomes, with just the same probabilities. But B describes those outcomes in terms of lives saved, while D describes those outcomes in terms of lives lost. It seems painfully obvious that whatever rational basis there can be for preferring A to B, or vice versa, obtains equally well for the choice between C to D. But over and over again, experimenters find the choice between equivalent scenarios to be highly sensitive to the way in which the choice is framed.

Our sensitivity to the way a set of alternatives is "framed," together with our insensitivity to that which is invariant across different ways of framing the same set of alternatives provides powerful leverage for purveyors of spin, propaganda, and bull. To take a not altogether fanciful example, imagine two politicians, Smith and Jones. Smith wants to convince the voters that program A (that is, C) ought to be pursued. She wants to do so because program A will be highly beneficial to a pharmaceutical company that has made significant contributions to her campaign. On the other hand, because a certain medical supply company will benefit highly from program D (that is, B) Jones wants to convince the voters that program D (that is, B) ought to be pursued. Smith knows that if she succeeds in framing the choice in terms of potential lives saved, she has a better chance of swaying the voters. Jones knows that if she succeeds in framing the issue in terms of potential lives lost, her arguments have a better chance of swaying the voters. Neither has an incentive to point out the frame-invariant regularities. Both have an incentive for exploiting our susceptibility to framing effects. To that extent, they co-operate in jointly misleading the voter into thinking that he has been subject to a real debate about competing options fairly and dispassionately considered. In reality, he has been no more than fodder in a war over the framing of the issues.[6]

Another kind of framing effect has to do with simple if-then reasoning. Human beings have a complex understanding of the causal structure of the world, more so than any other creature on this planet. It would not be unreasonable to expect that we as a species must be rather adept a simple if-then reasoning. Not just our understanding of the causal structure of the physical world, but all of social life would seem to be founded on our capacity for if-then reasoning. But, surprisingly, we are not as adept at such reasoning as one might antecedently have expected. Consider the so-called Wason selection task. That task tests for the ability to falsify conditional hypotheses. Here is a

---

[6] George Lakoff has recently diagnosed American political discourse as a war over frames. See his *Moral Politics: How Liberals and Conservatives Think* (Chicago: University of Chicago Press, 2002).

typical experimental set-up. Subjects are given four cards. They are told that each card has a number on one side and a letter on the other. They are asked to name those cards and only those cards which should be turned over in order to determine whether the following rule is true or false of these four cards:

If a card has the letter D on one side, it has the number 3 on the other

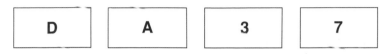

Applying straight-forward propositional logic, the correct cards are the D card and the 7 card. If a D is on the other side of the 7, then the rule is falsified. If anything other than a 3 is on the other side of the D card, the rule will be falsified again.

Subjects perform remarkably poorly on this task. Typically, less than twenty-five percent of subjects give the correct choice. Indeed, in some version of Wason's original experiment this was as low as five percent. The most frequent choices are that only the D card need be turned over or that the D card together with the 3 card should be turned over. The 7 card is *seldom* chosen by subjects. Moreover, subjects are remarkably resistant to training on this task. If shown the correct response for a particular run, they get the point, but they seem to lack the ability to generalize to new runs of essentially the same task.

Notice that turning over the 3 card cannot falsify the rule. Whatever is on the other side of the 3 card is consistent with the rule. So there is a weak sense in which the 3 card might be thought to "confirm" the rule. Perhaps that is why subjects tend to turn it over. So we may be seeing our old friend confirmation bias rearing its head again.

The persistent inability of subjects to perform well on this and other tests that would seem to require little more than a certain minimal logical acumen has tempted many to conclude that human cognition is irredeemably irrational. But that conclusion is hasty and crude. For one thing, whatever can be said for the rational powers of this or that individual mind, our amazing cognitive achievements as a species suggest that human cognition, taken as a whole, must be one of natural selection's most consequential innovations. Only the first advent of sexual reproduction, I suspect, was more consequential. I do not mean to deny that most of us probably are destined for some degree of cognitive mediocrity. But the real key to our cognitive success as a species rests, I conjecture, on our evolved capacity for culture. Where cultural mechanisms function to spread the benefits of one or more individual's cognitive innovations and successes to others, it is not necessary that everyone be an Einstein, Newton or Leonardo. In effect, our shared capacity for shared culture enables the many to free-ride on the cognitive achievements of the few. This is a fortunate fact indeed and another testament to natural selection's sheer brilliance at mind-design.

Even granting that many or most of us may be cognitive free-riders on the astounding cognitive achievements of the few, it would still be a mistake to conclude too hastily that human minds are *irredeemably* irrational. Sometimes, in fact, our sensitivity to framing effects works to give our minds a greater semblance of rationality. For example, performance on Wason Selection Tasks is known to improve dramatically when the conditional in question is "re-framed" in terms of something like a social contract. You are a bartender. Your task is to see that there is no underage drinking. That is, you must see to it that the following conditional is true: If someone is drinking beer, then she must be older than 21. Which cards should you turn over?

drinking beer	drinking coke	25 years old	16 years old

From a purely logical point of view, this problem has exactly the same structure as the earlier one. Nonetheless, subjects perform significantly better on the second version of the task than on the first.

Some evolutionary psychologists have concluded on the basis of this sort of data that natural selection has endowed the human mind with a special purpose "cheater detection" module.[7] Since the making and enforcing of social contracts of vary-

---

[7] See L. Cosmides and J. Tooby, "Cognitive Adaptations for Social Exchange," in Barkow, Cosmides, and Tooby, eds., *The Adapted Mind: Evolutionary Psychology and the Generation of Culture* (Oxford: Oxford University Press, 1992) for an example of this approach.

ing scope and complexities is no doubt a core human competence, it would not be at all surprising if we were somehow naturally and specially adapted to be able to determine swiftly and
reliably whether a contract was being respected or violated. Still,
it is striking that we are apparently unable to generalize, to
transport what works in a given problem domain to different but
structurally similar problem domains. The evolutionary psychologist concludes, partly on the basis of such inability, that our
minds are not general-purpose problem solving machines.
Rather, they were specifically adapted to solve specific cognitive
problems that were of recurring significance in the environments for which we are evolved. Often those recurring problems came with what we might call built-in frames that enabled
certain structures in our mind to quickly and effortlessly recognize the kind of reasoning that had to be applied. In his book,
How the Mind Works (New York: Norton, 1997), Stephen Pinker
puts it nicely:

> No organism needs content-free algorithms applicable to any prob-
> lem no matter how esoteric. Our ancestors encountered certain
> problems for hundreds of millions of years—recognizing objects,
> making tools, learning the local language, finding a mate, predict-
> ing an animal's movements, finding their way—and encountered
> certain other problems never—putting a man on the moon, grow-
> ing better popcorn, proving Fermat's last theorem. The knowledge
> that solves a familiar kind of problem is often irrelevant to any
> other one. The effect of slant on luminance is useful in calculating
> shape but not in assessing the fidelity of a potential mate. The
> effects of lying on tone of voice help with fidelity but not with
> shape. Natural selection does not care about the ideals of liberal
> education and should have no qualms about building parochial
> inference modules that exploit eons-old regularities in their own
> subject matters. (p. 304)

If this is right, then it is not altogether surprising that at least
some framing effects actually improve the functioning of the
human mind. And that conclusion provides some grounds for
hope that if we could always but frame matters rightly, much
cognitive detritus might well be swept away. Once again, we
see that for good or for ill, he who controls the frame may well
control all.

Reclaiming the Public Square

Our all-too brief examination of just a few of the many cognitive foibles of the human mind supports both a bleak conclusion and a more hopeful one. The hopeful conclusion is that our minds appear to be finely tuned instruments, well adapted for solving the plethora of recurrent cognitive challenges that were endemic in the information processing environments of our hunter-gather progenitors. To the extent that contemporary information processing environments match those in which we were designed to function, our cognitive capacities serve us well. Unfortunately, the modern world subjects human cognition to stresses and strains unlike anything encountered on the ancient savannah. We are bombarded with information and misinformation in a dizzying variety, often intentionally framed in ways unsuited for our natural cognitive capacities. The mismatch between our cognitive capacities and the informational environments in which we now find ourselves partly explains both why there is so much bull, spin, and propaganda about, and why we are so often taken in by it.

Now it bears stressing that the fundamental cognitive architecture of the human mind was fixed eons ago on the ancient savannah. So my claim is not that contemporary humans, as such, are any more or less susceptible to bullshit and other forms of misrepresentation than humans have ever been. Our minds are as they have always been. Only our circumstances have changed. Nor do I wish to deny the evident powers and achievements of the evolved human mind. The long march of human history has decisively established what a wondrous instrument the human mind is. It has scaled great cognitive heights. It has peered deeply into the innermost secrets of the natural world; it has given rise to cultures and to social formations complex and various; and it has even plumbed the depths of its own operations.

Lest I be accused of nostalgia for some bygone cognitive order, let me stress that I am fully aware that in every age and epoch, the mind has produced a profuse abundance of cognitive detritus. In every age of humankind, superstition, illusion, and falsehood of every variety has existed along side the highest art and deepest knowledge that the age has mustered. Moreover, we are blessed to live at a time when human beings collectively have scaled greater cognitive heights than humans ever have before. We see far more deeply into the workings of everything natural and human. So how could it possibly be that there is more cognitive detritus about in our own times?

The answer is, I think, twofold. First, the masters of bullshit, propaganda, and spin have paradoxically been aided by our improved the understanding of the workings of the human mind. In our times, the masters of the dark arts are astute students of the enduring foibles of the human mind. Second, the means of public representations and persuasion available to the masters of the dark arts have a vastly greater reach and efficacy than they have ever had. Consequently, in our own times, the masters of the dark arts are vastly more effective than their predecessors could have dreamt of being.

I don't mean to say that those who seek a hearing for sweet reason in the public square have no weapons of their own. The battle must be waged on at least two different fronts. First, it must be waged in the trenches of education. We must seek to instill in our children distaste for all dogma, an enduring suspicion of all easy and comforting falsehoods. We must instill in them an insatiable appetite for unyielding argument, a propensity to seek out and confront even the most disquieting evidence, even if doing so would undermine their or our most cherished beliefs. They must learn never to take at face value frames that are merely given. They must learn the skills of reframing, the habit of asking after that which is invariant across alternative frames. If our children are educated in this way, their minds will provide far less fertile ground for the spread of bullshit.

Though such a mind-by-mind slog in the trenches of education is necessary, it will not suffice. In addition, we must reconfigure the very means of public representation and persuasion. In our times, a narrow, self-serving elite, interested mostly in its own power, wealth and prestige enjoys a certain privileged access to the means of public representations and persuasion. We must seek to diminish that access by all the ways and means available to us—via the fragmented and unregulated internet, via politics, in still unoccupied small niches of the mass media. The purveyors of institutional and official bullshit will of course not yield easily. They are powerful, clever, and determined. Moreover, experience bears ample witness to the fact that good discourse does not spontaneously drive out bad. Neither, however, will bad discourse wither on its own. If bullshit is to be driven from the public square, only those who seek more than bullshit can drive it out. So let the battle be joined.

5
Bullshit and Personality

SARA BERNAL

Some bullshit is public and political. Other bullshit is more private, arising in interpersonal interactions. Yet other bullshit is more private still, arising within a single individual: people sometimes bullshit themselves.

Many of those of us who oppose the war in Iraq see the present cultural moment as one particularly rich in bullshit. But in this era of heightened public bullshit, private bullshit should not be overlooked. It seems to me that bullshit is at the core of many of the problems encountered and created by those afflicted with so-called *personality disorders*—those who have certain severe problems with navigating the social world.[1] Accordingly, I will propose an analysis of bullshit that may be usefully applied to the psychology of personality disorders, and perhaps more widely in psychiatry.

My analysis takes Harry Frankfurt's justly famous account as a point of departure. The departure is rapid: I disagree with his main contention, that bullshit is essentially unconnected to a concern with truth. I think many core cases of bullshit are better captured by an account on which bullshit has a stronger connection to the truth than Frankfurt countenances. What's more, applying this notion of bullshit to personality disorders tells us

---

[1] I do not mean to suggest that impairment of social cognition is unique to personality disorders—impaired social cognition of various sorts is characteristic of autism, schizophrenia, and psychopathy, among others. But a personality disorder is, in the first instance, a certain kind of difficulty with navigating the social world.

something interesting about why their core features lead to social difficulties, and sheds light on them in other ways as well.

Does the Bullshitter Pay Attention to the Truth?

Frankfurt claims that an "indifference to how things really are" is of the essence of bullshit. Bullshitters say whatever they need to say to achieve a certain purpose, without regard for the truth of what they say. Thus for him, bullshit is very different from lying:

> Both in lying and in telling the truth people are guided by their beliefs concerning the way things are . . . Someone who lies and someone who tells the truth are playing on opposite sides, so to speak, in the same game . . . The bullshitter . . . does not reject the authority of the truth, as the liar does, and oppose himself to it. He pays no attention to it at all. (*On Bullshit*, pp. 59–61)

While this may be true in some instances, Frankfurt fails to acknowledge that in the typical case, the bullshitter is strongly connected to the truth *via* a desire to obscure a specific part of it. This desire may be more or less conscious. The bullshitter may have that part of the truth in mind clearly or fuzzily, or it may be in some mental compartment to which she has no immediate conscious access.

Consider a prototypical case of bullshit: the undergraduate who knows that she has nothing thoughtful or deep to say on an assigned essay topic, and that her opinions are not as well informed by the course material as they should be, but who aims to prevent her instructor from realizing all this by throwing up a screen of verbiage. She may be clearly aware of the awkward facts behind her screen. Or she may just know "deep down" that there is a mess behind it, so that she is not surprised if her ruse fails and her grade is poor. Undergraduates do sometimes bullshit with malice aforethought. Sometimes, however, a student may proceed less calculatingly, but still be motivated by a desire to get an A that she knows is not really deserved. In such cases we cannot make sense of the student's behavior except by reference to this unconscious (or partially conscious) motive.

The bullshitter in this example, in both its variants, is like a liar in that she seeks to conceal from her audience some part of the truth (the mess behind her screen). She is *unlike* the liar in that she need not be clearly aware of this goal. She is unlike the liar also in that her method is *indirect*: she does not directly deny the truth behind her screen, but rather contrives various ways of implicating the contrary of that truth. Her bullshit is contained not in any single assertion within her essay, but rather by things like a pompous tone, a reluctance to get to the point, and general windiness. Thus her method bears out Frankfurt's observation that a lie is a "more focused act" than an instance of bullshit.

One may bullshit not only by using indirect means to get one's audience to believe the opposite of some part of the truth that one finds inconvenient, but also by simply distracting the audience from that part. In this second type, the bullshitter is again concerned with the truth in that she is motivated by a desire to conceal a specific part of it, and again this desire may be conscious or not.

Two Modes of Bullshit

Advertising and politics are replete with the two kinds of bullshit I've just distinguished. Two examples follow.

a. Indirect Implication of Falsehood

Newport cigarettes are advertised with the phrase "alive with pleasure." This phrase is emblazoned on billboards along with images of young, beautiful and (so far as I know) mostly African-American people in situations of luxurious leisure, such as on a yacht.

This ad campaign aims to plant in its audience the belief that representative smokers of Newports are healthy, vibrant, and wealthy, and that smoking Newports is a badge of membership in this select group. The truth is that representative smokers of Newports are poor, unhealthy African-Americans who live in the rough neighborhoods in which these billboards are so obnoxiously displayed.

b. Distraction

The Bush administration used dubious intelligence reports about Iraqi efforts to obtain yellowcake uranium from Niger, suggestions that Saddam Hussein was somehow connected with 9/11, and various other red herrings to direct our attention away

THE UNDERSTANDING, AND THROW ALL INTO CONFUSION, AND LEAD ME

from a key fact: they had an antecedent intention, and perhaps something like a plan, to invade Iraq no matter what.

I do not imagine that these are all the kinds of bullshit there are, but they are two kinds worth paying attention to. Before moving on to further illustrations, I should note some features of this two-part conception.

First, as I've said, bullshit is connected to the truth in a way that Frankfurt does not acknowledge. The bullshitter must *at some level* pay attention to the truth, or else her bullshit is not likely to succeed. The "indirect means" of type (a) must, in order to be effective, be somehow vetted for their ability to jointly implicate a specific falsehood. The distractors of type (b) must lead the audience away from a particular bit of truth, so the bull-shitter—or *something in her*—must be cognizant of what that bit of truth is, or she may end up with something that leads towards it rather than away. Bullshit of both types must be framed in sensitivity to a certain painful bit of the truth, or it will conceal that bit only by dumb luck.

That said, I can agree with an emended version of Frankfurt's claim that the bullshitter "pays no attention at all" to the truth. For a bullshitter can say anything and everything that distracts her audience—except, of course, the truth that she wants to hide! Or she can say anything and everything that jointly impli-cates the opposite of the truth she wants to hide. That is, her utterances must be checked (at some level) not for their corre-spondence with the facts, but for their tendency to distract from, or to implicate the contrary of, certain key facts. So the emended version of Frankfurt's claim is this: the bullshitter must pay atten-tion to just one key part of the truth, namely the part she wants to hide. Call this her target.

Second, bullshit on my conception is related to lying as fol-lows. The bullshitter always differs in her method from the liar: she never denies the target directly and explicitly, but instead distracts or contrives to indirectly implicate the contrary of the target. In the case of fully conscious bullshitting, the differences end there. Just like the liar, one who bullshits consciously has clearly in mind a target truth that she knows she wants to hide. That cannot be said of one who bullshits unconsciously, who therefore differs from the liar in more than her method. Thus the similarity to lying of any given case of bullshit depends on where it falls on the spectrum of conscious awareness. (Recall that I am countenancing degrees of awareness, so that "fully conscious" and "unconscious" are two ends of a spectrum.)

Third, since the bullshitter as I've painted her may not be aware of her wish to obscure her target, my story depends crucially on the assumption that there are unconscious motives. In the typical case, like that of the bullshitting student, she is at least dimly aware of her motive (and hence of her target) as she frames her bullshit, and may become more clearly aware of it in hindsight—after she gets a poor grade on her essay, for instance. But again, the bullshitter may be completely unaware of her obscuring motive.

I cannot describe the operation of the bullshitter's unconscious motive, but I can say a bit more to defend the claim that it is there, however it operates. The idea of an unconscious motive is of course not new. Neither is it the exclusive property of Freudians who would associate the motive with some bodily orifice. It is an idea with some currency in the neuroscience of today: it is commonly held that the bizarre confabulations of some neurology patients can be understood only by reference to unconscious motives.

Consider, for instance, some fascinating and well-known results about *split-brain patients*.[2] These are patients whose corpus callosum has been surgically severed in order to treat their severe epilepsy. The corpus callosum is a thick band of fibers connecting the two hemispheres of the brain. When it is cut, the hemispheres cannot communicate with each other, which can result in bizarre internal conflicts for the patient. One sort of test that was done on these patients was to show a picture to one hemisphere and ask for a report from the other. This is done by showing a picture to one side or the other of a patient's visual field: pictures on the left project to the right hemisphere, and *vice versa*.[3]

It is the left hemisphere that talks—that side is primarily responsible for language. Thus when a split-brain patient sees

---

[2] See M.S. Gazzaniga, *The Bisected Brain* (New York: Appleton-Century-Crofts, 1970); and "The Split Brain in Man" *Scientific American* 217 (1967), pp. 24–29.
[3] More specifically, the picture is *flashed* for an interval of less than one-quarter of a second. This ensures that there is no time to saccade, so we can be sure that the picture is shown to just one hemisphere.

a picture in her left visual field, and she is asked to say what she sees, she has a problem: the information is "stuck" in the non-talking (right) hemisphere. Patients in this situation reacted in a number of different ways: some would just frown and shake their heads; others could at least say what the picture was *not* of. Some, however, would make up stories about their own reactions to what they were shown: they would *confabulate*. It is these cases that are relevant to the present point.

To take just one example, a picture of a naked woman was presented to one patient's left hemisphere, then her right. When it was presented to the left hemisphere, the patient giggled, then accurately described what she saw. When it was presented to the right hemisphere, she smiled mischievously and began to giggle. When asked what was so funny—and this is the startling part—she said, "I don't know . . . nothing . . . Oh, that funny machine" (Gazzaniga 1970, p. 106). Such confabulations are often understood by neuroscientists in terms of an overarching unconscious motive to maintain a stable and internally consistent world-view.[4]

What incoming information might threaten the stability or consistency of the giggling split-brain patient's world view? She has just giggled unaccountably. To uphold her belief that she is a sane, rational person who does things for reasons, and reacts appropriately to situations, she must somehow explain away the fact that she has just giggled slyly for no apparent reason, like a madwoman. Her target, then, is that she has just done something that appears crazy, nonsensical, bizarre. She has an overarching motive—an unconscious one—to maintain her image of herself as a sane, rational person. Her unexplained giggling threatens that world view, since it looks like the behavior of a madwoman. So she has a second motive, derived from the first, to explain her giggling as something quite sane and rational (Who wouldn't laugh at "that funny machine"?). It is commonly accepted that patients who confabulate in this way have some such unconscious motive, though there is as yet no fully worked-out, generally accepted story about how this motive

---

[4] V.S. See Ramachandran and S. Blakeslee, *Phantoms in the Brain* (New York: Morrow, 1998).

operates. Thus my own claim of unconscious motives is in good company—in this regard at least.

Fourth, while bullshit à la Frankfurt seems to be a largely verbal affair, the misleading and distracting of bullshit as I construe it may be achieved by non-verbal as well as verbal means.[5] The photos that appear in Newport ads provide one example; I'll discuss further examples below.

Fifth, bullshit as I construe it may occur *intra*personally. That is, you can bullshit yourself in either of the ways I've distinguished. The person who distracts from a painful part of the truth and the distractee may be one and the same; the person who contrives to implant a belief contrary to that truth may be the same person in whom the belief is implanted. Such self-bullshitting is a species of self-deception. Indeed, it may be all that self-deception is. Whether that is so is a large question on a rich topic (self-deception), and I cannot answer it here.

There are, however, some differences between self- and other-bullshitting. *Conscious* self-bullshitting is less straightforward than conscious bullshitting of others, if indeed it is possible at all. This is so for the same reason that explicitly lying to yourself is impossible. To do that you would have to be fully aware of some proposition p and at the same time assert not-p to yourself with the intention of getting yourself to believe not-p—an endeavor that would seem futile in the face of your established belief that p. To consciously self-bullshit you would have to deviously attempt to get yourself to believe not-p, though you are fully aware of p's truth, either by implicating not-p or by distracting from p. This may be possible,[6] but your own clear awareness of p introduces a difficulty with self-bullshitting about p that is absent from other-bullshitting about p. But having noted this complication, I can set it aside, as the cases of self-bullshitting I shall consider are not fully conscious.

---

[5] Frankfurt notes in passing that *humbug*, as glossed by Max Black—a precursor to his own notion of bullshit—"may be accomplished by words or by deeds" (pp. 10–11). But it is not clear that this is meant to be a feature of bullshit as he construes it.

[6] You could start out with a clear awareness of p, but still succeed in distracting yourself from that painful truth, without actually unseating your belief; or you could in implicating the contrary of p get yourself to question your previous confidence in p.

Finally, it is an advantage of my account that, unlike Frankfurt's, it has application in psychiatry. In particular, it nicely frames some key features of personality disorders.

Bullshit and Personality Disorders

Some people have bullshit deeply embedded in their personalities. Everyone knows that politics and advertising are replete with bullshit. It is not as widely appreciated that certain problematic personalities are also goldmines of bullshit. Indeed, so far as I know the concept has never been applied in any systematic way to personality psychology (or elsewhere in psychiatry, for that matter). Yet if you examine the strategems that characterize personality disorders, the bullshit fairly leaps out at you.

What Is a Personality Disorder?

A personality disorder is defined in the DSM-IV (the current *Diagnostic and Statistical Manual*, the bible of psychiatry) as "an enduring pattern of inner experience and behavior that deviates markedly from the expectations of the individual's culture."[7] To count as having such a disorder, one must have difficulties in two or more of the following areas: perception of the social world and one's place in it; appropriateness and range of emotional responses; social interaction; and impulse control. The problematic pattern must be inflexible, and must be manifest in a broad range of situations. It is especially distinctive of personality disorders, among psychiatric disorders, to cause trouble and pain not just for the afflicted but for those around her as well.

Personality disorders are standardly characterized as encompassing *maladaptiveness* in several domains. First, they comprise maladaptive *traits*. These traits are normal, healthy traits taken to an extreme degree, and sometimes combined in especially problematic ways. Thus, conscientiousness taken to an extreme degree becomes obsessive-compulsiveness; very low trust combined with high hostility becomes paranoia. The mal-

---

[7] R. Larsen and D. Buss, *Personality Psychology* (New York: McGraw-Hill, 2005), p. 608. American Psychiatric Association, *Diagnostic and Statistical Manual of Mental Disorders-IV*, 1994.

adaptive *motivation* characteristic of personality disorders is exemplified in the antisocial personality's complete lack of motivation for intimacy. Maladaptive patterns in perceiving, interpreting, and planning—aspects of *cognition*—are also ubiquitous in personality disorders. The afflicted are especially challenged when it comes to perceiving and interpreting the social world: each personality disorder is marked by distorted perception of others and impaired social judgment. Each personality disorder is also characterized by some abnormal and maladaptive pattern of *emotion*: extreme volatility, perhaps, or an extreme of one emotion such as anger. Finally, the *self-concept* of a disordered personality tends to be out of whack: often, she doesn't know quite who she is, lacking a clear, stable sense of herself; or her self esteem is either excessive or deficient.

The *DSM-IV* lists ten personality disorders, arranged into three clusters: the *erratic* cluster, often characterized by unpredictable or violent behavior; the *anxious* cluster, characterized by fear and distress; and the *eccentric* cluster, characterized by social awkwardness or disengagement. Brief descriptions of the disorders, drawn mostly from the *DSM-IV*, are supplied below. Sub-types are sometimes recognized, but the *DSM-IV* lists only the basic or "pure" type.

Here's a clue to where the bullshit lurks in the following list. Where the afflicted is herself out of touch with some key aspect of reality, or where her stock behavior tends to lead others to false beliefs, bullshit is often found.

> *Antisocial personality disorder (erratic).* These people have little concern for others. They are generally impulsive and irresponsible, and often violent. They feel no guilt over the suffering they cause to others. The textbook case of antisocial personality disorder is a violent, crafty, and remorseless criminal. They need not be violent, however: the Enron crew, for example, exhibit antisocial behavior in spades.[8] They are con artists of a sort, and many con artists are diagnosable as antisocial. Antisocials often possess a glib, superficial charm, which allows them to take advantage of the unwary.

---

[8] Thanks to Tom Oltmanns for pointing this out to me.

Borderline personality disorder (erratic). The borderline personality is always riding some kind of roller coaster: her emotions, relationships, and self-image are all marked by wild instability. They can shift rapidly from idealizing to demonizing a partner or friend. They are terrified of abandonment, and can become very aggressive when they see it on the horizon. They are also prone to harming themselves in the face of real or imagined impending abandonment Suicidal gestures are common in this type; *threats* of suicide ("if you go, I'll kill myself") are still more common.

Histrionic personality disorder (erratic). Histrionics are recognized by their frantic attention-seeking, inappropriate sexual provocativeness, and excessive displays of emotion. They are generally uncomfortable when they are not the center of attention. They are seductive and flirtatious in situations where such behavior is inappropriate— in professional settings, for instance. The textbook case is a female undergraduate who often visits male professors during office hours, devoting her time there to talking about herself in a general way, rather than to legitimate academic business.[9] Histrionic women often wear too much makeup, and dress in clothes that are too sexy and bright. Histrionic men, for their part, are often hyper-macho, boasting of success at work or sexual exploits. Histrionics are shallow in various ways: opinions, friends, and projects may be taken up with great enthusiasm, then quickly dropped. But their enthusiasm can be magnetic: they often possess a kind of meretricious charm.

Narcissistic personality disorder (erratic). The narcissist has an inflated sense of her own importance and accomplishments. Correspondingly, she undervalues the accomplishments of others. When their accomplishments threaten to outshine her own, she responds with violent

---

[9] See *Personality Psychology* and also Theodore Millon, Seth Grossman, Carrie Millon, Sarah Meagher, and Rowena Ramnath, *Personality Disorders in Modern Life, Second Edition* (Hoboken: Wiley, 2004).

envy. She has a strong sense of superiority, and she is elitist: the only people worthy to be her associates are those
whose gifts and accomplishments are in the same exalted
realm as her own. She requires admiration and special
treatment from those around her. She expects lavish
praise and recognition, and may angrily mete out punish-
ment to those who deny her her rightful obeisance. Self-
centered as she is, she has little attention left over for the
needs and desires of others, into which she lacks insight.
Narcissists are often wildly ambitious, and better-func-
tioning ones can be quite successful.

Avoidant personality disorder (anxious). Avoidant personalities have an inferiority complex. They believe
steadfastly that they are inadequate. They cannot abide
criticism—it calls attention to their shortcomings, which
they imagine to be severe—and will go to great lengths
to avoid it. This results in their leading very restricted
lives: potentially rewarding activities and relationships
are shunned out of fear that they will open the door to
criticism.

Dependent personality disorder (anxious). These individuals believe that they are incapable of taking care of
themselves. They require constant reassurance from others, which makes it difficult for them to work independently. Since they depend so heavily on others, they will
generally take a submissive line, suppressing any dissent
they might feel, in order to keep the peace. In extreme
cases this can lead to their withstanding physical abuse in
order to hang on to a "caregiver."

Obsessive-Compulsive personality disorder (anxious).
Obsessive-compulsives are preoccupied with order: rules,
lists, schedules, and all manner of details are very often
on their mental front page. Their perfectionistic pursuit of
order leaves little time for relations with others, which
relations are stunted by this neglect. Leisure activities
have little appeal. Obsessive-compulsives are hard-working to a fault. Their own standards are so high that they
have difficulty delegating tasks to others, who are likely

ANOTHER SUCH DECEPTION IS TO MISTAKE A MERE DIFFERENCE IN THE C

to aim for a lower standard. They are generally very stubborn in their insistence on their own hyper-orderly way.

Schizoid personality disorder (eccentric). Schizoids are intensely solitary, eschewing friendship, often drifting out of contact even with immediate family, and taking jobs that minimize their contact with others. Their emotional lives are very restricted: they come off as cold and affectively flat, and take pleasure in few activities (if any). Sexual relations with others hold no interest for them. They appear indifferent to praise and criticism: if reprimanded for some aspect of their job performance, for instance, they'll return a "does not compute" sort of response.

Schizotypal personality disorder (eccentric). Schizotypals are close relatives of schizoids.[10] But while the schizoid is indifferent to the social world, the schizotypal regards it with suspicion and fear that verges into paranoia. This does not conduce well to social relations with others, which are generally absent from their lives. While the schizoid evinces no affect at all, the schizotypal tends to evince inappropriate affect: a smile in response to a sad story, for instance. Schizotypals are recognized by their odd beliefs and superstitions, clairvoyance and telepathy being special favorites. They often report unusual perceptual experiences, such as seeing the future.

Paranoid personality disorder (eccentric). The paranoiac needs no introduction. Universal distrust is her signature. Utterly benign social gestures may be interpreted as insulting, threatening, or otherwise sinister. Imagined slights become the occasion for grudges that are held indefinitely. A paranoiac's romantic partner has her work cut out for her, as she will often be the object of pathological jealousy. Those who question the irrational beliefs

---

[10] The two disorders are thought to lie on a continuum, known as *schizotypy*, with schizophrenia. There is some evidence for genetic links among the three. Schizotypals are thought to be closer to schizophrenics.

of paranoiacs generally meet with extreme hostility and combativeness, which may turn violent.

This, then, is our cast of colorful characters. Notice that it is of the essence of a personality disorder to be *rigid*. Afflicted individuals will try the same strategy over and over, regardless of its success or failure in the past. Since the strategy is deployed reflexively, rather than with sensitivity to the situation at hand, it tends to fail. Thus for them life becomes like a "bad one-act play that repeats again and again" (*Personality Disorders*, p. 14).

Some of the disorders are diagnosed more frequently in men, others in women: thus diagnosed antisocials are much more likely to be men, dependents and histrionics to be women. But it is not clear that these patterns of diagnosis reflect the truth, since the evidence regarding the epidemiology of personality disorders is questionable.[11] Also, at least some of these patterns are changing: diagnoses of antisocial personality disorder in women appear to be on the rise. For these reasons I have chosen to treat the disorders as gender-neutral.

Some Examples of Bullshit in Personality Disorders

Recall that bullshit of both the types I've identified may be directed to others or to oneself. I'll lay out examples of other-directed bullshit first, then move on to the self-directed variety.

Other-Bullshitting. I'll start with the first type of bullshit I identified, in which the bullshitter contrives some indirect means of implicating, by word or deed, the contrary of the target truth that she would like to hide. The glib charm typical of the antisocial provides an especially dangerous example. Her charm tends to lead people to believe that she is a nice person, while she is in fact a dangerous, nasty piece of work. She does not come right out and say "I am not a nasty piece of work," of course; her charm is what leads her hapless victims to believe that, and to implicitly trust her. This makes it easier for her to take advantage of them.

The suicidal gestures of borderline personalities provide a second example. Consider the standard case, in which a suicide

---

[11] Thanks to Tom Oltmanns for this point.

attempt is provoked by a real or imagined threat of abandonment by a romantic partner. With this maneuver, the borderline seeks to make her partner believe something like: *my relationship with you in particular is so important to me that life without it is not worth living for me.* The partner who believes that would presumably be less likely to leave. The truth is that, since borderlines often vacillate between idealizing a romantic partner and holding him in contempt, the person who is supposedly so important as to be utterly indispensable may be ridiculed and rejected shortly thereafter. And the relationship is not likely to last; the partner will likely soon be replaced with another, with whom the pattern will be repeated.

Histrionic personality disorder is marked by "shallow opinions." A typical histrionic may, for instance, declare a certain writer to be brilliant, despite having little knowledge of her work. Easy come, easy go: she'll relinquish the opinion before too long. In an unwary audience, such declarations might implant the belief that the histrionic is a deep thinker, while she is in fact the opposite.

The case of narcissism is a bit trickier than the others in the Erratic cluster, but a certain sub-type of the disorder, *compensating narcissism*, provides an illustration. While the pure narcissist has a genuinely high opinion of herself, this type seeks to conceal a core of low self-esteem with a charade of superiority. She will, for instance, tirelessly inflate and call attention to her own accomplishments, but unlike the pure narcissist she lacks the conviction that they amount to such a big deal. She depends on accolades from others to counteract her own self-doubt. Thus her charade of superiority, her demands for obeisance and special treatment, can be seen as indirectly implicating the contrary of the painful target truth: that she is not such a grand personage. She generally has some glimmering of her own *modus operandi*; this painful truth is something she tends to be dimly aware of.

As for bullshit of the distracting variety, the sexual provocativeness of the histrionic furnishes a clear illustration. By such means as revealing clothing, body language, eye-batting, veiled invitations, flattery, or coy double-entendres, the histrionic distracts attention from her own flaws. The titillation she achieves in this way serves to blind her audience to the fact that she is getting more than her rightful share of attention—more than she would get if her audience saw things clearly. Unfortunately for the histrionic, this sort of behavior can make her especially vulnerable to sexual victimization.

Self-Bullshitting. I'll begin, again, with the falsehood-implicating type, which in the case of self-bullshitting is the less common variety. There is a type of paranoid known as a *fanatic* who is a close cousin of the compensating narcissist. They are described as having "run hard into reality," a collision which shatters their narcissistic self-image. They cope with the pain that results by retreating into fantasy: they portray themselves as superheroes pitted against an evil world. Their target, then, is the fact that they are not extraordinary. The fantasies they construct contain implicit denials of this fact. The construction of such a fantasy can also distract them from a from harsh reality; thus both types of bullshit are perhaps combined in this instance.

The self-bullshitter excels particularly at self-distraction. Two types of avoidant personalities supply illustrations. The *phobic* species of avoidant combines "pure" avoidant with some dependent features. Being dependent, she invests her trust and her sense of self in some significant other, and lives in terror of the loss of that relationship. The phobic strategy is to displace her anxiety from its true object—the significant other, possible loss of same—to some concrete object or situation: the dog next door, elevators, drowning, what have you. This distracts her from her real problem.

The *self-deserting* avoidant deals with her intense social discomfort by retreating into fantasy. This allows her to escape from immediate discomfort, and when the strategy is deployed generally it allows her to escape herself, which she finds to be pathetically inadequate. Strangely, such avoidants are generally aware to some extent of using such tactics, and their use of fantasy gradually becomes less effective in shielding them from what they believe to be the painful truth of their inadequacy. Like the use of fantasy found in the fanatic paranoid, this one arguably combines both types of bullshit.

Self-distracting is also popular with dependent personalities. For instance, in the interest of securing and maintaining a valued relationship, dependents of an *accommodating* sort contrive to distract themselves from any doubts or grievances they might have about the relationship, which would lead to inner conflict. So distracted, they are able to put a happy face on things, and avoid acknowledging the conflict.

Finally, one function of the obsessive-compulsive's preoccupation with details, rules, lists, and the like is to distract her from her own anxiety about big-picture issues that might be the source of legitimate concern. By immersing herself in details, she distracts from larger issues: the compass of her anxiety is only as big as the niggling little thing she's presently focused on. In this way she can lose the dangerous forest for the (relatively unthreatening) trees.

Patterns in Personality Bullshit

Here are some things to notice in this survey. I have identified an example of bullshitting for eight of ten disorders—multiple examples, in some cases. The bullshit-strategems I have described are, in most of the foregoing cases, defining characteristics of the personality disorder in question. That is, the glib charm of the antisocial, the provocativeness and shallow opinions of the histrionic, the obsessive-compulsive's devotion to rules and details, etc., are all what you might call first-rank symptoms of personality disorders, and if I am right they may be understood in terms of bullshit. In the remaining cases the strategems identified are defining characteristics of one or more sub-types of the basic disorder.[12] Thus, while "each of us contributes his share" (*On Bullshit*, p. 1) to the collective bullshit of our culture, as Frankfurt says, pathological personalities are notably reliable and generous in their contributions.

However, bullshitting is notably absent from most of the Eccentric cluster. I can see no examples of either type, self- or other-directed, in the behavior of the schizoid or the schizotypal.[13] Happily, plausible explanations of this gap are not far to seek. First, in the case of the schizoid at least, there is a marked flatness of affect: she comes across as cold or emotionally absent. In all the cases of bullshit I've just described, the bull-

---

[12] The sub-types I refer to in the foregoing are not officially recognized by the American Psychiatric Association in the *DSM-IV*. I lean heavily here on *Personality Disorders in Modern Life*, where they *are* recognized.

[13] Indeed, insofar as the "fanatic paranoid" is just paranoid, he is not a bullshitter; it is really his narcissist streak that contributes the bullshit.

shitter is motivated by a desire to avoid the pain she would feel upon meeting her target truth full in the face. If you lack the capacity to feel that sort of pain, then you have no motive for bullshitting. Second, successful bullshitting requires a certain level of "mindreading" facility: you need to have some capacity to predict what effects your words and deeds will have on the beliefs of your audience, and you need to choose words and deeds that will have the desired effect. Schizoids and schizotypals may lack the requisite mindreading facility: they may be too socially disengaged to bullshit.[14]

Bullshitting of others is most characteristic of the Erratic cluster, while self-bullshitting is most characteristic of the Anxious cluster. The other-bullshitting is more likely to be of the falsehood-implicating type, while the self-bullshitting is more likely to be of the distracting type. This is not terribly surprising, since people don't like getting bullshitted by others, and those in the Erratic cluster are easiest to dislike. That said, remember that a person with a personality disorder is *afflicted*; harmful and infuriating as her bullshit may be, it is also a personal tragedy for *her*.

Perfect Partners: Bullshit and Distorted Social Perceptions

The paranoiac imagines threats and insults where there are none; the histrionic inhabits a world full of ardent admirers; the borderline sees abandonment on the horizon; the schizoid seems not to understand praise and blame. Each personality disorder is marked by some distortion or other abnormality in the perception of the intentions, desires, and feelings of others—of social reality. Now, if your perceptions are distorted or otherwise inaccurate, or very dim, then you will be farther from the truth than you would be if you saw things clearly. Meanwhile, the bullshitter may put distance between herself and the truth *intentionally*, depending on how aware she is of her target and her interest in obscuring it. Thus impaired perceptions and bullshit both serve to distance one from the truth. Since both are characteristic of

---

[14] This story does not, I'm sorry to say, cover the apparent near absence of bullshit from paranoid personality disorder.

personality disorders, it's natural to wonder whether these two ways of distancing oneself from the truth somehow reinforce each other. I think there is reinforcement in both directions.

Poor social perception can increase one's opportunities for relatively low-effort bullshitting, as follows. Owing to distortions, gaps, and other problems with her perception, the disordered personality simply sees less of social reality than normal people do. Remember that on my story, the bullshitter may be clearly aware of her target, dimly aware, or quite unaware, and all grades in between. Recall also that in the first case the bullshitter is just like the liar in having a deceptive intention (though her method is different). Unless you are given to intentional deception, it is *easier* to bullshit if you are not aware of your target than if you are. For if you are not aware of it, you can frame distractions and ways of implicating the contrary without feeling the sting of conscience that willful deception would ordinarily provoke. (That is, anyhow, what it would provoke in the case of other-bullshitting. In the case of self-bullshitting, awareness of your target would tend to provoke cognitive dissonance, since what you are trying to hide from yourself is staring you right in the face.) Among the parts of the social truth the disordered personality does not see are parts that are potentially painful and inconvenient—parts that she might have an interest in obscuring. So she has more "easy targets" than a normal person would.

In just the same way, it is easier to bullshit about something you are only dimly aware of than something you are clearly aware of. In addition to just *missing* parts of social reality to a greater-than-average degree, and to systematically distorting remarks, actions and gestures, it is common for disordered personalities to perceive only dimly those parts of social reality that they *do* see—to have glimmerings of the truth. Two instances of bullshit already discussed provide illustrations: the compensating narcissist has some glimmering that she carries on a charade of superiority, and the self-deserting avoidant has some glimmering that she is escaping into fantasy.

If this story about facilitation is correct, then some substantial fraction of the bullshit that is found in disordered personalities is causally downstream of their distorted social perception. Notice further that this is a two-way street: bullshit—of the self-directed kind, at least—can worsen the impairment of social perception. For if you hide from yourself those parts of the social truth that you can see at first, your social perception gets even worse, in that you then simply see less of social reality.

The Threat Posed by Bullshit

My findings about bullshit in personality disorders have some notable implications concerning the kind of threat bullshit poses. First, bullshit threatens good social relations.

I have claimed that pathological personalities are especially good bullshitters, generally speaking. They are also known for their distorted perceptions of social reality—which, like bullshitting, serve to distance them from the truth. Meanwhile, their relations with others are especially likely to be messed up in some systematic way: the antisocial exploits people, the borderline lurches wildly from one unstable relationship to the next, the dependent is a burden to those around her, the paranoiac imposes pathological jealousy on her partner, and so forth. Indeed, some such impaired social functioning is of the essence of personality pathology; what better criterion to use in deciding whether a personality is pathological?

The disordered personality's problems with the truth contribute greatly to her problems with people. Her bullshitting, and the distorted perceptions that help it along, are surely key contributors to her messed-up social relations. This is just a bit of common sense. People do not like getting bullshitted, so those who are given to bullshitting others easily become *personae non gratae*; it can be very exasperating to deal with someone in the grips of self-directed bullshit; and it is difficult to communicate with someone who is given to distorting what you say and do.

It's a platitude, though one that is forgotten all too often, that good, sound human relationships thrive on *truthfulness*. But this suggests a stronger principle: good relationships thrive on *truth*.[15] If either party fails to see things clearly—basic, important things concerning who she is and what she wants, and the same basic facts about the other party—then the relationship is likely to flounder. This can result not only from deliberate deception, but also from the involuntary disconnection from the truth that poor perception brings. If either party wittingly *or unwittingly*

---

[15] Thanks to Philip Robbins for helping me distinguish these two.

hides some such important parts of the truth through bullshit or outright lying, the relationship is gravely threatened.

Personality pathology is marked by lousy social relations, and the bullshitting of the disordered personality helps explain why her relations with others are lousy. I promised at the outset that applying my notion of bullshit to personality disorders could shed some light on how their core features can lead to social difficulties. I have now made good on that promise: impaired social cognition, a core feature of personality pathology, facilitates bullshit, which—among other elements of the disordered personality's behavior—tends to ruin her social relations.

Among the most interesting and provocative claims about bullshit that Frankfurt makes is that it is a greater enemy of the truth than lies are. This is supposed to be because "through excessive indulgence in [bullshitting], which involves making assertions without paying attention to anything except what it suits one to say, a person's normal habit of attending to the ways things are may become attenuated or lost" (*On Bullshit*, p. 60). Since I think the bullshitter *does* pay attention to the truth—at some level, in any case—I cannot agree. Still, like Frankfurt I think bullshit is an enemy of the truth in a way that lies are not—but a different sort of enemy than he described.

The threat I have in mind stems from the fact that bullshitting can be unconscious while lying cannot. The habitual liar, like the habitual bullshitter, gradually obscures more and more bits of the truth. But generally speaking, *it is easier to make a habit of bullshitting than of lying*, because outright deception ordinarily provokes a sting of conscience. Where bullshitting is less than fully conscious, this sting is less than fully sharp, and is therefore a weaker deterrent.

Bullshit thus poses a sort of threat to the truth that lying does not pose, or does not pose to the same degree. This does not imply that the *total* threat it poses to the truth is greater than that posed by lying, for lying may pose threats to the truth that bullshit does not pose. But these are questions about the comparative moral status of bullshit and lies, and that is a topic for another day.[16]

---

[16] Many thanks to Tasmin Astor-Jack, Gary Hardcastle, Tom Oltmanns, and especially Philip Robbins for helpful feedback on an earlier version of this paper.

6

Performing Bullshit and the Post-Sincere Condition

ALAN RICHARDSON

Mission Statement

This essay, aspiring to be one of the world's best philosophy essays, will prepare readers to become exceptional theorists of bullshit, promote the values of a rigorous and sustainable philosophical community, and be an example of outstanding research serving the people of British Columbia, Canada, and the world.

Harry Frankfurt's goal in *On Bullshit* was "to articulate, more or less sketchily, the structure of [the] concept" of bullshit (p. 2). But, he left many things for his followers to do. For one, he set aside the question of attitude (theoretically if not practically)— that is, he expressed various attitudes toward bullshit even as he left unanswered the question of why our attitude toward it differed from our attitude toward lying.

Frankfurt left "as an exercise for the reader" the "problem of understanding why our attitude toward bullshit is generally more benign than our attitude toward lying" (p. 50). He also did not "consider the rhetorical uses and misuses of bullshit" (p. 2). This essay attends to these unconsidered points, since bullshit's rhetorical purposes are exactly where its value lies and where we must seek to illuminate our attitudes toward it. Bullshit is, as we know, all well and good in its proper place. But it tends to transgress that place and crowd out other aspects of life.

Shitty Attitudes: On the Use and Misuse of Bullshit in Life

Let's begin by using a charming anecdote of Frankfurt's to amend his own account of bullshit. It is a story of Ludwig Wittgenstein as friend, offered by Fania Pascal (p. 24):

> I had my tonsils out and was in the Evelyn Nursing Home feeling sorry for myself. Wittgenstein called. I croaked: "I feel just like a dog that has been run over." He was disgusted: "You don't know what a dog who has been run over feels like."

Frankfurt does not exhibit much patience with Wittgenstein's sour and unsympathetic response, but the anecdote does aid in his diagnosis of bullshit as speech unconcerned with truth; Frankfurt finds Wittgenstein's annoyance to lie in Wittgenstein's sense that Pascal speaks in full knowledge that she does not know what she is talking about.

Fair enough. If Wittgenstein had been a cruder man, the conversation could have gone this way:

FP: I feel just like a dog that has been run over.
LW: Bullshit! You don't know what a dog that has been run over feels like.

But, notice that Pascal, in the context of a discussion about her health, had to utter *something* about her physical discomfort for Wittgenstein to get upset in this way—simply uttering something she was not in a position to know ("I feel just like the oldest living inhabitant of the nearest planet to Alpha Centauri," for example) would not have induced such a response. Wittgenstein's response, warranted or not, is attuned to the way in which the specific thing Pascal did say not only went beyond what she could know *but also sought to elicit sympathy for her suffering*. Indeed, the more given Pascal is to complaint or hypochondria, the more sympathy we have for Wittgenstein. The declarations of suffering among such people are often bullshit. (Indeed, it is only in rare cases, such as when a doctor asks us to describe a pain, that our reports of how much pain we are in are primarily information reports.) Bullshit is not simply any speech unconcerned with truth, then, but rather speech the truth of which is irrelevant but which aims to evoke some sort of positive attitude toward the speaker.[1]

If we take up the first-person situation, we get similar results. In planning to write a joint grant proposal, I can say to a colleague: "Here we have to add some bullshit about the training opportunities the grant will afford to graduate students. I have some boilerplate on that that I can import from another grant I have written." I am willing to call this portion of our proposal bullshit precisely because it is meant to express a positive attitude toward the education of graduate students and, thus, to get the adjudicators to like the proposal, even though my own attitude for or against graduate education need not be accurately expressed by what I write. Or, again, consider the following sort of exchange, after a department meeting:

> **GARY:** (*nervous and pale, his upper lip trembling*) I didn't know that you thought so highly of the Dean.
>
> **ALAN:** Oh, that was just bullshit; I wanted to appeal to the high opinion others have of him in order to pass the motion on hiring that Thomist I want to hire.

Here we see a key difference between lying and bullshitting. If I was praising the Dean in order to win over his fans in my department for my side of an argument about hiring, I am not really lying in expressing something that is not my true attitude toward the Dean. My attitude toward the Dean was not the point of what I was saying about the Dean; I was engaged in something else entirely. Knowing my intention, you could not successfully accuse me of lying.[2] Nonetheless, the remarks made about the Dean are relevant to the situation; I couldn't have recruited support for my favored candidate by saying nice things about the local ice hockey team, even if my colleagues like the team better than they like the Dean, the team being irrelevant in the situation at hand.

---

[1] Even false humility or self-abnegation is bullshit precisely to the extent that we are meant to value the speaker as humble via the act of uttering something falsely humble or self-abnegating. But more on performative bullshit below.

[2] That is, if you did accuse me of lying, I would rebut the charge by reminding you of what you already know, namely, my intention. As George Reisch has stressed in Chapter 3 of this volume, there's more to bullshit than semantics.

Similarly, when I complain that the son of a friend does not know how to disguise his disappointment at the presents I give him, I am complaining that this child has not learned courtesy conventions that are the nearest kin to bullshit. The sort of honesty involved in saying, straight-away, "I hate this stupid sweater" is not warranted in the gift-receiving situation, if the gift was itself offered in good faith. (Compare the case of your older brother, who seems to give you only joke presents. After thirty years of this, you might say, "Why do you keep giving me this bullshit?" He has failed the sincerity conditions of gift giving; his is a series of bullshit acts, raising questions about the nature of your relationship.) We don't want him to lie and say "Thank you for this sweater; I love it," but we'd like him to be courteous and say "Thank you for this sweater."

So, the sort of bullshit that one recognizes as bullshit and seeks (as Wittgenstein did in relation to Pascal) to deflate is more than saying X without being a position to know that X. In addition, X and the utterance of X are meant somehow to reflect well on the speaker. This contrasts with the sort of bullshit that is offered as entertainment or to kill time among those who mutually understand the conversation they are in not to be an attempt to convey accurate information. Thus, I think, contrary to Frankfurt (p. 11), that at least the sort of bullshit that evokes "That's bullshit" as a response does have pretentiousness as a constitutive element. But, not all bullshit is liable to evoke that response. Indeed, some bullshit is stock-in-trade and when well-crafted discharges a legitimate function.

Bullshit as a Condition of Life

Bullshit, therefore, is vastly more widespread than straight-out lying. Bullshit is a sort of misdirection; lying is direct and to the point. Students lie when they say they tried to turn in their papers but the office was closed; they bullshit when they come to office hours to offer up excuses for why they could not possible turn in their papers on the due date. What they say in such circumstances is rarely evidently false (if it were, it wouldn't work), it is simply a story put together in such a way as to get them what they really want, which is an extension. They do this by evoking sympathy for their circumstances, which have to be plausibly true and, importantly, hard to check.

Bullshit is in fact so ubiquitous that one cannot engage in some activities *without* engaging in bullshit. Consider grant proposals again. These require a sort of breathless discussion of how ground-breaking and exciting your research is, how it requires a hundred thousand dollars to do, how fabulous it will be to have research assistants (who will do your photocopying and be paid fifteen thousand a year for the privilege), and so on. Proposal writers know that this is all bullshit, but generically-necessary bullshit; proposal readers know it, too. Readers discount and ignore exactly what the writers put in as the bullshit component. But, no one will succeed if she does not put in the bullshit. One must *perform* certain values in a grant proposal even though they count for nothing. (It is like figure skating, which requires compulsory figures but doesn't count them.) This is the equivalent of Frankfurt's pompous Fourth of July speaker (pp. 16–18): patriotism is the order of the day on the Fourth of July in the United States, and no one takes expressions of patriotism offered on that day seriously precisely because on that day they are utterly *pro forma*. Nonetheless, no Fourth of July orator can safely set patriotic themes aside. That would be a spectacular mistake in judgment and value, a confession of a profound ignorance of the very genre.

The grant proposal and the Fourth of July oration are, indeed, bullshit *genres*. Another bullshit genre, perhaps the most important in academic life, is the letter of reference. All letters of reference are unreliable as guides to the genuine virtues of the applicants. Yet straight-out lying ("Mortimer invented the Internet, and his oils hang in the Louvre") would be counter-productive. Confident assertions of bullshit have to be on points on which legitimate disagreement is widely accepted and on which standards of evidence can be expected to diverge. Thus, I can write that "Mortimer's Ph.D. thesis offers a counterfactual account of causation that is a significant contribution to our understanding of causation" without fear that I have engaged in gratuitous and counter-productive bullshit. Indeed, if I am Mortimer's advisor, I am supposed to write this, even though the number of Ph.D. theses in philosophy that are significant contributions to anyone's understanding of anything is vanishing small.

A reader's bullshit detector might start sounding if I say, however, something like "Mortimer's contribution is the most significant contribution to the understanding of causation since Hume." Such a claim is almost always over-the-top even within a genre in which bullshit is expected; I have here entered the terrain of gratuitous and damaging bullshit. I must write bullshit but not induce my readers to say "That's bullshit" in response.[3]

So, we have the beginning of an answer to one question Frankfurt left as an exercise for his reader: Our attitude toward bullshit is more benign because there are various things we do in which we cannot succeed without the right amount of bullshit. Moreover, there are other activities in which attitudes and acts that are close kin to bullshit (courtesy, for example) are necessary for the maintenance of civility. Honesty is rarely the best policy in cases in which honesty is not the whole point of the enterprise. That is why bullshit is everywhere; it is dishonesty without tears.

The interesting questions begin just when we recognize bullshit's ubiquity. Letters of reference are a bullshit genre, so in order to write a good letter of reference for Mortimer I will have to bullshit. Yet, it is, it seems, not hard to imagine a world in which a letter of reference is simply an honest appraisal. Such a world might seem more functional than our world, since it is harder to evaluate bullshit accurately and effectively than it is to evaluate the truth. So how did the letter of reference become a bullshit genre? This, it seems to me, is a question for sociology and for rhetoric. Philosophers should be a bit chary about venturing *a priori* answers to such questions, but there are real conceptual difficulties that a bit of philosophy can help with here, even if it cannot wholly sort them out.

An answer that suggests itself immediately appeals to freeriders. If everyone else is truthful about his or her students while I bullshit about mine, mine will do better on average than they ought to do (provided I bullshit well). So the letter of reference genre tends towards bullshit. But this is not sufficient. My students might do better in *getting into* graduate school than they should if I bullshit and no one else does. But, my bullshit will

---

[3] The most curious cases within the letter of reference genre are cases in which the sort of bullshit offered is outside what is acceptable, not by being over the top but by violating the genre conventions. If one reads in a letter of reference that "Mortimer is like a cool breeze on a warm summer evening," one's reaction is "What sort of bullshit is this?," suggesting that at the minimum it is the *wrong sort* of bullshit.

not make them *succeed* in graduate school.[4] So, if my assessments are bullshit while everyone else's are not and, thus, my students get in to better schools than they should, the sanction should quickly come to rest on me—my students are worse than my letters let on, and my letters will quickly come to be regarded as bullshit.[5]

At this point, now that we have seen that bullshit often matters and may be unavoidable, I begin to want to distance myself even more from Frankfurt's account of bullshit. Bullshit in bullshit genres like letters of reference is, as Frankfurt concedes (pp. 22–23), well-crafted. I write letters that are dishonest in a sense, but I do not write things that are false; I do care that my claims are "true enough" or, to use Stephen Colbert's coinage, "truthy." I write "Mortimer will be an asset to any PhD program that accepts him; I recommend him without reservation" precisely because if I were honest that I do worry that his personal reticence will make him ill-suited to the pressure cooker of some departments, he will not get in—not just to those departments but to others in which he will do well. I tick the "top ten percent" box if it is the highest one available or the "top five percent" box if that one is, because I am not certain what either really means when the issue is "takes initiative" and the damage of putting Mortimer in the second rank is much higher than the damage of over-estimating him. Indeed, letters of reference can be extraordinarily well-crafted. Sometimes I wish my "without reservation" to be seen as bullshit. But I do not write my reservations into the letter; they appear in precisely how I do and do not say some things.

So, I do not think that free riding is the origin of bullshit genres—since it is counter-productive. Much more likely, it seems to me, is the fact that the letter of reference has not multiple audiences but multiple interested parties. I need to be able to say with plausibility to the student that I have written him a good letter, to the departments that receive the letter that I have

---

[4] For that their own bullshit must suffice.

[5] If we are tempted to go for evolutionary explanations, we might analogize bullshit to altruism and try to copy evolutionary explanations of altruism. Bullshit as biological adaptation, however, seems extraordinarily unlikely. I do not doubt that somewhere someone is writing up "The Function of Bullshit in a Hunter-Gatherer Society," however; such is the way of bullshit.

written them something that accurately expresses (not, reports) the strengths and weaknesses of the candidate, and to myself, that I have not lied or been dishonest (in any way that goes beyond the dishonesty of the genre itself). My ability to say these things with a plausible modicum of truth requires just the right amount of bullshit in the letter. Bullshit often arises in this way: I wish to recruit my colleagues to a cause, so I appeal to *their* values in arguing for the cause; thus, I offer an argument I myself do not believe or endorse. I have to craft this just right, however, so that I don't lose, say, my colleagues who distrust the Dean when appealing to those who do trust him. The better I can do this, the more well-honed is the performative nature of argument. I have learned to use arguments I neither endorse nor believe to recruit people into doing what I want to happen for other reasons entirely. I have become a highly effective bull-shitter—a politician, a courtier.

Thus, given the nature of the act and to whom that act is responsible, the fate of reference letter writing to be a bullshit genre is sealed—and our imagined world of honest letters of reference disappears. The details of how bullshit will be deployed are still open. British letters are rhetorically less inflated than American letters. They still strongly smell of bullshit, however, although of a more genteel and institution-based variety. (The candidate is less praised than her American counterpart; but, her college at Oxbridge, good heavens, has been pumping out intellectual deities for centuries.) Moreover, the enormity of the American system and its diffuseness mean that letter readers often do not know the letter writers and the bullshit quota goes up the more personal trust goes down. (If I know Professor X and know that he knows me and we have a decent relationship, I can write in a more honest tone, relying on his ability to read my intent.)

The World as Will to Bullshit

So, in this our world, bullshit is unavoidable. So far that seems a depressing conclusion. But the most depressing aspect is yet to come. There is bullshit in the world, but it does not yet get to the core of what bothers so many today—the sense that bullshit is increasing, that a sort of smug dishonesty is overtaking everything, even where it is not needed.

One of my local video stores posts, prominently, the following customer service guarantee:[6]

Each of us at Ballbreakers is empowered, authorized, and committed to serving you.

The service there is not notably better than anywhere else in retail. If one has a complaint, moreover, the guarantee does not cause the staff to take you very seriously and seek to remedy the situation. No, the guarantee serves for them as evidence that they have already done all that could reasonably be expected and that you, the customer, must be a crank.

Another prominent example in the lives of many of the authors in this book is the recent rise of the university "mission statement" and "academic plan." Universities have existed for hundreds and hundreds of years, but within the past twenty or so, their administrators have come to feel that someone (who?) needs to know better what their universities are trying to do, hence, the university mission statement. Mission statements *cannot* be honest: "We aim to provide a good postsecondary education subject to the constraints under which we operate" just doesn't inspire. So, instead, we have hundreds of universities that "aim to be one of the leading universities in the world" or to be "world-class." Here, for example, is the mission statement of my employer, The University of British Columbia[7]:

UBC'S VISION FOR THE 21ST CENTURY

The University of British Columbia, aspiring to be one of the world's best universities, will prepare students to become exceptional global citizens, promote the values of a civil and sustainable society, and conduct outstanding research to serve the people of British Columbia, Canada, and the world.

OUR MISSION

The University of British Columbia will provide its students, faculty, and staff with the best possible resources and conditions for learning and research, and create a working environment dedicated to

---

[6] The name of the store is altered to preserve anonymity; the pledge was still up on 19th April, 2006.

[7] This is from http://www.ubc.ca/about/mission.html.

excellence, equity, and mutual respect. It will cooperate with government, business, industry, and the professions, as well as with other educational institutions and the general community, to discover, disseminate, and apply new knowledge, prepare its students for fulfilling careers, and improve the quality of life through leading-edge research.

The graduates of UBC will have developed strong analytical, problem-solving and critical thinking abilities; they will have excellent research and communication skills; they will be knowledgeable, flexible, and innovative. As responsible members of society, the graduates of UBC will value diversity, work with and for their communities, and be agents for positive change. They will acknowledge their obligations as global citizens, and strive to secure a sustainable and equitable future for all.

Everyone knows that very few universities can be "one of the world's best"[8]; everyone knows therefore that these missions are, by and large, impossible and often, as in the case of UBC's, just silly. More importantly, because everyone knows that, everyone knows that these are not really the missions of the universities at all. But every year huge pots of money go into carefully crafting more and more bullshit mission statements.

I have written to administrators of my home institution, objecting to some things in the academic plans. My missives look like this: "You say that a strong faculty is the university's chief asset and that, thus, you are committed to making the working conditions as good as they must be to attract and retain a strong faculty. Yet, you started knocking down the neighboring wing of my building in January—right at the beginning of our second term—and it is, in consequence, almost impossible for me to work in my office. Surely, what you say about a strong faculty is true but your actions are not in accord with your pledge." The response, should there be one, is invariably puzzled. The administrator, much like our video store employees noted above, seems to think that the commitment to doing what is best for the faculty, having been made, is automatically fulfilled. The response has the form: "We have made that pledge. Therefore, we are doing everything we can to retain a strong

---

[8] But suppose all universities are equally good, says one of my undergraduate philosophy students who has taken logic. Well, then, there is no particular reason to sort them into the very best and the also-rans.

faculty. You must be a crank and a *prima donna.*" The desire to make me see my own crankiness is so ingrained that almost invariably these responses go out of their way to say that "all other feedback received on this matter has been positive." That I know that, too, to be false (since I know my colleagues well enough to know I am not alone) is again not to the point. Increasingly, it is hard for me to figure what the point really is.

The video store and the university administration point to two phenomena. The first is the explosion of bullshit genres. University missions and customer service commitments have not been and need not be matters of bullshit; yet, now, increasingly they are. Even more disturbing than this explosion of bullshit is the phenomenon of self-fulfilling bullshit: "We have treated you well in the very act of pledging to treat you well; now, piss off." This last is an odd sort of new-fangled *performative bullshit.* Its mark is a commitment that is taken to be fulfilled simply in virtue of its having been made.[9]

Consider the video store employee who acts as if he has fulfilled his commitment to treating you with respect because it says on the prominently-displayed pledge that he will treat you with respect. If he genuinely believes this, then he does not understand that the conditions under which commitments are undertaken are different from those under which they are fulfilled. A commitment involves conditions both for its proper issuance and for its fulfillment, but these are (except in a few self-referential cases like "I hereby promise to make a promise") distinct. You have not treated me well by saying that you will. You have placed yourself under an obligation to treat me well, which obligation you might not otherwise have had. I do not have complete say over whether that obligation has been fulfilled, but my sense that it has not is, on the face of it, evidence that it has not been. Moreover, no one whose commitment to treat me well is genuine will cite the fact that they pledged to treat me well as evidence that they have.

Performative bullshit has the form of a commitment, but it is not a real commitment. There are two options, however, regarding its dishonesty. In the first case, the person performing bull-

---

[9] My remarks on performative bullshit owe much to John Austin's classic, *How to Do Things with Words* (Cambridge, Massachusetts: Harvard University Press, 1962).

shit might genuinely believe that she is making a real commitment. I am not certain that this ever happens. The second case,
so it seems to me, is thus universal or nearly so. In this case, the
person knows he has not really made the commitment but acts
as if it is in effect in order to make it impossible to get anywhere. Thus, the video store employee does not really believe
that he has treated you well because he has pledged to do so.
However, if he takes his good treatment of you to have been
discharged in the pledge to be good to you, then there is no
place from which you can issue a complaint that he need take
seriously. If a university administrator acts as if pledging to do
everything it takes to retain her faculty is itself doing everything
that it takes, then no faculty member may properly complain to
her about mistreatment. Mistreatment continues as before, but
the ground has shifted so that it becomes illegitimate to claim
mistreatment.

Performative bullshit is the source of much of the sense
many of us have that the world is making us crazy. Whereas a
public performance of a genuine commitment would precisely
make it easier to demand that it be fulfilled, the pseudo-com-
mitment of performative bullshit removes the ground for that
demand. And the realm of performative bullshit goes well
beyond commitments of various sorts.[10] As applied to arguments, performative bullshit directs that an argument be taken
as a good argument by virtue of having been offered as a good
argument.

Thus, if George W. Bush argues on the basis of fabricated
intelligence that Saddam had weapons of mass destruction and,
thus, that the USA has to go to war against Iraq, he attempts to
defuse any objections to the argument simply by pointing out
that the argument was offered as a good argument.[11] If it is discovered that the intelligence was false, this does not touch the
argument, performed as bullshit, which remains good because it

---

[10] Examples can be multiplied: Canada, as a nation, seems to engage in performative
courtesy-bullshit, according to which the universal belief (or claim) among Canadians
that they are courteous is taken as evidence that they have been courteous in any given
case: "No, sir, I cannot have been rude to you; I am Canadian."
[11] I do not know whether Bush is utterly insincere, although the smirk would indicate
that he is. Leaving Bush aside, the insincerity of the American media, both right and left,
is palpable. Could anyone maintain sincere outrage, night in and night out, for years the
way our friends on Fox News and its rivals do? It's not possible.

was the proffered reason. For those for whom it is impossible to maintain that a false reason is a good reason, another bullshit reason can be fabricated (defeating Al-Qaeda, expanding freedom and democracy—take your pick). The entire sequence of reasons, whose truth does not matter and whose connection to whether the USA should go to war does not matter, has caused the deaths of countless people and destabilized the entire region. It has, moreover, further damaged the whole business of honestly and sincerely offering and demanding reasons for political action. True reasons might be able to contend with faulty reasons, but in a world of performative bullshit, all bets are off. The sincere person ends up diligently sifting through arguments that were never meant to be taken seriously in the first place.

We live in a world in which arguments are proffered which not only do not present the genuine reasons an action was undertaken but also deny the very existence of genuineness in the realm of reasons. We live in a world in which commitments are publicly made not only without any intention to fulfill them but also with the intention that the public issuance of them will prevent anyone from claiming that they were not fulfilled. In such a world, sincerity is not even possible. Indeed, irony in the strict dramatic sense is not possible, for, having become the spectators in the drama of our own lives, the emptiness of our own gestures is clear to us. Even cynicism, since it posits ulterior motives, is not possible—there are only pseudo-motives, lacking even sincere self-interest.

Overcoming Overwhelming Bullshit

In a bullshit world, no one succeeds like the bullshitter. I mean the person whose very being is constituted from bullshit. There are such people. Consider the administrator whose whole job is to craft and then endorse the bullshit mission statement for a university. Whatever the university does, it does. But then someone adds the imprimatur of The Mission, which says of what was done that it was done so that the university will be "world class." The whole professional being of this person is to add the bullshit that serves as the locus of value of the acts of the university. Absent the bullshit, this person would have no role. The bullshit being present, this person creates our contemporary replacement for genuine value, the pseudo-value that inheres in actions that must, constitutively, have value simply for having been done. This person does not hide what she really wishes to do beneath the smokescreen of the mission; there are simply actions and then the ritual claim that they were done for the mission.

Our problem is not that a bullshit world is unstable, but precisely that it is inherently stable. If every employee-customer interaction is an instance of good customer relations because the bullshit pledge of customer satisfaction proclaims it so, then disrupting this situation is very difficult. Customers, who began only by asking for something more from the person who is "helping" them, come to be seen as subject to "rage," and this provides one more opportunity to serve the customer by not serving her.

Suppose, however, you are not happy about living in a bullshit world. Are there any remedies? If sincerity has been drained out of a situation, can it be put back in? There is one strategy in the field that seems to be of some consequence: flat-out, self-evident bullshit that outperforms its covert competitors. This is the Jon Stewart gambit: We will offer a news show that clearly is made-up and that yet does a better job of presenting the news than most of its alternative "serious" sources. Here bullshit comes full circle: By self-consciously flouting the conventions of truth-telling and making it clear that he does not care about the truth—and yet doing a better job at revealing that truth, Stewart reminds us what those conventions were for and reveals something about how they've been perverted. Bullshitters in covering themselves with faux virtue are notable for their lack of humor. In a bullshit world, humor becomes the sincerest form of unconcern for the truth, the only form of concern for the truth still available.

But, what if bullshit or comedy are for you an insufficiently inspiring pair of alternatives. Suppose you would like more options than the insincere sincerity of Fox News and the sincere insincerity of *The Daily Show*. I can think only of one option. Consider the university mission statement and imagine what it would be like to take the task of writing one seriously. Imagine you genuinely believe that in light of the current world situation the mission of higher education needs to be rethought. You might have questions such as these in mind: Is it possible to export democracy to parts of the world in which fundamental religious beliefs preclude the possibility that, in the words of the Declaration of Independence, "governments are instituted among Men, deriving their just powers from the consent of the governed"? Or, given that the principles of higher education have derived, since the eighteenth century, from Enlightenment ideals, can we either recover Enlightenment ideals we can endorse or reorient higher education in a post-Enlightenment world?

Crafted with such questions in mind, a mission statement would not look like a corporate pledge to maximize profits or a sports team's pledge to win a championship. It would seriously have to enunciate a new cultural mission for higher education and seek to make that mission both palatable and possible to our citizens. If we cannot sincerely endorse currently culturally available values, then we must fundamentally rethink those values. If we lack the courage or the ability to do that, then all we are left with, and all we deserve, is bullshit.[12]

---

[12] Thanks to Judy Segal for comments on the earlier draft. Thanks to the editors for relevant inspiration and detailed comments on earlier, shittier drafts.

7

The Importance of Being Earnest: A Pragmatic Approach to Bullshitting

CORNELIS DE WAAL

One of the tasks Frankfurt sets himself in *On Bullshit* is to sketch, as he phrases it, "the structure of [bullshit's] concept" (p. 2). Frankfurt's approach is largely that of an ordinary-language analysis of what people are trying to say—or do—when they use the word. I agree with Frankfurt when he says that 'bullshit' is a generic term of abuse that is applied to a very vague and open-ended range of epistemic phenomena, but I aim to explore, further than does Frankfurt, that most interesting aspect of bullshit: the intention with which it is created. This is a paper on bullshitting rather than bullshit.

To get a better grip on bullshitting I will compare it with situations where people are genuinely interested in figuring out how things really are, and situate it among other epistemic ventures that are illicit or unproductive. Part of the reason behind the prevalence of bullshitting and the ease with which it is accepted is a lack of confidence that genuine inquiry is worth pursuing, or even possible. Admittedly there are other reasons why people bullshit, such as epistemic sloth or the need to voice one's opinion on matters one is only marginally familiar with. But contrasting bullshitting with the modest but honest attempt to figure out how things really are seems to me profitable. In brief, what distinguishes bullshitting from genuine inquiry is a difference of intention.

Two Tauroscatological Schools

G.A. Cohen's excellent article, "Deeper into Bullshit" (Chapter 8 in this volume) marks the beginning of two distinctive schools in bullshit thinking. Cohen separates what he calls Cohen-bullshit from Frankfurt-bullshit. He also observes, not without satisfaction, that one doesn't need a Frankfurt bullshitter to generate Cohen bullshit. Cohen points to several differences between the bullshit he is interested in and the bullshit he sees Frankfurt addressing.

The key difference between the two, however, is that whereas Cohen focuses on bullshit as a product, irrespective of how it is generated, Frankfurt concentrates on the act of bullshitting itself. I will call these two approaches to bullshit the *structuralist* school and the *intentionalist* school because of their respective emphasis on structure and intention. Since in the intentionalist school we are speaking of the *act* of bullshitting, intention refers to the reason, motive, or purpose with which the act is engaged in, like courting a woman with the intention to marry her, or approaching a tourist with the intention to steal her purse.

Within the intentionalist school the focus is on the bullshitter, not the bullshit. The essence of bullshitting is that the bullshitter does not care about the truth of his statements, because he is indifferent to how things really are, or because he believes that whatever he says doesn't really make a difference. Often, but not always, the bullshitter tries to hide his indifference to truth. When the bullshitter is publicly hostile to "those old-fashioned prigs who still hold on to the notion of truth"[1]—a view that is in vogue in certain relativist, postmodernist, and neo-pragmatist circles—this indifference may even be openly flaunted. Within the intentionalist school the bullshit that results is only of secondary interest; it is simply what we get when people bullshit. What counts is the intention of the producer.

At face value it seems that intentionalists fail to appreciate that one person's bullshitting can generate another person's insight. This suggests that intention doesn't guarantee bullshit, as the intentionalists claim. We may call this the insight problem.

---

[1] Richard Rorty, *Essays on Heidegger and Others* (Cambridge: Cambridge University Press, 1991), p. 86.

I think, though, that the insight problem is best treated as a case of unintended consequences—like someone dodging an unpleasant task by reading this essay instead is an unintended consequence of me writing it. The intentionalist can argue that just as I cannot take any credit for having helped someone dodge a particular task, the bullshitter cannot take any credit for what value others might see in what he excretes. I will return to this a bit later.

Within the structuralist school, in contrast, the focus is squarely on the bullshit. On this view whether something counts as bullshit has little to do with the intention with which it is generated, but depends wholly on its intrinsic features. For instance, a piece of writing that is "unclarifiably unclear," Cohen observes, is bullshit, no matter what its author's intentions were or what went through his head when he wrote it (p. 130). To determine whether a certain text is bullshit, one must analyze the text, not speculate about the intentions of its author. True, those intentions may explain how the bullshit came to be, but in the end those intentions are irrelevant to the question what makes something bullshit. Bullshitting and bullshit are on this view logically independent. Someone who is bullshitting may unwittingly produce brilliant insights, while someone who is genuinely concerned with truth but who happens to have been hanging around with the wrong crowd, may become a veritable fountainhead of jargonistic bullshit. For the structuralist, what counts as bullshit is determined by its structure, or the lack thereof, and not by how it is produced.

There are a few, admittedly rather uneven reasons why I feel more attracted to the intentionalist school. One of these is that much has already been written about Cohen bullshit, albeit under different names, and that various strategies have already been developed to separate bull from knowledge. These include, among others, Descartes's insistence on clear and distinct ideas, the verificationist principle of the logical positivists, and the pragmatists' pragmatic maxim. To these can now be added the Cohen-Brown test, on which something is bullshit when it is just as plausible as its negation (p. 132). The intentionalist school, in contrast, brings in something important that till now has been almost entirely ignored.

A second reason for favoring the intentionalists' approach is that although I agree with Cohen that the bullshitter can generate genuine knowledge, even if only by accident, I am not so sure that this exempts it from being bullshit. Take a physician and a sham astrologer who respectively make a false and a true prediction about the death of a certain celebrity—the physician after physically examining her and studying her medical record, the astrologer by consulting Tarot cards which he does not really believe in and which he doesn't quite know how to read. Should we abstain from calling the astrologer's conclusion bullshit simply because it turns out his prediction was the right one? My view is that we should still call it bullshit because of how the claim was generated. That the claim happens to be true, or that important segments of the argument are innovative, carefully crafted, or make sense, is another matter. Even when the bullshitter just happens to get it right, it remains bullshit until someone who is not bullshitting has gone over it, affirmed it, *and thereby transformed it into knowledge.*

This gets us back to the insight problem. Precisely because the focus is on intention, the product of one person's bullshitting *can* be another person's insight, just as one person's trash can be someone else's treasure. The claim that a certain chair cannot be at once trash and treasure mistakenly assumes that these are qualities intrinsic to the object, on a par with the chair being wobbly or the chair being extended in space. The structuralist school takes this stance: calling something bullshit is very much like calling a chair wobbly. The intentionalist school denies this. Just as calling something trash has to do with the attitude that is taken towards it, calling something bullshit has to do with the intention with which it is generated, and not with any of its intrinsic qualities. Just as no chair is trash in and of itself, no claim or argument is bullshit in and of itself. In fact, the discovery that one's bullshitting is taken by someone as genuine insight can come as quite a shock to the bullshitter, as happened with William Perry's undergraduates who bullshitted their way through an exam and later discovered that they got an A for it.[2] Of course none of this means that no claim or argu-

---

[2] William G. Perry, Jr., "Examsmanship and the Liberal Arts: A Study in Educational Epistemology," *Harvard College: A Collection of Essays by Members of the Harvard Faculty* (Cambridge, Massachusetts: Harvard University, 1967), pp. 754–765; my conception of bullshitting differs from Perry's "bull," however, in that the intention isn't quite the same.

ment can be plain nonsense in and of itself. But nonsense need not be bullshit.

The Epistemic Imperative

To get a better grip on bullshitting, I will contrast it with *genuine* inquiry. For the purpose of this paper I will interpret inquiry (including, but not just including, genuine inquiry) as any activity that leads to knowledge claims that are in some aspect new to those participating in the activity. Now it may be argued that the bullshitter, who doesn't care about the truth of what she is arguing for, cannot possibly be engaged in inquiry, so that contrasting bullshit with inquiry is misguided. However, because bullshitting and inquiring are alternative ways of responding to questions that are posed or problems that are raised, the two can be compared and contrasted. Someone who is bullshitting about whether cigarette smoking causes lung cancer, or whether homosexuals should be allowed in the army, stands in the same arena as those who really seek to know whether something is true or whether something should be allowed. To the untrained ear the genuine inquirer and the bullshitter may be indistinguishable. In fact, the bullshitter, who is far more flexible because she is much less restricted in what she can say, may even be the most convincing. In short, bullshitting and inquiring are sufficiently similar to warrant comparison.

There is another reason why contrasting bullshitting with genuine inquiry is insightful. Even the most avid bullshitter is not likely to accept bullshit from others in matters that are of real importance to him. For instance, when he is feeling sick he wants not bullshit, but the doctor to genuinely inquire into his ailment. Bullshitting, prevalent as it may be, is essentially a free-rider problem. Bullshitters are like people that hop on the bus without buying a ticket. One can only do this as long as others pay for the busses to go. The same is true for bullshitting. With the exception of areas of no practical importance (such as metaphysics or literary criticism), bullshitting can flourish only in an environment that is secured by people who do more than just bullshit.

Contrasting bullshitting with genuine inquiry also puts us on track to cure it. A general loss of faith in the very possibility of genuine inquiry, or in the possibility of genuine inquiry in certain areas (often extending to everything except the hard sciences), is an important cause of the prevalence of bullshit.

To understand genuine inquiry we ought to turn to the pragmatists, and especially to Charles Sanders Peirce, whose philosophical importance is increasingly recognized. For the pragmatists, knowledge is generated through our interaction with a world that poses real problems that generate living doubt. Hence, inquiry takes the form of problem-solving, and any conception of knowledge that banishes knowledge from the world in which we live is firmly rejected. Because of its focus on action, pragmatism is a natural fit for the intentionalist school.

Following Peirce, I define *genuine* inquiry as any inquiry that is fueled by the desire to find true answers to the questions one is asking, or involved (perhaps indirectly) in asking. Peirce defined science that way.[3] To define science in terms of the scientific method, as was done traditionally, was for Peirce to put the cart before the horse. If inquiry is conducted with the right attitude, methods that further that inquiry will evolve naturally in the course of that inquiry. The use of scientific method by itself doesn't guarantee that inquiry is conducted with the right attitude, as the pseudo-inquirers may be more successful in reaching their goals when they use methods developed by scientists. In short, what makes something scientific is not the correctness of the conclusions, nor the methods employed, but the attitude with which it is conducted. The resulting conception of science is a very broad one. It includes *any* inquiry that is engaged with a genuine desire to find true answers to the questions one is asking. Thus conceived, it encompasses the work of homicide detectives who want to find the murderer, philologists who seek to recover the meaning of an ancient text, politicians who want to know which health plan best serves the public, and car mechanics who are looking for the cause of a suspicious rattle.

What characterizes *genuine* inquiry is neither its methods, nor its results, but the attitude with which it is conducted. Inquiry should be engaged in with a genuine desire to find true answers to the questions that are being asked. Taking this posi-

---

[3] Charles S. Peirce, *Collected Papers* (Cambridge, Massachusetts: Harvard University Press, 1931–58), 1:44 (referenced by volume and paragraph number).

tion does not commit us, however, to the view that we can solve all the questions we can possibly ask. It doesn't even commit us to say that any particular question we ask must be solvable merely because we were able to formulate the question. All it commits us to is that when we try to answer a particular question we proceed from the notion—or the postulate, if you will—that that question can be answered, and hence that we direct our inquiry in such a way as to find that answer. One possible outcome of that inquiry might be that the question was ill-posed, which may lead to its abandonment or point to a new question that seems to have better prospects. Formulating better questions is one way of advancing our knowledge.

To truly counter the bullshitter, however, we must show that genuine inquiry is not a pipedream, but something attainable. One thing that keeps genuine inquiry within our reach is that its aim is not something grand and abstract, like "discovering the whole truth," but, modestly, finding answers to the questions that are actually being asked. This raises the question of what it is to answer a question. Staying close to the intentionalist stance, we can say that a question is answered (or resolved) when the doubts that initiated the question have been satisfied. This may raise an eyebrow or two, since at least on the face of it the correctness of an answer seems independent of what the inquirer believes it to be, something that is borne out by the fact that occasionally (if not to say often) people are quite satisfied with a wrong answer.

Several things can be said about this. Whether the answer he comes up with is mistaken or not, once the inquirer has satisfied himself that he has found the answer, he will stop inquiring. Put differently, the satisfaction of the inquirer brings the inquiry to conclusion. Subsequent doubts about this answer can cause the same inquirer, or others, to reopen the investigation until everyone is again convinced that the right answer has been reached, and then inquiry once again comes to a close. Such new doubt can emerge when new facts come to light, or when the question is looked at with fresh eyes. For many of our questions this is a long and torturous process, sometimes involving generations of inquirers.

This account of inquiry also points at something else: inquiry is a deeply social enterprise. Given our assumption that the inquirer is really interested in uncovering the right answer, reasonable doubt expressed by others, especially when they are peers, is powerful fuel for rekindling doubt. In fact, interaction with others is often the only way that personal biases, quirks, lacunae, etc., can be ironed out.

The above claim that the answer to the question must be *independent* of what the inquirer thinks it to be is misleading. What is really meant is that the answer is not *determined* by what the inquirer believes it to be. However, we can maintain the opposite: the *answer* that solves the puzzle will determine, or at least influence, what the inquirer is going to conclude if he is interested in finding that answer and if he is given enough time to complete the inquiry. Put differently, whereas the doubt that generates the question can be seen as the efficient cause of inquiry, the answer can be considered its final cause; it is that toward which genuine inquiry directs itself. Pragmatists even go a step further. Rejecting any view as meaningless on which truth is made into something that is in principle unattainable, they argue that the answer that would be agreed upon in the long run by the community of all inquirers is the truth with respect to that question.[4] There is no more to truth than that. It is called the final opinion, in that neither new facts nor fresh eyes can elicit any doubt that the answer that has been reached is indeed the right one. We do not need to go that far for our purpose—which is merely to show that wherever the outcome matters genuine inquiry is superior to bullshitting—but it does show that a robust theory on which genuine inquiry is truth-indicative is possible.

Remaining with the pragmatists a little, we can say that although for countless questions the moment a final opinion could be reached lies infinitely far in the future, there are also countless questions for which we have already reached such an opinion or for which such a final opinion is in our reach. However, at the same time, since we are human and hence fallible, there is no guarantee that in any actual case the answer we have reached, and have come to agree upon, is correct. Hence, though we can say that many of our answers must be true (how else could we survive?), we cannot point at any single one of them and say with certainty that the answer to that

---

[4] *Collected Papers*, 5.407.

particular question is true. Consequently dogmatism, which maintains that there are certainties we can identify and build upon, goes out the window.

This, however, by no means forces us into skepticism, as is often assumed. The skeptic concludes from the fact that we can doubt *any* of our answers that we can doubt *all* our answers. But that simply doesn't follow. From the fact that a passenger can occupy any vacant seat in the train it does not follow that she can occupy them all. The viable third option that presents itself here is that of the fallibilist, who argues that though we can trust many of our beliefs to be true, we cannot single out any particular belief as true. The fallibilist is like someone who is building a house in a swamp. Though none of the foundation poles hit solid ground, all of them combined keep the house firmly in place. Hence, whereas skepticism undermines the very possibility of knowledge, fallibilism does not.

The above, very brief discussion of inquiry allows us to recast the scientific attitude in terms of a general epistemic imperative:

> When engaging in inquiry we should always proceed upon the hope that there is a true answer to the questions we ask and act from a desire to find that answer.

The Problem with Bullshitting

Where there's an imperative there are ways it can be violated. Bullshitting is one such violation, but there are others. Let us look at a few. Peirce, who inspired the imperative, directed most of his own criticism against what he called "sham reasoning." In sham reasoning, the intent is not to find true answers to the questions asked, but to find facts that will support a conclusion that is already believed. Creationism, which uses science specifically to support the preconceived notion that the universe is created literally as explained in the *Old Testament,* is a paradigm case of sham reasoning. The creationist already knows the answer. His attention is focused on finding the facts that support it and refuting the arguments that deny it. The creationist, however, genuinely believes that the theory of evolution is wrong. It has to be wrong because its conclusions are wrong. Hence, the creationist isn't bullshitting. In contrast to the bullshitter, the creationist cares about how things really are. However, he is not a genuine inquirer either, because the conclusion is set beforehand and isn't negotiable.

A different type of violation—one that Susan Haack has dubbed "fake reasoning"—occurs when the inquirer is not concerned with finding the right answer, but with some ulterior goal, one that is related to the inquiry but is in essence extraneous to the question that is being inquired into.[5] An inquirer who receives funding from a large corporation has a strong incentive to produce work that gives the results her sponsors want hear. Someone who is working toward a conclusion, not because he thinks it is the right answer, but because it will give him fame, save his career, bring in research money, land him votes, etc., is a fake reasoner. A marketing campaign that tailors claims about the benefits of a product to scenarios that maximize the company's profit is engaged in fake reasoning as well. A special kind of fake reasoning is that which is designed to absolve the reasoner of responsibility. We can find this with cold-blooded murderers who plea temporary insanity, corporations that seek to avoid damage claims, and politicians that smooth over the gap between what they promised and what they actually did.

Note that the fake reasoner need not actively doctor the results. The influence of ulterior goals can take place at a subconscious or even at an unconscious level. The fake reasoner is also not a bullshitter. The issue is not that he doesn't care about the truth, as with the bullshitter, but that there are certain other goals that he cares about more. He is not a genuine inquirer either, as finding the right answers is not his highest priority. Sure, his reasoning may be shaky, he may twist language, massage his statistics, or embrace logical fallacies with vigor, but all that does not make him a bullshitter, at least not in the intentionalist school. The fake reasoner *per se* still believes in genuine inquiry and departs from it only because of other reasons more pressing in his eyes—the inquiry being only one of several balls that are being juggled.

A third violation is that of prematurely dismissing the inquiry as going nowhere, so that the answer to the question we are

---

[5] See for example Susan Haack, *Manifesto of a Passionate Moderate* (Chicago: University of Chicago Press, 1998), pp. 189–191.

asking is a defeatist "we'll never know." This is the approach of the skeptic. But there is a difference between being convinced that there is no truth and not caring whether what one says is true. Consequently, the skeptic too is no bullshitter.

So, what then is bullshitting? What makes someone a bull-shitter—at least in the intentionalist school of Frankfurt and others—is that he doesn't care about the truth or the correctness of his statements, either because of a total indifference to how things really are, or because of the belief that whatever he says makes no difference at all, his voice being only one in a sea of others, many of which more powerful, and all clamoring for attention.[6] The sales clerk who doesn't care about the company she works for, and who tells her customer that the shoes she is trying really look great on her without paying any attention to whether they do or not, is bullshitting. There is no motivation to get things right, nor to deceive; there isn't even any ulterior motive. In bullshitting claims are made, judgments cast, arguments presented, all with the unbearable lightness of those who are free of any responsibility or commitment, even if it is a freedom that is rooted in a profound sense of impotence or insecurity.

A lack of faith in genuine inquiry, intellectual laziness, being forced to speak on issues one knows too little about, all contribute to a culture of bullshitting. And it is a culture that can very well feed on itself. Bullshitting invariably invites more of it. It would be a mistake, however, to limit one's search for bull-shitting only to spent scientists, oily politicians, or slick marketers. When philosophy itself is boldly identified, per Richard Rorty, with "carrying on the conversation" and truth is defined as "what your peers will let you get away with," even the perennial search for wisdom is being reduced to mere bullshitting. What this means is not just that what some philosophers say is jargonistic, obscure, or meaningless, but that even philosophers are not immune to losing the desire to really search for answers to the questions they are raising. The temptation to just blurt out what sounds good and the power of whatever sounds good to find willful ears (generally including one's own) is just too great.

---

[6] *On Bullshit*, pp. 33–36.

Not all violations of the epistemic imperative are so simple and straightforward. They can be blended, and even combined, with genuine inquiry. The fake reasoner who doesn't care what people think, or who has lost all respect for his audience, may resort to bullshitting when trying to bridge the gap between the results he needs and the results inquiry would bring him. He makes factual claims and explanations without caring whether they are true or false, whether they make sense or not, or whether they are even convincing. The same can be said for the sham reasoner who seeks to defend his holy truths in a political arena where he is faced with an audience that steadfastly refuses to see things as he sees them. Also the genuine inquirer may engage in bullshitting when playing the game of keeping corporate sponsors, university administrators, or grant agencies happy, furnishing them with facts, findings, and arguments he doesn't himself believe. One can even bullshit about bullshitting.[7] It's important, however, to keep such second-order bullshitting separate from first-order bullshitting. Otherwise one runs the risk of losing the child with the bathwater, as when one would dismiss excellent research because of the bullshitting with which its findings were made public.

In light of the above, one might still argue that there are some situations where bullshitting is productive, and that even within genuine inquiry there is a proper place and time for it. Frankfurt's discussion of the bull session points in this direction (pp. 34–37). Bullshitting could be interpreted as creating the right atmosphere for inquirers to vent new hypotheses they feel unsure about or draw wild analogies that contain a potential key for further progress. However, there remains an important difference between brainstorming, however creative, and bullshitting. Returning once more to the central premise that drives the intentionalist school—that what makes something bullshit is the *intention* with which it is generated—we can say that what distinguishes a brainstorm session from an evening of bullshitting is that the participants in the former are interested in discovering something, a desire that is altogether absent among bullshitters. Bullshitting lacks the openness of mind and the ability to adapt in face of new insights that are essential for anything to

---

[7] Though not in the present volume. —Eds.

be taken seriously or as worth pursuing. True, what bullshitters excrete may on occasion prove useful to others, but that's an accidental and unintended consequence. Taken in that way, listening to someone bullshit is no more part of inquiry than serendipitously hitting upon some insight while browsing tabloids or while mindlessly driving through town.

So Why Bullshit?

Having distinguished bullshitting from genuine inquiry as well as from sham and fake reasoning, and having said something about why people engage in those activities, the question remains: Why do people bullshit? Why do people make epistemic claims without caring whether they are true? Leaving pure epistemic sloth aside and with no pretense of being exhaustive, I will say a little about two (mutually reinforcing) reasons why people bullshit: the social pressure to speak on any issue (often combined with the notion that whatever one says makes no difference), and a lack of faith in the possibility—or the usefulness—of genuine inquiry. Because I have separated bullshitting from sham and fake reasoning, some motives often attributed to the bullshitter properly belong to the sham or the fake reasoner.

Within a liberal democratic society, as Frankfurt notes, every individual is expected to be a responsible citizen who is able to instantly voice an opinion on countless pertinent and not so pertinent issues (p. 63). This expectation goes back to the Cartesian rejection of authority and the Enlightenment's appeal that everyone should think for himself. However, when the situation is such that one is forced, or conditioned, to speak with conviction on many issues one knows little about, one will be unable to always speak from a genuine desire to find true answers. For one thing, there simply isn't the time. Moreover, in cases where one is not directly affected there is little motivation to do so. Being relatively detached from the issues one is voicing opinions about, and finding that one's voice is just one among many, has the liberating effect that what opinion is being voiced does not make any difference. Hence, there's no real need to be concerned about the truth of what one is saying.

In addition to the feeling that one does not need to engage oneself in genuine inquiry for many of the issues one is asked or feels compelled to voice an opinion about, there is the belief that genuine inquiry is far too romantic an ideal to be worthy of actual pursuit. Generally, such a prophylactic pessimism follows the disillusion caused by a failed search for certainty. I hope that the above account of genuine inquiry, which makes no reference to something like "Truth with a capital T," and with its fallibilistic stance, makes a sufficient case to counter this type of bullshitter.

When addressing the issue of the prevalence of bullshit it may be fair to say that the Enlightenment's narrow focus on individuals has made bullshit its natural outcome, as it leaves every individual to fend for himself in an overwhelming epistemic landscape. Put differently, one way of looking at the prevalence of bullshit is that it is the price we are paying for the Cartesian-style epistemic emancipation that developed into a linchpin of the ideology of modernity, an ideology that situates knowledge within the individual and makes any appeal to authority suspect.

Hence, the best way to counter bullshitting is to restore confidence in genuine inquiry and insist that people be in earnest when they make epistemic claims. Confidence in genuine inquiry also alleviates the need to be able to speak on any and every issue, as it allows one to rely on the work of others. Scientists work like this. Unless there is good reason to doubt the work of their colleagues in other fields of research, they take the results they obtained at face value, assuming that they are the product of genuine inquiry.

Now one might object that by focusing on inquiry I did not cast my net wide enough, because there is more to life than inquiring into things, even if we include sales clerks helping customers find the right shoes. May there then not be some other function of bullshitting that is not a violation of the epistemic imperative? Take, for instance, the formulaic "It's nice to see you!," which is not intended to reveal or conceal the speaker's real feelings, nor to convince the addressee about the true nature of those feelings, but rather to make the addressee feel at ease. It could be argued that the claim's truth value doesn't matter for that, so there's is no need for any of those involved to concern themselves with the claim's truth value, thereby making bullshitting permissible.

In response to this, it might be suggested that this is not a case of pure bullshitting but that it is bullshitting for a cause, and that the claim "It's nice to see you!" is in effect a purported product of inquiry, even if this inquiry amounts to little more than a reflection upon one's feelings. With the formulaic "It's nice to see you!" this inquiry is simply not engaged in because no matter what the inquiry would reveal about our feelings toward that person, the best strategy remains to say "It's nice to see you!" That is what best serves the purpose that is deemed more important, which is to ease our interaction with that person—making it technically a case of fake reasoning. What this comes down to is the belief that it is not always best to be earnest. Just as there may be situations where it is better to lie, there may be situations where it is better to bullshit.

Alternatively, take the case of a few friends that are just having a good time by horsing around a bit for fun. Their bullshitting serves no other purpose than that they enjoy doing it; it plays a role not unlike that of playing Scrabble or some other game. However, since we are still dealing with a situation that involves passing off claims as knowledge, however casually, it satisfies the broad definition of inquiry given before, on which inquiry encompasses any activity that leads to knowledge claims that are in some aspect new to those participating in the activity. Such cases of horsing around can be defended, though, by arguing that in situations where the conclusions reached do not matter, the enjoyment of the activity can overrule the epistemic imperative. Yes, bullshitting too has its aesthetic appeal.

The fact that these two cases can be interpreted in terms of inquiry doesn't prove that all cases of bullshitting can be satisfactorily interpreted that way. Personally, I doubt that this can be done. What it does show, however, is that looking at bullshitting from the perspective of inquiry gives us a viable framework through which to interpret and evaluate bullshitting. A better understanding of bullshitting may be a first step, not only towards detecting and identifying bullshit, but also towards countering or preventing it when it is inappropriate.

II

The Bull by the Horns

Defining Bullshit

8
Deeper into Bullshit

G.A. Cohen

bullshit n. & v. *coarse sl.* - *n.* **1** (Often as *int.*) nonsense, rubbish. **2** trivial or insincere talk or writing. - *v. intr.* (**-shitted, -shitting**) talk nonsense; bluff. bullshitter *n.*

—*Oxford English Dictionary*

It is just this lack of connection to a concern with truth—this indifference to how things really are—that I regard as the essence of bullshit.

—Harry Frankfurt, *On Bullshit*, pp. 33–34

1 Without the Shit of the Bull

Harry Frankfurt's essay "On Bullshit" is a pioneering and brilliant discussion of a widespread but largely unexamined cultural phenomenon. Upon being honored by an invitation to contribute to a volume that celebrated his work,[1] I decided to focus on Frankfurt's work on bullshit, partly because it is so original and so interesting, and partly because bullshit, and the struggle against it, have played a large role in my own intellectual life.

---

[1] This chapter appeared originally in Sarah Buss and Lee Overton, eds., *Contours of Agency: Themes from the Philosophy of Harry Frankfurt* (Cambridge, Massachusetts: MIT Press, 2002), pp. 321–339. For comments on an earlier draft, I thank Malcolm Anderson, Annette Barnes, Jerry Barnes, Sarah Buss, Paula Casal, John Davis, Jon Elster, Cécile Fabre, Diego Gambetta, Grahame Lock, Ian Maclean, David Miller, Alan Montefiore, Michael Otsuka, Lee Overton, Derek Parfit, Rodney Peffer, Mark Philp, Saul Smilansky, Alan Sokal, Hillel Steiner, Tracy Strong, and Arnold Zuboff.

AT SOMETIMES -- AND SUCH IS THE CASE WITH RACISM -- AN IDEOLOGY HAS

They have played that role because of my interest in Marxism, which caused me to read, when I was in my twenties, a great deal of the French Marxism of the 1960s, principally deriving from the Althusserian school.

I found that material hard to understand, and, because I was naive enough to believe that writings that were attracting a great deal of respectful, and even reverent, attention could not be loaded with bullshit, I was inclined to put the blame for finding the Althusserians hard entirely on myself. And when I managed to extract what seemed like a reasonable idea from one of their texts, I attributed to it more interest or more importance (so I later came to see) than it had, partly, no doubt, because I did not want to think that I had been wasting my time. (That psychological mechanism, a blend, perhaps, of "cognitive dissonance reduction" and "adaptive preference formation," is, I believe, at work quite widely. Someone struggles for ages with some rebarbative text, manages to find some sense in it, and then reports that sense with enthusiasm, even though it is a banality that could have been expressed in a couple of sentences instead of across the course of the dozens of paragraphs to which the said someone has subjected herself).[2]

Yet, although I was for a time attracted to Althusserianism, I did not end by succumbing to its intoxication, because I came to see that its reiterated affirmation of the value of conceptual rigor was not matched by conceptual rigor in its intellectual practices. The ideas that the Althusserians generated, for example, of the interpellation of the individual as a subject, or of contradiction and overdetermination, possessed a surface allure, but it often seemed impossible to determine whether or not the theses in which those ideas figured were true, and, at other times, those theses seemed capable of just two interpretations: on one of them they were true but uninteresting, and, on the other, they were interesting, but quite obviously false. (Failure to distinguish those opposed interpretations produces an illusory impression of interesting truth).

---

[2] As Diego Gambetta has pointed out to me, a mechanism merits mention that is different from the "sunk cost" one that figures above. You can be so happy that you've got *something* (after whatever amount of labour, or lack of it, you've expended) from someone who is reputed to be terrific that you overvalue it. In both mechanisms you misattribute the pleasure of getting *something* to the quality of the text you got it from.

No doubt at least partly because of my misguided Althusserian dalliance, I became, as far as bullshit is concerned, among the least tolerant people that I know. And when a set of Marxists or semi-Marxists, who, like me, had come to abhor what we considered to be the obscurity that had come to infest Marxism—when we formed, at the end of the 1970s, a Marxist discussion group which meets annually, and to which I am pleased to belong, I was glad that my colleagues were willing to call it the Non-Bullshit Marxism Group: hence the emblem at the head of this article, which says, in Latin, "Marxism without the shit of the bull." (The group is also called, less polemically, and as you can see, the September Group, since we meet each September, for three days.)

2 Two Species of Bullshit

I should like to explain how this chapter reached its present state. I read Frankfurt's article in 1986, when it first appeared. I loved it, but I didn't think critically about it.

Having been asked to contribute to the present volume, I reread the article, in order to write about it. I came to realize that its proposal about the "essence" of bullshit worked quite badly for the bullshit (see Section 1 above) that has occupied me. So I wrote a first draft which trained counter-examples drawn from the domain of the bullshit that interests me against Frankfurt's account. But I then realized that it was inappropriate to train those examples against Frankfurt, that he and I are, in fact, interested in different bullshits, and, therefore, in different *explicanda*. Frankfurt is interested in a bullshit of ordinary life,[3] whereas I am interested in a bullshit that appears in academic works, and, so I have discovered, the word "bullshit" characteristically denotes *structurally* different things that correspond to those different interests. Finally, and, belatedly, I considered, with some care, the *Oxford English Dictionary* (OED) account of "bullshit", and, to my surprise, I discovered (and this was, of course, reassuring) that something like the distinct *explicanda* that I had come to distinguish are listed there under two distinct entries.[4]

---

[3] His essay begins as follows: "One of the most salient features of our culture is that there is so much bullshit. Everyone knows this. Each of us contributes his share" (p. 1).
[4] Frankfurt himself cites the OED, but mainly with respect to meanings and uses of the

So, instead of citing cases of the bullshit that interests me in disconfirmation of Frankfurt's account, I now regard it as bullshit of a different kind.[5] Which is not to say that I have no criticism of Frankfurt's treatment of the kind of bullshit that interests him.

Frankfurt is partly responsible for my original, misdirected, approach. For he speaks, after all—see the second epigraph at the beginning of this article—of the "essence" of bullshit, and he does not acknowledge that the *explicandum* that attracted his interest is just one flower in the lush garden of bullshit. He begins by saying that the term 'bullshit' is very hard to handle, analytically, but, as we shall see, he rather abandons caution when he comes to offer his own account of it.

Consider, then, the OED reading of 'bullshit':

> bullshit n. & v. *coarse sl.* - *n.* 1 (Often as *int.*) nonsense, rubbish. 2 trivial or insincere talk or writing.[6] - *v. intr.* (-shitted, -shitting) talk nonsense; bluff. bullshitter *n.*

The bullshit that interests me falls under definition 1 of the noun, but the bullshit that interests Frankfurt is closer to what's defined by definition 2 of the noun. And that is because of the appearance of the word 'insincere' in that second definition of 'bullshit'. In definition 2 of the noun 'bullshit', bullshit is constituted as such through being the product of discourse governed by a certain state of mind. In this activity-centered definition of bullshit, the bull, conceptually speaking, wears the trousers: bullshit is bullshit because it was produced by a bullshitter, or, at any rate, by someone who was bullshitting at the time. Bullshit is, by nature, the product of bullshitting, and bullshitting, by nature, produces bullshit, and that biconditional, so

---

word 'bull': he touches on its definition of "bullshit" only in its use as a verb. I disagree with his discussion of the entries he cites, but it would be an imposition on the reader's capacity to endure tedium to explain why.

[5] Four differences between the kinds of bullshit that exercise Frankfurt and me are listed in footnote 26 below. The import of those differences will emerge in due course, but the reader will probably follow me better if he or she glances ahead now to footnote 26.

[6] 'Trivial' is very different from 'insincere', partly because it has weaker implications for the state of mind of the speaker or writer. I shall take 2 with the accent on 'insincere'.

understood that 'bullshitting' enjoys semantic primacy, is true of Frankfurt's view of the matter.[7]

Definition 1, by contrast, defines 'bullshit' without reference to the bullshit-producer's state of mind. The defect of this bullshit does not derive from its provenance: almost any state of mind can emit nonsense or rubbish, with any old mix of sincerity and its lack. Here the shit wears the trousers, and *if* there are indeed "bullshitters," and "bullshittings," that correspond to the bullshit of definition 1, then they are defined by reference to bullshit: but it may be the case, as I meant to imply by that '*if*', that the words 'bullshitting' and 'bullshitter' don't have a stable place on this side of the *explicandum* divide.[8] However that may be, definition 1 supplies an output-centered definition of the noun: the character of the process that produces bullshit is immaterial here.

Note, moreover, how the alternatives in the brief entry on the verb 'to bullshit' match alternatives 1 and 2 in the definition of the noun (even though that entry isn't, as it perhaps should have been, sub-numbered '1' and '2'). One can "talk nonsense" with any intentions whatsoever, but one cannot unknowingly or inadvertently "bluff": bluffing is a way of intending to deceive. (I'm not sure, by the way, that the dictionary is right in its implication that it suffices for bullshitting, in the non-bluff sense, that you produce bullshit, in sense 1: innocent producers of bullshit might be said not to be bullshitting when they produce it.[9])

It is a limitation of Frankfurt's article that, as we shall see, he took for granted that the bull wears the semantic trousers: he therefore focused on one kind of bullshit only, and he did not address another, equally interesting, and academically more significant, kind. Bullshit as insincere talk or writing is indeed what it is because it is the product of something like bluffing, but talking nonsense is what it is because of the character of its output,

---

[7] Frankfurt certainly believes that a person bullshits if he produces bullshit, since he thinks it a necessary condition of bullshit that it was produced with a bullshitting intention. He (in effect) raises the question whether that intention is also sufficient for bullshit at p. 9. But, although he doesn't expressly pursue that question, his definition of 'bullshit' (pp. 33–34), and its elaboration (pp. 54ff), show that he holds the sufficiency view as well. It is because Frankfurt asserts sufficiency that he can say (pp. 47–48) that a piece of bullshit can be true.

[8] See, further, the last two paragraphs of Section 4 below.

[9] See, once again, the last two paragraphs of Section 4 below.

and nonsense is not nonsense because of features of the non-sense-talker's mental state.

3 Bullshit and Lying

At the beginning of his article, Frankfurt describes a complexity that afflicts the study of bullshit:

> Any suggestion about what conditions are logically both necessary and sufficient for the constitution of bullshit is bound to be somewhat arbitrary. For one thing, the expression *bullshit* is often employed quite loosely—simply as a generic term of abuse, with no very specific literal meaning. For another, the phenomenon itself is so vast and amorphous that no crisp and perspicuous analysis of its concept can avoid being procrustean. Nonetheless it should be possible to say something helpful, even though it is not likely to be decisive. Even the most basic and preliminary questions about bullshit remain, after all, not only unanswered but unasked. (pp. 2–3)

I have no problem with Frankfurt's first remark, to wit, that "bullshit" has a wide use in which it covers almost any kind of intellectual fault. To circumvent this problem, to identify a worthwhile *explicandum,* we could ask what 'bullshit' denotes where the term does carry (as Frankfurt implies that it sometimes does) a (more or less) "specific literal meaning," one that differs, in particular, from the meanings carried by words that are close to 'bullshit', but instructively different in meaning from it, such as the word 'horseshit', which, at least in the United States, denotes, I believe, something characteristically produced with less deviousness than characterizes the production of (OED-2) bullshit. And I think that, for one such meaning, Frankfurt has provided an impressively discriminating (though not, as we shall see, fault-free) treatment: much of what he says about one kind of bullshit is true of it but false, for example, of horseshit.

Frankfurt's second remark, about the difficulty caused by the fact that "the phenomenon itself is so vast and amorphous," is more problematic. Notice that this remark is meant to be independent of the first one (hence the words 'For another . . .'), as indeed it must be, since no *phenomenon* could be thought to correspond to 'bullshit' where it is an undifferentiated term of abuse. In making this remark, Frankfurt must suppose, if, that is, he supposes, as he appears to do, that he will command the reader's agreement, that the reader has some "specific, literal meaning" of 'bullshit' implicitly in mind. But that is extremely doubtful, partly because it is a gratuitous assumption (and, indeed, as the OED reveals, a false one) that 'bullshit' has some *single* "specific, literal meaning." In a word: how can we be expected to agree, *already*, that bullshit is "vast" and "amorphous," when no specification of 'bullshit' has yet been provided?

However that may be, Frankfurt leaves these preliminary problems behind, and plunges right into his subject, by reviewing, refining, and developing a definition that Max Black once gave of 'humbug' (which is close to bullshit of the OED-2 kind), and then by commenting on an example of real or feigned rage expressed by Ludwig Wittgenstein against (putative) bullshit uttered by Fania Pascal.

Emerging from the Black and Wittgenstein discussions, Frankfurt very surprisingly says, that "the essence of bullshit . . . is . . . lack of connection to a concern with truth— . . . indifference to how things really are" (pp. 33–34), where that indifference (see the Frankfurt passage quoted in the paragraph that follows here) is concealed by the speaker. It's the word 'essence' that surprises me here: it seemed to be implied by Frankfurt's preliminary remarks that the term 'bullshit', considered comprehensively, denotes no one thing whose essence one might try to specify,[10] and Frankfurt had not in the interim indicated a particular *region* of bullshit, whose bullshit might, perhaps, be identified by an essence.

Frankfurt later elaborates his definition as follows:

> This is the crux of the distinction between him [the bullshitter] and the liar. Both he [the bullshitter] and the liar represent themselves falsely as endeavoring to communicate the truth. The success of each depends upon deceiving us about that. But the fact about himself that the liar hides is that he is attempting to lead us away from a correct apprehension of reality; we are not to know that he

---

[10] Does Frankfurt think that the phenomenon of "indifference to how things really are" is "vast and amorphous"? Surely not. Then *what*, again, is he asserting to be "vast and amorphous," in his second preliminary remark, which I criticized two paragraphs back?

wants us to believe something he supposes to be false. The fact about himself that the bullshitter hides, on the other hand, is that the truth-values of his statements are of no central interest to him; what we are not to understand is that his intention is neither to report the truth nor to conceal it. This does not mean that his speech is anarchically impulsive, but that the motive guiding and controlling it is unconcerned with how the things about which he speaks truly are. (pp. 54–55)

Notice that, when Frankfurt elaborates what is supposed to be a proposal about bullshit, he speaks not of "bullshit" but of the "bullshitter." This confirms that it is the bull that wears Frankfurt's trousers. But he wrongly takes for granted that that is the only important or interesting bullshit that there is.

Now, in the light of the semantic promiscuity of 'bullshit' that was discussed at the outset of this section, it was, so I have suggested, unwise of Frankfurt to cast his claim as one about the "essence" of bullshit, as he does in the pp. 33–34 passage. He should have submitted his indifference-to-truth thesis as an attempt to characterize (at least) one interesting kind of bullshit, whether or not there are other interesting kinds of it. Let us assess his thesis as such, that is, not with the ambitiously generalizing status that Frankfurt assigns to it, but as an attempt to characterize one kind of bullshit, and, in particular, an activity-centered kind of bullshit. I return to the distinct bullshit-*explicandum*, which corresponds to OED definition 1, in Section 4 below.

Consider Frankfurt's statement, with which we may readily agree, that

> The realms of advertising and of public relations, and the nowadays closely related realm of politics, are replete with instances of bullshit so unmitigated that they can serve among the most indisputable and classic paradigms of the concept. (p. 22)

I find it hard to align this remark with Frankfurt's proposal about the essence of bullshit: advertisers and politicians are often very concerned indeed "to lead us away from a correct apprehension of reality" (p. 55) and to design what we might well call "bullshit" to serve that end (yet the quoted p. 55 words are used by Frankfurt to characterize the purpose of liars *as opposed* to bullshitters). Is it not a problem for Frankfurt's proposal about the essence of bullshit that those whom he designates as paradigm bullshitters engage in a great deal of what is not, for Frankfurt, bullshitting?

Frankfurt might say (as he must, to sustain his proposal) that, when advertisers and politicians seek to cover up the truth, they are doing something *other* than bullshitting. But when we are inclined to agree with Frankfurt that advertising and politics supply paradigms of bullshit, it is not the subset of their doings to which his proposal points that induces our inclination to agree. I think we are induced to agree partly because we recognize at least some lying to be also bullshitting.[11] Frankfurt's contrast between lying and bullshitting is malconstructed, and he erred, I believe, because he failed to distinguish two dimensions of lying, which we must separate if we are to determine the relationship between lying and Frankfurt's bullshitting.

Standardly, a liar says what he believes to be false: let us call all that his standard *tactic* (or, for short, his tactic). Liars also standardly seek to deceive their listeners about some fact (other than the fact that they disbelieve what they say): we can call that the liar's (standard) *goal*. And normally a liar pursues the stated *goal* by executing the stated *tactic*: he says something that he believes to be false *in order to* induce his listener to believe something false. (Usually, of course, what I have called the liar's "standard goal" is not also his ultimate or final goal, which may be to protect his reputation, to sell a bill of goods, to exploit his listener, or whatever.[12] But the liar standardly pursues such further goals by pursuing the goal which liars (as I have said) standardly seek. None of these further goals *distinguish* the liar from non-liars.)

Now, what I have called the "standard tactic" and the "standard goal" of lying can come apart. Consider what was one of Sigmund Freud's favorite jokes:

Dialogue between two travelers on a train from Moscow:
"Where are you going?"

---

[11] I suppose all lying is insincere talk, and I do not think all lying is bullshitting: at least to that extent, the OED-2 definition is too wide. But *some* lying is undoubtedly also bullshitting, so Frankfurt's definition of activity-centred bullshit is too narrow.

[12] Few liars care about nothing more than inducing false beliefs: that is the ultimate goal of only one of the eight types of liar distinguished by St. Augustine: see Frankfurt, p. 55.

"To Pinsk."

"Liar! You say you are going to Pinsk in order to make me believe
    you are going to Minsk. But I *know* you are going to Pinsk. So
    whom are you trying to fool?"[13]

Suppose that the first traveler's diagnosis of the purpose of the
second traveler's uttering 'To Pinsk' is correct: let us therefore
call the second traveler 'Pavel' (because of the 'P' in Pinsk), and
let us call the first traveler 'Trofim'. On the indicated supposi-
tion, Trofim is right to call Pinsk-bound Pavel a liar, since, as
Frankfurt says, the liar is someone who tries "to lead us away
from a correct apprehension of reality" (p. 55), and that's what
Pavel is trying to do to Trofim. The peculiarity of the present
example is that Pavel here seeks to deceive by telling the truth.
Pavel does not, in my view, lie, on this occasion, but he nevertheless proves himself to be a liar. Pavel's goal is the standard
goal of the liar, but his tactic, here, is to speak the truth. (The
important and entirely non-verbal point is that the standard goal
and the standard tactic of lying lose their normal association
here, not whether Pavel is lying, or telling a lie, etc.)

A converse case, in which the standard tactic subserves a
non-standard goal, would go as follows. Pavel knows that
Trofim knows that Pavel habitually lies, at any rate when it
comes to disclosing his intended destinations. But, on the present occasion, it is very important to Pavel that Trofim should
believe the truth about where Pavel is going. So Pavel, once
again traveling to Pinsk, says that he is going to Minsk, precisely
because he wants Trofim to believe the truth, which is that Pavel
is going to Pinsk. I don't know, or very much care, whether
Pavel thereby lies, but he is not here "attempting to lead [Trofim]
away from a correct apprehension of reality," save with respect
to his own state of mind: he wants him to think he's trying to
get Trofim to believe something false, when he's not.

We must, accordingly, distinguish two respects in which liars
characteristically traffic in falsehood. Liars usually intend to utter
falsehoods, while intending that they be thought to be speaking
truthfully; but that is quite separate from their standard goal, which
is to cause a misrepresentation of reality in the listener's mind.

---

[13] See *Jokes and their Relation to the Unconscious*, in *The Basic Writings of Sigmund
Freud* (New York: Modern Library, 1965).

What is the bearing, if any, of this distinction, on Frankfurt's distinction between lying and bullshitting?

The root difficulty for Frankfurt's bullshitting-lying distinction, the difficulty underlying the problem with his advertiser example, is that, while Frankfurt identifies the liar by his goal, which is to mislead with respect to reality, he assigns no distinctive goal to the bullshitter, but, instead, identifies the bullshitter's activity at the level that corresponds to what I have called the liar's tactic. The standard liar pursues his distinctive goal by asserting what he believes to be false and concealing that fact. Frankfurt's bullshitter asserts statements whose truth-values are of no interest to him, and he conceals *that* fact. But Frankfurt assigns no distinctive goal to the bullshitter that would distinguish him from the liar. And, in fact, Frankfurt's bullshitters, as he identifies them, have no distinguishing goal: they have a variety of goals, one of which can be precisely to mislead with respect to reality, and that, indeed, is the goal of bullshit advertising.[14] Advertisers and politicians spew a lot of bullshit, and they indeed seek to induce false beliefs about reality, but those are not, as Frankfurt must have it, separate but, typically, coincident activities on their parts.

The failure to distinguish the level of tactic from the level of goal runs throughout the discussion. Frankfurt writes at p. 47 (my emphasis):

> Bluffing too is typically devoted to conveying something false. Unlike plain lying, however, it is more especially a matter not of falsity but of fakery. This is what accounts for its nearness to bullshit. For the essence of bullshit is not that it is *false* but that it is *phony*.

The problem is that this falsehood is at the level of tactic, whereas phoniness is at the level of goal. If bluffing is like bullshit, that is partly because bullshitting, too, is often devoted to conveying something false—although often not by saying that false thing itself.

As Frankfurt says, the bullshitter may not care whether or not what he says is true. But Frankfurt has confused that with the

---

[14] It is not, of course, the ultimate goal of that advertising, which is to cause (some of) its audience to buy what's advertised.

bullshitter's not caring whether his audience is caused to believe something true or false. That explains an error that Frankfurt makes about the Fourth of July orator whom he describes at pp. 16–18 (my emphases)[15]:

> Consider a Fourth of July orator, who goes on bombastically about "our great and blessed country, whose Founding Fathers under divine guidance created a new beginning for mankind." This is surely humbug . . . the orator is not lying. He would be lying only if it were his intention to bring about in his audience beliefs which he himself regards as false, concerning such matters as whether our country is great, whether it is blessed, whether the Founders had divine guidance, and whether what they did was in fact to create a new beginning for mankind. But the orator does not really care what his audience thinks about the Founding Fathers, or about the role of the deity in our country's history, or the like. At least, it is not an interest in what anyone thinks about these matters that motivates his speech.
>
> It is clear that what makes Fourth of July oration humbug is not fundamentally that *the speaker regards his statement as false.* Rather . . . the orator intends these statements to convey a certain impression of himself. *He is not trying to deceive anyone concerning American history.*

The orator's unconcern about truth is, mistakenly, identified at the level of his goal, rather than, in line with p. 55, merely at the level of his immediate tactic. For the bullshitting orator, as Frankfurt describes him, might well care a lot about what the audience thinks about the Founding Fathers.[16] If the orator had been Joseph McCarthy, he would have wanted the audience to think that the "new beginning" that the Founding Fathers "created" should persuade the audience to oppose the tyranny supposedly threatened by American Communism. The fact that it is not "fundamental" that "the speaker regards his statements as false" in no

---

[15] Strictly, the orator's oration is presented as an example of humbug, rather than bullshit. But it's clear that Frankfurt would also say that he is a bullshitter, precisely in virtue of what makes him a purveyor of humbug, whatever difference between humbug and bullshit Frankfurt might want to affirm.

[16] I do not think Frankfurt means to be *stipulating* otherwise: we are meant to agree with what he says about the orator on the basis of his initial, first-sentence of the passage, description of him. 'Surely', in the second sentence, would otherwise make no sense.

way implies that "he is not trying to deceive anyone concerning American history." (Similarly, advertisers may not care whether or not what they say is true, but they do care about what their audience is caused to believe, or, rather, more generally, about the thought-processes that they seek to induce in people.[17])

4 Bullshit as Unclarifiable Unclarity

Unlike Frankfurt's bullshitting, lying is identified in terms of the defect at which it aims, namely, falsehood. We clarify what a liar is by reference to falsehood, rather than the other way around; we do not, that is, when asked to characterize what falsehood is, say that falsehood is what a liar aims to say. In parallel, we might, unlike Frankfurt, seek to clarify what a bullshitter is by reference to what he aims at, to wit, bullshit. We might start with the shit, not with the bull. And that would induce us to consider OED definition 1 ("nonsense, rubbish") the one that fits the bullshit that interests me, rather than the bullshit that interests Frankfurt. My bullshit belongs to the category of *statement* or *text*. It is not primarily an activity but the result of an activity (whether or not *that* activity always qualifies as an activity of bullshitting.[18])

A liar who tries to say something false may inadvertently speak the truth, whether or not he is then lying, and whether or not what he then says is a lie. And there is also the opposite case in which an honest person, by mistake, speaks falsely. The bullshit that interests me is relevantly parallel. I countenance a bullshitter who has tried, but failed, to produce bullshit—what comes out, by accident, is good sense—and I also countenance a lover of truth who utters what he does not realize is bullshit. A person may avow, in full honesty, "I'm not sure whether what I'm about to say is bullshit." These are not possibilities for the bullshit that interests Frankfurt. But they are possibilities. So the bullshit that interests Frankfurt doesn't cover the waterfront.

A person who speaks with Frankfurtian indifference to the truth might do so yet *happen* to say something true, and, in at least one sense of the term, the one that interests me, what he

---

[17] Although this is not, again (see the text to footnote 12 above), their ultimate goal.
[18] See the final paragraph of this section.

says could not then be bullshit.[19] And, oppositely, an honest person might read some bullshit that a Frankfurt-bullshitter wrote, believe it to be the truth, and affirm it. When that honest person utters bullshit, *she's* not showing a disregard for truth. So it is neither necessary nor sufficient for every kind of bullshit that it be produced by one who is informed by indifference to the truth, or, indeed, by any other distinctive intentional state.

The honest follower, or the honest confused producer of bullshit, may or may not count as a bullshitter,[20] but she is certainly honest, and she certainly utters (one kind of) bullshit. There exists bullshit as a feature of utterances that does not qualify as bullshit by virtue of the intentional state of the utterance's producer (although that state may, of course causally explain why the bullshit is there, and/or why what's there is bullshit).

But what *is* that feature of utterances? *One thing it can be*, at least to a first approximation, is what the OED calls it, to wit, *nonsense*. But what particularly interests me is a certain variety of nonsense, namely, that which is found in discourse that is by nature *unclarifiable*, discourse, that is, that is not only obscure but which cannot be rendered unobscure, where any apparent success in rendering it unobscure creates something that isn't recognizable as a version of what was said. That is why it is frequently an appropriate response to a charge of bullshit is to set about trying to clarify what was said. (Think of attempts to vindicate Heidegger, or Hegel. The way to show that they weren't bullshitters is not by showing that they cared about the truth, but by showing that what they said, resourcefully construed, makes sense. Those who call them bullshitters do not doubt that they cared about the truth, or, at any rate, it is not *because* of any such doubt that they think Hegel and Heidegger were bullshitters.[21] That Frankfurt issue isn't the issue here.)

---

[19] Perhaps in contrast with Frankfurt's sense, and certainly in contrast with what Frankfurt says about that sense (see pp. 47–48).

[20] That question is addressed in the penultimate paragraph of this section.

[21] For the record, I do not believe that Hegel was a bullshitter, and I am too ignorant of the work of Heidegger to say whether or not he was a bullshitter. But I agree with my late supervisor Gilbert Ryle that Heidegger was a *shit*. I once asked Ryle whether he had continued to study Heidegger after he had written a long review of *Being and Time* that was published in *Mind*. Ryle's reply: "No, because when the Nazis came to power, Heidegger showed that he was a shit, from the heels up, and a shit from the heels up can't do good philosophy." (Experience has, alas, induced me to disagree with the stated Rylean generalization.)

Something is unclarifiable if and only if it cannot be made clear, but I shall not try to say what "clear" means in this essay. (I'm inclined to think it's not possible to do so, in an illuminating way.) Note, however, that there are relevantly different forms of unclarity, all of which have bearing here. There is the unclarity of a sentence itself, and then there is the unclarity as to why a certain (possibly perfectly clear) sentence is uttered in a given context: So, for example, the meaning of Wittgenstein's "If a lion could speak, we would not understand him" is in one way perfectly clear, but it might nevertheless be judged obscure, and unclarifiably obscure, by one who doubts that it carries, in context, a graspable point. There is also the unclarity of why one statement should be taken to lend credence to another statement. And there are no doubt other pertinent unclarities too.

Note that it is not an objection to the proposed sufficient condition of bullshit that different people might, in the light of different background beliefs, impose different standards of clarity, and, therefore, identify different pieces of texts as bullshit. Some of the people might, of course, be wrong.

I emphasized "one thing it can be" three paragraphs back because defects other than unclarifiable unclarity can suffice to stigmatize a text as bullshit. I focus on this variety of the phenomenon because it commands a greater academic following than other varieties do. In the various varieties of bullshit, what is wanting, speaking very generally, is an appropriate connection to truth, but not, as in Frankfurt's bullshit, as far as the state of mind of the producer is concerned, but with respect to features of the piece of text itself. Unclarifiably unclarity is one such feature. Rubbish, in the sense of arguments that are grossly deficient either in logic or in sensitivity to empirical evidence, is another. A third is irretrievably speculative comment, which is neither unclear nor wanting in logic, such as—David Miller's excellent example—"Of course, everyone spends much more time thinking about sex now than people did a hundred years ago."

I focus on unclarifiable unclarity in particular in preparation for a further inquiry into bullshit that addresses the question why so much of that particular kind of bullshit is produced in France. This kind of academic bullshit, unlike the two contrasting types of bullshit, be they academic or not, mentioned in the previous paragraph, comes close to being celebrated for its very unclarity, by some of its producers and consumers. What some of them certainly celebrate is a disconnection with truth: in what perhaps ranks as the consummation of the development of unclarity-type bullshit, a consummation that Hegel might have called "bullshit risen to consciousness if itself", truth is, in much post-modernism, *expressly* disparaged.

Although I foreswear a definition of 'clarity', I can offer a sufficient condition of unclarity. It is that adding or subtracting (if it has one) a negation sign from a text makes no difference to its level of plausibility:[22] no force in a statement has been grasped if its putative grasper would react no differently to its negation from how he reacts to the original statement. The deliberate bullshit published by Alan Sokal[23] no doubt comes out as unclarifiable, by that criterion. Note that this test does not apply to the different sorts of bullshit reviewed a couple of paragraphs back, and, being a merely sufficient condition of unclarifiability, it does not characterize *all* cases of the latter either.

An objection that faces my account is that it appears to classify good poetry that isn't bullshit as bullshit, since a piece of good poetry may be unclarifiable. A tempting way of acquitting such poetry of the charge of bullshit is by reference to its designation *as* poetry, rather than *as* some sort of contribution to knowledge in a more straightforward sense. But then the same text would be bullshit or not according, Frankfurt-like, to its, as it were, intentional encasement, and I am trying to characterize an intention-independent sense of the term.

An unclarifiable text can be valuable because of its suggestiveness: it can stimulate thought, it can be worthwhile seeking to interpret it in a spirit which tolerates multiplicity of interpretation, and which therefore denies that it means some one given thing, as a clarifiable piece of text does. So let us say, to spare good poetry, that the bullshit that concerns me is not only unclarifiable but also lacks this virtue of suggestiveness.[24] (I am

---

[22] This criterion of bullshit was devised by Professor Arthur J. Brown, to whom I am indebted.

[23] In his wonderful spoof, "Transgressing the Boundaries: Towards a Transformative Hermeneutics of Quantum Gravity"—which was published as a non-spoof in the thereby self-condemning *Social Text* 46–47 (Spring–Summer, 1996), pp. 217–252.

[24] I am allowing that the unclarifiable may be productively suggestive, but I would not

sure that many academic bullshitters get away with a lot of bull-shit because *some* of their unclarifiabilia are valuably suggestive, and therefore not bullshit. Their readers then mistakenly expect more, or most, of it to be so.)

So much by way of a preliminary attempt to identify the *bullshit* that interests me. But what reading of 'bullshitter', if any, corresponds to the bullshit that I have tried to identify? Producers of Cohen-bullshit are clearly not by nature bullshit-ters, in Frankfurt's sense, though Frankfurt-bullshitters often produce Cohen-bullshit, at least in the academy. Rather, I would say that the word 'bullshitter' that corresponds to my bullshit has two readings. In one of its readings, a bullshitter is a person who is *disposed* to bullshit: he tends, *for whatever rea-son*, to produce a lot of unclarifiable stuff. In a second accept-able reading of the term, a bullshitter is a person who *aims* at bullshit, however frequently or infrequently he hits his target.[25] (Notice that other nouns that signify that their denotations engage in a certain activity display a similar pair of readings: a killer may be a being that tends to kill, with whatever intention or lack of it (a weed-killer, for example, is a killer, and a merely careless human stomper on flowers is a (flower-) killer); or he may be a being who intends to kill, whether or not he ever

---

go as far as Fung Yu-lan does: "Aphorisms, allusions, and illustrations are . . . not artic-ulate enough. Their insufficiency in articulateness is compensated for, however, by their suggestiveness. Articulateness and suggestiveness are, of course, incompatible. The more an expression is articulate, the less it is suggestive - just as the more an expres-sion is prosaic, the less it is poetic. The sayings and writings of the Chinese philosophers are so inarticulate that their suggestiveness is almost boundless" (*A Short History of Chinese Philosophy* [New York: Macmillan, 1960], p. 12).

[25] Michael Otsuka comments insightfully on a familiar academic "case in which the two come apart: that is, in which someone is disposed to unclarifiable unclarity without aim-ing at it. Many academics (including perhaps an especially high proportion of graduate students) are disposed to produce the unclarifiable unclarity that is bullshit, not because they are aiming at unclarifiable unclarity, but rather because they are aiming at profun-dity. Their lucid utterances are manifestly unprofound, even to them. Their clarifiable unclear utterances can be rendered manifestly not profound through clarification. But their unclarifiably unclear utterances are unmanifestly not profound. Hence it is safe for them to think that they are profound. These utterances are not profound either because they are meaningful (in some subtle way, should there be one, that is consistent with their unclarifiable unclarity) but unprofound or because they are meaningless. They are *unmanifestly* not profound because it is hard to demonstrate that they are not profound, given their unclarifiability. By aiming at profundity, these academics tend to produce obscurity. But they do not aim at obscurity, not even as a means of generating profun-dity" (Private communication, 2nd September, 1999).

does). Aim-(Cohen)-bullshitters *seek* and *rely* on unclarifiability, whereas innocent speakers of bullshit are merely victims of it. Aim-bullshitters resort to bullshit when they have reason to want what they say to be unintelligible, for example, in order to impress, or in order to give spurious support to a claim: the motives for producing bullshit vary. (And just as a person might sometimes kill, without being a killer in either of the senses I distinguished, so a person who is in neither of the senses I distinguished a bullshitter might, on occasion, produce bullshit.)

What about the verb, 'to bullshit'? Does the producer of my bullshit, always bullshit when she produces bullshit, as Frankfurt's does? I see no reason for saying that an innocent does, especially if she's not even a disposition-bullshitter. But an aim-bullshitter who produces bullshit indeed bullshits.[26]

5 Bullshit as Product and Bullshit as Process

It matters that bullshit can come in the non-intention-freighted form by which I am exercised. For there is, today, a great deal of my kind of bullshit in certain areas of philosophical and semi-philosophical culture, and if, as we should, we are to conduct a struggle against it, the sort of struggle that, so one might say, Alan Sokal has inaugurated,[27] then it is important not to make false accusations, and not, therefore, for example, to charge possibly innocent traffickers in bullshit of lacking a concern for truth, or of deliberately conniving at obscurity.[28] Our proper

---

[26] Let me now list some central differences between the two kinds of bullshit that I have distinguished:

	Typical Context of Utterance	Corresponding OED Definition	Primary Locus	Essence
Frankfurt's bullshit	everyday life	2	activity	indifference to truth
Cohen's bullshit	the academy	1	output	unclarifiability

[27] Initially in the article referenced in footnote 23, and then more comprehensively in *Intellectual Impostures*, which he wrote with Jean Bricmont (London: Profile, 1998).
[28] Consider this sentence from the work of Étienne Balibar: "This is precisely the first meaning we can give to the idea of dialectic: a logic or form of explanation specifically adapted to the determinant intervention of class struggle in the very fabric of history" (*The Philosophy of Marx* [New York: Verso, 1995]). If you read that sentence quickly, it can sound pretty good. The remedy is to read it more slowly, and you will then

polemical target is bullshit, and not bullshitters, or producers of bullshit, as such. So while it's lots of fun, for people like me, who have a developed infantile streak, to talk about bullshit, and even just to write 'bullshit', over and over again, in an academic article, there is nevertheless, in my opinion, something important at stake here, and the character of what is at stake makes the bullshitter/bullshit distinction important.

To prevent misunderstanding, let me add that I do believe that there is quite a lot of *aiming* at obscurity in the production of philosophical bullshit, and a lot, to boot, in this region, of lack of concern with truth.[29] But these moral faults should not be our primary focus. For reasons of courtesy, strategy, and good evidence, we should criticize the product, which is visible, and not the process, which is not.[30]

---

recognize it to be a wonderful paradigm of bullshit: yet I know Balibar to be an honest thinker.

[29] The evidence assembled in Sokal and Bricmont's *Intellectual Impostures* proves, so I think, the truth of those beliefs.

[30] We may hope that success in discrediting the product will contribute to extinguishing the process. I try to contribute to the project of discrediting the product in an unpublished and unpublishable discussion of "Why One Kind of Bullshit Flourishes in France," a draft of which will be supplied upon application to me.

9
The Unity of Bullshit

GARY L. HARDCASTLE

Our topic is bullshit, of course, and it goes almost without saying that in reflecting on our bullshit-rich practices, and on the various concepts we use to describe them, we'll be making use of philosophy. Since reflection and tinkering with concepts is part of our practice as well, in thinking philosophically about bullshit we have every chance (and by 'we' I mean 'I') of actually engaging in bullshit (that is, "bullshitting"). Perhaps without even knowing it, or, perish the thought, caring. So there's not just philosophy afoot, but irony as well. Fair warning.

Yet think about bullshit we must. Not just because this is a volume of essays on bullshit, and not just because I'm a contributing editor to that volume facing, for this very paper, a ridiculous deadline, the missing of which will obligate me to purchase a very expensive French dinner for another of the volume's contributors (nor has it escaped my attention that these conditions are themselves ideal for the promulgation of bullshit, so the bullshit-risk I'm running in even *attempting* this essay is, shall we say, immense).

No, the reason we must talk about bullshit is simply because (a) it's a fixture in our lives, and (b) we'd rather it wasn't. That is, we find bullshit—not always, but often enough—obnoxious and, occasionally, intolerable. And under exactly these conditions arises, inexorably, that oldest genre of talk: *complaint.* As in, "What's *with* all this bullshit?!" (but in Sumerian).

Fortunately, not all our bullshit talk is complaint. Everyone, from me to all but the most cynical among us, nurses the hope that with a bit of care, a bit of insight, a bit of resolve, and a bit

137

of luck, we could reduce, nay, eliminate, the amount of bullshit in our own lives, nay, in the lives of everyone we deal with, nay, in *everyone*. Or, if not eliminate, maybe *overcome* the bullshit. And it's that hope that sends us off, personally, in our families, and occasionally in our communities, on anti-bullshit campaigns of various scales, with limited success but nearly unlimited expectations of success. Preliminary to these campaigns, and usually in conjunction with them as well, we settle on what it is exactly we'd like to eliminate. And that involves a certain amount of talk very different in kind from complaint. It involves marshalling examples, crafting definitions, designing a strategy, anticipating resistance, measuring success, and articulating some sort of exit strategy (that last one optional in the United States).

The talk is usually just *thought*, of course—talk to ourselves. But occasionally someone climbs on stage, takes a deep breath, and lets the rest of the world, or at least everyone who is listening, in on her plan. When one too many "Customer Service Specialists" consigned the earnest and hard-working Laura Penny, a Canadian writer and writing instructor, to one too many "Automated Customer Service Facilities," the result was an anti-bullshit declaration pedestrian in sentiment but celestial in eloquence. The ending of Penny's *Your Call Is Important to Us: The Truth About Bullshit* genuinely touches me:

> You, Gentle Reader, are probably not one of the powerful male-factors of great bullshit, so all of this huffing and puffing is kind of like chastising kids for poor attendance at school. The kids who are congenitally un-there aren't around to hear you chew them out.
>
> But in the event you are a perpetrator (and you know in your heart of hearts if you are), I say unto you: Shame. Shame! Have you no sense of decency? You take names in vain, and send legions of vain names into the world. And when you fuck with English, you are money-changing in my temple.[1]

How much bullshit do you suppose it takes to get a writing instructor to write *that*? A lot, I'm imagining. Go Laura!

It's been some time since a philosopher worked up a comparable head of steam, but let's note that this sort of talk about

---

[1] Laura Penny, *Your Call Is Important to Us· The Truth about Bullshit* (New York: Crown, 2005), p. 223.

bullshit—devising definitions, crafting strategies, countering resistance, and so on—is one thing philosophers *do regularly*, as a matter of profession and sometimes as a matter just of professional habit. And every so often one philosopher makes such headway against bullshit, or at least comes to believe that such headway has been made, that his or her particular anti-bullshit project attracts the attention not just of other philosophers but of regular people. This happened most recently with Harry Frankfurt's *On Bullshit*, a *bona fide* bestseller.

On Bullshit is a charming (if skinny) book with a catchy title, and partly because of this, no doubt, it enjoyed twenty-six weeks on the *New York Times* bestseller list, where dashes demurely obscured its title's naughty bit. And since Frankfurt's book had circulated as a paper for some years before its promotion to book, other philosophers—notably G.A. Cohen, whose "Deeper Into Bullshit" is included in this volume (pp. 117–135)—had something to say about bullshit. Philosophically speaking, 2005 was a very good year for bullshit, and so was 2006.

We should celebrate both *On Bullshit*'s enormous success, and the immanent delivery of yet more related philosophical work (including the book you're holding right now), to the public that professional philosophy all too often forgets. We should celebrate it not as the long-awaited return of the philosopher kings to the public debate (or even to *Rolling Stone*) but simply as an occasion for philosophy to join the discussion taking place more or less all the time outside the realm of philosophy departments, classrooms, and conferences. If Frankfurt's book shows anything, it's that philosophers, as much as anyone else, want to know what's with all the bullshit. Actually, we even have a few ideas.

Frankfurt's idea (as many, if not all, the chapters in this volume will point out) is that bullshit is a certain kind of negligence, specifically, negligence of truth. This notion is well-expressed in a distinction Frankfurt draws between bullshit and lying: the liar *cares* about the truth (and wants to steer us *away* from it), while the bullshitter doesn't give a hoot about the truth so long as she can bullshit her way through to the promotion, the donation, the grade, the vote, the sale, or sometimes—let's be honest—just the end of the conversation. The bullshitter's utter disregard for the truth Frankfurt deems more offensive than the liar's perverse regard for the truth. "Bullshit," as Frankfurt puts it, "is a greater enemy of the truth than lies are" (*On Bullshit*, p. 61) because, Frankfurt seems to believe, our living together in relative peace and harmony demands of each of us that we mind the truth.

Incidentally, this leaves Frankfurt with the puzzle of why we seem, at a first glance at least, to be so much *more* tolerant of bullshit than lying (a puzzle several others take up in this very volume). If bullshit is *so* corrosive, one would think it would get the blunt end of our moral cudgel; yet we let a lot of bullshit slide. As to the different question of why there is so much bullshit, Frankfurt suggests that we in the democratic West have backed ourselves into having to have a view about everything, no matter how little informed we might be, and that under these conditions a disregard for the truth becomes a rather attractive strategy for getting through the day (for an extensive discussion of this point, see Mark Evans's contribution to this volume). Democracy, it appears, breeds bullshit.

Frankfurt's ideas about bullshit are not the only ones on the table. There's also G.A. Cohen's. Cohen finds fault with Frankfurt's "indifference thesis" insofar as the various aims attached to bullshitting *include* some that require misdirection with respect to reality, that is, lying. And if some lying is bullshitting, Frankfurt's claim that bullshitting is entirely different from lying must be, well, wrong. Cohen cites advertisers (whom Frankfurt tags producers of classic, paradigm bullshit) as bullshitters, and notes that, like liars, they are keen to steer us away from the truth. The mistake, as Cohen has it, lies in confusing the bullshitter's not caring "whether or not what he says is true" with his "not caring whether his audience is caused to believe something true or false" (pp. 127–28). Cohen claims that the bullshitter's negligence of the truth of what he says sits alongside an obsession for the truth about what others believe. Advertisers, to continue the example, care *not at all* if the new Ford Humiliator *is* the best-built or most reliable SUV but *loads* about the truth of what *we* believe about it.

A second complaint of Cohen's cuts deeper. He claims that Frankfurt's account of bullshit is *incomplete*. It misses out on an important, and different, *kind* of bullshit. In focusing "on one kind of bullshit only," writes Cohen, Frankfurt did not address another, equally interesting, and academically more significant, kind. Bullshit as insincere talk or writing is indeed what it is because it is the product of something like bluffing, but talking nonsense is what it is because of the character of its output, and nonsense is not nonsense because of features of the nonsense-talker's mental state. (pp. 121–22)

On Frankfurt's concept of bullshit, the bull, to borrow Cohen's expression, "wears the trousers"; bullshit is whatever we get from the bull. What we need, according to Cohen, is a bullshit-(rather than a bull-) centered account of bullshit—an account of bullshit or nonsense *independent* of facts about the person serving it up (such as, for example, her mental state). And Cohen delivers an admittedly preliminary account of bullshit in this sense, one that emphasizes as a sufficient condition of bullshit its "unclarifiable unclarity" (p. 131). Something, a sentence for example, is unclarifiable "if and only if it cannot be made clear." It's disappointing that Cohen declines to say what 'clear' means —and, indeed, he lets on that he doesn't think it's even "possible to [say what 'clear' means], in an illuminating way" (p. 131). But it's an ironic disappointment, so at least we have that.

Frankfurt and Cohen each have some ideas about bullshit, then, and, not surprisingly, they are at odds. My *own* idea about bullshit consists, I hesitate to divulge, in adding yet *more* ideas about bullshit to the mix, in the hope of resolving what appear to be irresolvable differences between Frankfurt's idea and Cohen's. This strategy of simplifying the conceptual stew by adding more things to it strikes many (my students especially) as a bit perverse. But it is in fact a reliable (and, partly for that reason, quite popular) way to actually make progress in these sorts of matters, especially when the ideas added to the mix have garnered decent reviews on the intellectual stage; when they have, that is, a respectable intellectual ancestry. Determining this strategy's success in the *particular* instance of this paper I leave as an exercise for the reader.

The ideas I'll be bringing to bear on the schism between Cohen and Frankfurt are the ideas associated with logical positivism—the premier, passionate, remarkably successful, and altogether thoroughly entertaining anti-bullshit philosophical program of the 1920s and 1930s (its end met, tragically but not surprisingly, at the hands of two of the twentieth century's pre-

mier *bullshit* programs, European fascism and the Red Scare[2]).
There are clear parallels between logical positivism and contemporary anti-bullshit programs,[3] and, in fact, I'm surprised that
so far so few, Frankfurt included, have either noticed the parallel or drawn upon it to add to the current discussion.[4] But no
matter; perhaps this book, and even this essay, is a start.

The logical positivists were not shy about bringing the ham-
mer down on bullshit, but as often they described what they
were up to in the appropriately positive terms of promoting
unity among all the domains of genuine knowledge. *Their* idea
was that the unity of science meant making clear the connec-
tions various domains of knowledge bore to one another, and
that *that* led to eradication of the hidden depths and dark
recesses that could serve as massive underground bullshit
bunkers. "Unity of science!" they sang, warbling 'science' in its
very general, distinctly German, sense. So using the logical positivist's own ideas about bullshit, its source, and its eradication
to *unify* Frankfurt and Cohen's accounts, as I intend, invokes, it
seems to me, good anti-metaphysical karma.

---

[2] The good single-volume intellectual history of logical positivism before World War II
is still to be written, but see V. Kraft, *The Vienna Circle: The Origin of Neo-positivism: A
Chapter in the History of Recent Philosophy* (New York: Greenwood, 1953); Michael
Friedman, *A Parting of the Ways: Carnap, Cassirer, and Heidegger* (Chicago: Open
Court, 2000); and A. Richardson and R. Giere, eds., *Origins of Logical Empiricism*
(Minneapolis: University of Minnesota Press, 1998). For the period after World War II see
G. Hardcastle and A. Richardson, eds., *Logical Empiricism in North America*
(Minneapolis: University of Minnesota Press, 2003), and George A. Reisch, *How the Cold
War Transformed Philosophy of Science: To the Icy Slopes of Logic* (Cambridge:
Cambridge University Press, 2005).

[3] Ayer was logical positivism's Laura Penny. Whether Frankfurt is Rudolf Carnap and
Cohen Hans Reichenbach (or *vice versa*) I leave as an extra credit exercise for Alan
Richardson, subject to his agreement that we are all waiting for Gödel.

[4] Although Cohen, in the last pages of an unpublished addition to his "Deeper Into
Bullshit" devoted to the prevalence of bullshit in French intellectual culture, alludes off-
handedly to logical positivism's alleged failure to attract French adherents. For that matter, it has been suggested that Rudolf Carnap's 1932 "Überwindung der Metaphysik
durch Logische Analyse der Sprache," (*Erkenntnis 2* (1932): pp. 219–241) ("Overcoming
Metaphysics through the Logical Analysis of Language"), an essay famously representative of logical positivism and one to which I will turn to below, ought to have been titled
"Overcoming *Bullshit* through the Logical Analysis of Language," (presumably: "Überwindung der *Mist* durch Logische Analyse der Sprache"). Carnap's essay was reprinted
as "The Elimination of Metaphysics through Logical Analysis of Language" in A.J. Ayer,
ed., *Logical Positivism* (New York: Free Press, 1959), pp. 60–81; I follow recent practice
in preferring 'overcoming' for 'Überwindung'.

No Bullshit, Please, We're Austrian

Now the logical positivists railed against metaphysics rather than bullshit. If you happen to be worried that the positivist's metaphysics isn't Frankfurt's (or Cohen's) bullshit, then I aim to allay your worries by showing how the logical positivist's metaphysics *unites* Frankfurt's, and Cohen's, bullshit. The most famous instance of positivistic railing against metaphysics, I believe, is Rudolf Carnap's 1932 "Overcoming Metaphysics through the Logical Analysis of Language."[5] Philosophers know this essay as the one in which the young Rudolf Carnap takes the then far-better established German philosopher Martin Heidegger to task for writing, on p. 34 of his 1929 *Was Ist Metaphysik?*, "Das Nichts selbst nichtet," that is, 'The nothing *noths*'.[6] Here was a choice bit of metaphysics, Carnap noted, and just the sort of thing that we ought to *overcome* (rather than ponder, examine, debate, or refute) by sober, and rather elementary, logical analysis of the sentence itself. Carnap's essay is hardly the only instance of a logical positivist assault upon metaphysics, but (recall my ridiculous deadline) it's the only one I'll consider here. There is on the ontological horizon a succession of interesting articles and books with titles like "Neurath on Bullshit," "Reichenbach on Bullshit," "Quine on Bullshit," and so on, and someone (other than myself) ought to write them.

Carnap's target, and the target of the logical positivists generally, was meaningless utterances, but not *just* meaningless utterances. Carnap is interested in the much more interesting topic of meaningless utterances that can be, and often are, presented as and widely understood to be meaningful—their utterers might, for example, present them (falsely) as though they had a meaning, or the people who read or hear such utterances might believe (again, falsely) that they have a meaning. Such utterances are *pseudo-sentences*, and Carnap's claim is that metaphysics consists precisely of such pseudo-sentences. Spelling this out means, first, giving an account of what it is for an utterance to have meaning (thereby identifying what it is for it to be *meaningless* as well) and, second, explaining how it is that meaningless utterances could ever be confused with mean-

---

[5] In Ayer, *Logical Positivism*, pp. 60–81.
[6] Martin Heidegger, *Was Ist Metaphysik?* (Frankfurt A.M.: Klostermann, 1929).

ingful ones—how, we might say, metaphysics happens. Perhaps it's not hard, having said even just this little, to see how Carnap's approach to metaphysics might incorporate both Cohen's bullshit-centered notion of "unclarifiable unclarity" and Frankfurt's idea that bullshit is a certain intention, characterized by the disregard for the meaning of what one says (and, by that fact, for the truth). Both are afoot in the metaphysics Carnap begs us to overcome.

Examples work wonders for Carnap. He invites us to imagine an encounter with someone using the word 'teavy', a new word, or at least a word new to us:

> In order to learn the meaning of this word, we ask him about its criterion of application: how is one to ascertain in a concrete case whether a thing is teavy or not? Let us suppose to begin with that we get no answer from him: there are no empirical signs of teavyness, he says. In that case we would deny the legitimacy of using this word. If the person who uses the word says that all the same there are things which are teavy and there are things which are not teavy, only it remains for the weak, finite, intellect of man an eternal secret which things are teavy and which are not, we shall regard this as empty verbiage. (p. 64)

The meaninglessness of 'teavy' stems, Carnap holds, from the fact that what Carnap calls the term's *elementary* sentences—sentences with the form "x is teavy" (such as 'This world is teavy' or 'My brother is teavy')—cannot be deduced from other sentences. At the time, this meant for Carnap that the elementary sentences could not be verified.[7]

Utterances, as opposed to terms, can be meaningless as well, even when all the terms they contain are meaningful. There are trivial cases (Carnap offers 'Caesar is and'), but also cases like 'Caesar is a prime number', which might at first glance be taken as meaningful. This latter category contains *pseudo-statements*, things that aren't statements but might initially be taken to be (in Carnap's world, margarine, which isn't butter but can be passed off as butter, would be *pseudo-butter*). Meaningfulness for utter-

---

[7] Few would raise an eyebrow at an allegation of meaningless leveled at the made-up 'teavy', but Carnap is happy to note some other terms that are "in the same boat" as 'teavy' as far as meaninglessness goes. These include, 'principle', 'essence', 'the Ego', 'the Infinite', and (in one common use, at least) 'God' (p. 67).

ances, as for words, amounts to a certain disconnectedness to other claims: we cannot, in principle, bring evidence to bear on the meaningless expression, either for it or against it. Carnap offers as examples of these Heidegger's 'We find the nothing' and 'We know the nothing'; 'The nothing noths' wins *special* Carnapian exasperation points for being not just a meaningless arrangement of terms, but for having among its terms a meaningless one to boot, the pseudo-verb 'to nothing' (p. 71).

A Little Carnap in Everyone

Carnap's notion of meaninglessness, his main diagnostic tool in his battle against metaphysics, is a much more precise rendering of "unclarifiable unclarity," Cohen's main diagnostic tool in *his* battle against bullshit. This is why I am genuinely surprised that Cohen doesn't mention Carnap or, for that matter, any of the logical positivists. I believe the parallel is confirmed by a careful, sustained, reading of Cohen's paper alongside Carnap's; but, really, that's the sort of thing one ought to do in private.

But I will offer a consilience that bolsters my claim. Cohen offers nonsense as an example of bullshit, and by 'nonsense' he means not merely unclear discourse but discourse that *can't be made clear*: the mark of such unclarity is that "any apparent success in rendering it unobscure creates something that isn't recognizable as a version of what was said" (p. 130). This manner of identifying the unclarifiable by its *disconnectedness* to other statements or texts is just Carnap's strategy for isolating the meaningless. For Carnap, it is not as though there are antecedently meaningful sentences, and connecting a new sentence to one of these somehow infects the former with the latter's meaning. The idea, rather, is that something is meaningful just *in* bearing the right (presumably, logical) relation to other assertions or texts. And it's the same for Cohen: it's not as though there are clear sentences out there, the clarity of which seeps into other sentences if we position the latter correctly. Clarity is a matter of bearing the right relation to other claims. So it's a demonstration of profound *un*clarity if, in trying to show a sentence's connection to others, you inevitably mangle the claim with which you began into "something that isn't recognizable as a version of what was said." This shows that there was no such connection to begin with.

On Carnap's account, then, our language holds, for us, its users, a danger. For in allowing for the formulation of nonsense words and meaningless expressions it allows us to lapse into bullshit. Carnap frequently mentions the possibility of being "misled," or "seduced," by our language, and he means misled or seduced into metaphysics. But that is not the only danger. Because our language allows for the formulation of pseudo-words and pseudosentences, it is a powerful and effective tool that can be exploited by those whose aims are served by misdirection or the obfuscation of truth short of lying, that is, by bullshitters in the Frankfurtian sense. By the very fact that they present meaningless statements as meaningful they express their disregard for the truth, and by the fact that they utter meaningless statements they can't be lying; they are, after all, saying nothing.

In this regard, consider these two more passages from Carnap's essay, each of which emphasizes the intention of the metaphysician—the bullshitter, as I read it. The first invites us again to imagine a new term, 'toovy' this time, which, in contrast to 'teavy', is meaning*ful*:

> Let the sentence "this thing is toovy" be true if and only if the thing is quadrangular. . . . Then we will say: the word "toovy" is synonymous with the word "quadrangular." And we will not allow its users to tell us that nevertheless they "intended" something else by it than "quadrangular"; that though every quadrangular thing is also toovy and conversely, this is only because quadrangularity is the visible manifestation of toovyness, but that the latter itself is a hidden, not itself observable property. We would reply that after the criterion of application had been fixed, the synonymy of "toovy" and "quadrangular" is likewise fixed, and that we are no further at liberty to "intend" this or that by the word. (p. 64)

For Carnap, the example is intended to show that the meaning of a term is exhausted by the deductive relationships the term's elementary sentences bear to other sentences; anyone who claims for a term a meaning not captured by those deductive relationships cannot be offering us a meaning at all. But the example tells us as well about the intentions Carnap clearly thinks are tangled up with metaphysics. We too would dismiss anyone who continued to profess additional meaning for 'toovy' after its synonymy with 'quadrangular' had been laid bare.

What's her problem?!? Absent appeals to absurdity, comedy, or idiocy (three well-known bullshit-defeaters deserving of much more philosophical attention), such flagrant disregard for meaning can be explained only by concluding that it was never the toovy-talker's intention to convey information to us in the first place, or even steer us away from some information (to, that is, lie). She must have wanted to accomplish some other end for which uttering such pseudostatements would be of use. 'Toovy' was a meaningful term all along, but in her disregard for the term's meaning the toovy-talker was engaged in metaphysics . . . that is, bullshitting.[8]

The second passage I have in mind, in which Carnap comments on the intentions behind metaphysics, comes, interestingly enough, in the context of Carnap's answer to the question of why there is so much metaphysics, and why we seem to put up with it—confirmation, incidentally, of my view that Carnap and Frankfurt are talking about the same thing. "How could it be," Carnap asks, "that so many men in all ages and nations, among them eminent minds, spent so much energy, nay veritable fervor, on metaphysics if the latter consisted of nothing but mere words, nonsensically juxtaposed?" (p. 78). How, indeed? What's *with* all this metaphysics?

Carnap's answer is that metaphysics is a consequence of a desire to express some "general attitude towards life" (*Lebenseinstellung*) combined with a mistaken impression that an attitude (towards life or anything else) is a *state of affairs*, that is, the kind of thing that can be expressed by a declarative sentence. An attitude towards life *can* be expressed, but only in art, poetry, or music; to attempt its expression in assertions, as though the attitude were not an attitude but a state of affairs, is futile.[9] "Thus in the case of metaphysics," Carnap writes, "we find this situation:"

> Through the form of its works it pretends to be something that it is not. The form in question is that of a system of statements which

---

[8] The reader can construct her own contemporary version of this example by replacing 'toovy' with 'terrorist', another term the meaning of which has, I suggest, been toovied.
[9] Hence Carnap's otherwise puzzling yet stinging assessment of metaphysicians (especially Heidegger) as "musicians without musical ability" and his (otherwise equally puzzling but) laudatory endorsement of Friedrich Nietzsche for writing *Thus Spake Zarathustra* as poetry (quality, apparently, notwithstanding), p. 80.

are apparently related as premises and conclusions, that is, the form of a theory. In this way the fiction of theoretical content is generated, whereas, as we have seen, there is no such content. It is not only the reader, but the metaphysician himself who suffers from the illusion that the metaphysical statements say something, describe states of affairs. The metaphysician believes that he travels in territory in which truth and falsehood are at stake. In reality, however, he has not asserted anything, but only expressed something, like an artist. (p. 79)

On its face, this diagnosis renders metaphysics rather benign. That is a strength, of course, if the question is why we tolerate it. And as far as the parallel with bullshit goes, it gives us another answer to the question of why bullshit is both ubiquitous and tolerated. To wit: bullshit arises when people have something they want to get across and are confused, perhaps but not always culpably so, about what tools are appropriate to that task.

But alongside these somewhat contented observations about metaphysics, and bullshit, in our life, there is of course a critical current in Carnap, and Frankfurt, and we can't afford to miss it. Carnap describes the case in which the metaphysician as well as his audience is under the illusion that his utterances make sense, but there are, as Carnap was more than aware, cases in which the metaphysician, but not the audience, is under no such illusion. After all, metaphysics can only "pretend to be something that it is not" if behind the metaphysical utterance is a metaphysician pretending to say something, knowing at the same time that he is not. This is bullshit, Frankfurt-style, pure and simple. It's more egregious, of course, to the extent that the metaphysician-bullshitter propagates the illusion in his followers even after we've called him on his insolence regarding the meaninglessness of his utterances or, in Frankfurt's phrase, regarding the truth-value of his claims. Heidegger was a metaphysician before Carnap penned "Overcoming of Metaphysics through Logical Analysis of Language," but his metaphysical bullshit was more offensive after Carnap called him on it. Ditto, *mutatis mutandis*, for modern-day Frankfurt bullshitters. *On Bullshit*'s placement on the *New York Times* bestseller list not only sold a pile of books; it raised the moral stakes on people who don't care about the truth of what they say.

The Unity of Bullshit

Recall that Cohen employed a rather useful metaphor to distinguish his view from Frankfurt's: Frankfurt's account of bullshit focuses upon the bull, and his, Cohen's, starts from the bullshit. In light of our discussion of Carnap's anti-metaphysical program and my promise to unify Frankfurt's and Cohen's account, it will pay to return to the metaphor.

There is a certainly a distinction to be drawn between a bull and bullshit, and between bullshit and the bullshitter. But, my local veterinarians assure me, a bull that doesn't shit is no bull, at least not for long. And it takes, as David Hume might put it, no nice metaphysical head to realize that we get bullshit from a bull, not necessarily of course, but in fact, in this world and all the close possible ones. Cohen's metaphor not only serves his purpose, but it ought to remind us that the two sides of bullshit, Frankfurt's and Cohen's, are two sides of one thing. There are in this world those whose have ends that are served by a misuse of language, and whose desires trump or even eradicate any concern they might have had for the meaning or the truth of what they say. These are Frankfurtian bullshitters, and so be it. But we also have a tool, a language, that is amenable, perhaps even suited for, just the sort of misdeeds bullshitters have in mind. All of us have, or can, fashion Cohen-style bullshit on demand, and so be that. Combine the two and you have fodder for books like this one and Laura Penny's, and for that matter for the many, many, conversations held *today* that included the phrase "This is *such* bullshit." Carnap, of course, didn't know from Frankfurt and Cohen in 1932, but he knew bullshit. His approach to it gave us the intellectual goods on offer today from Frankfurt and Cohen, and then some.

Ah, but what to do? Is it any solace to have one account of bullshit over two, if our aim at the start was, implicitly at least, to get *rid* of the bullshit? The question of how to respond to bullshit is more pressing, and depressing, when we realize not just that the bullshit tide is rising, with no recess in sight, but that all those enthusiastic bullshit-eradication programs of yore, logical positivism included, have that rather embarrassing odor of ambition-cum-failure. In this context, the very end of Laura Penny's book might look at a first glance like the quintessential twenty-first century post-whatever reply to bullshit: a none-too-hearty "Oh, well."

But that's just a first glance. Here's a suggestion that may sound less antique and more plausible the more our intolerance for bullshit and its perpetrators grows. Our analysis of bullshit as one part tool (a language amenable to misuse) and one part intention (to put something over by means of that tool) invites a strategy oddly familiar to advocates of gun control: control the gun. In this case, of course, it's control the language, the tool that bullshitter's employ. No one, not Frankfurt, Carnap, Cohen, or Penny, suggests that we will eradicate from our midst those with *intent* to bullshit; indeed, sometimes that very enemy is us. Bullshitters are inevitable. But we can take in hand the tool the Frankfurtian bullshitter turns to, and needs: our language. This taking in hand need not be the fashioning of the ideal language that Carnap and many (though, notably, not all) of the Vienna Circle imagined, or even the conceptual clean up Cohen calls for.

Again, I'm moved by the last line of Penny's book, and I don't mean the choice verb. The language we use, English or whatever, is *ours*, together, and each of us bears responsibility for its misuse and abuse in our presence. When one of us misuses it, placing it in the employ of bullshit, it is no prissy matter of grammar or style that is at stake but a common temple being defaced. Your task, gentle reader, is to stand at the door of the temple. This can mean writing a book, or an essay, or a letter, or a blog, but it will also and more often mean holding a sign, raising a hand, casting a vote, or interrupting a conversation.

It's a daily, mundane, thankless, and unending task, but it will be the way out when the alternative becomes too much bullshit to bear. Take some heart that you will be joined, in spirit if not in corpus, with Carnap's robust colleague, Otto Neurath, who impressed upon his wide audience that the shape of the world around is the result not of reasons beyond our control—pseudorationalism, Neurath called this idea—but of our *own* choices.[10] It really is up to us.

---

[10] See Otto Neurath, "The Lost Wanderers of Descartes and the Auxiliary Motive (On the Psychology of Decision)," in Neurath, *Philosophical Papers 1913–1946* (Boston: Reidel, 1983), pp. 1–12.

10
Raising the Tone: Definition, Bullshit, and the Definition of Bullshit

ANDREW ABERDEIN

> I always love that kind of argument. The contrary of a thing isn't the contrary; oh, dear me, no! It's the thing itself, but as it *truly* is. Ask any die-hard what conservatism is; he'll tell you that it's *true* socialism. And the brewers' trade papers: they're full of articles about the beauty of true temperance. Ordinary temperance is just gross refusal to drink; but true temperance, *true* temperance is something much more refined. True temperance is a bottle of claret with each meal and three double whiskies after dinner.[1]

Bullshit is not the only sort of deceptive talk. Spurious definitions, such as those quoted above, are another important variety of bad reasoning. This paper will describe some of these problematic tactics, and show how Harry Frankfurt's treatment of bullshit may be extended to analyze their underlying causes. Finally, I will deploy this new account of definition to assess whether Frankfurt's definition of bullshit is itself legitimate.

Semantic Negligence

Frankfurt's principal contribution to the study of bullshit is the distinction he draws between the bullshitter and the liar. Whereas the liar represents as true something he believes to be false, the bullshitter represents something as true when he neither knows nor cares whether it is true or false (*On Bullshit*, p. 55). As Frankfurt amply demonstrates, this indifference is much

---

[1] Aldous Huxley, *Eyeless in Gaza* (London: Chatto and Windus, 1936) pp. 122–23.

of what we find most objectionable about bullshit. The liar has a vested interest in the institution of truth-telling, albeit a parasitical one: he hopes that his falsehoods will be accepted as true. The bullshitter may also hope to be believed, but he himself is not much bothered whether what he says is true, hence his disregard for the truth is of a deeper and potentially more pernicious character.

Our outrage is conditioned on our being the objects of a deception. When we know what the bullshitter is up to we can be much more indulgent. As the comic novelist Terry Pratchett observes of two of his characters, "they believed in bullshit and were the type to admire it when it was delivered with panache. There's a kind of big, outdoor sort of man who's got no patience at all with prevaricators and fibbers, but will applaud any man who can tell an outrageous whopper with a gleam in his eye."[2] The gleam in the eye is essential here: it is this complicity between bullshitter and audience which constitutes the "bull session" (*On Bullshit*, p. 34). Only when it escapes from the bull session and masquerades as regular assertion is bullshit deceptive; however, the insidious nature of this deception degrades the commitment to truth upon which public discourse depends.

One way of characterizing Frankfurt's innovation is as the introduction of a new category of linguistic misbehaviour, which we might call 'semantic negligence'. It is this concept which enables him to distinguish the bullshitter from the liar. In British and American common law, a civil claim for negligence arises when the defendant has a duty of care to the plaintiff which he neglects to exercise, thereby harming the plaintiff. Here the deceptive bullshitter has a duty to tell the truth; neglecting this duty harms his audience if they come to believe his false statements. His indifference as to the truth value of his statements, that is whether they are true or false, a meaning-related or semantic property, may thus be termed semantic negligence. Lying involves a higher degree of culpability, since the liar convinces his audience of falsehoods intentionally, not just foreseeably. Frankfurt's insight is that conventional accounts of deception provide no middle ground between this higher level of culpability and complete innocence, and therefore no room

---

[2] Terry Pratchett, *Going Postal* (London: Corgi, 2005) pp. 280–81.

for many familiar forms of deceit, such as bullshit. My contention is that semantic negligence may arise with respect to features of meaning other than truth value, and as such may be used to disentangle a wide variety of deceptive dialectical practices. Furthermore, semantic negligence is itself a matter of degree. The legal understanding of negligence acknowledges that the associated culpability can range from inadvertence to willful blindness. We may generalize Frankfurt's position further by recognizing that some instances of semantic negligence are worse than others. In assessing the gravity of semantic negligence we should ask questions such as 'How foreseeable was it that deception would arise?' and 'How much at fault is the speaker in not foreseeing this?'.

A Caricature History of Semantics

My argument will draw on themes from the philosophy of language, chiefly the pioneering German logician Gottlob Frege's disambiguation of the naive understanding of 'meaning'. In what may be considered the primal moment of analytic philosophy, Frege drew a threefold distinction between *Sinn*, *Bedeutung*, and *Färbung*, or sense, reference and tone. The sense of a term is what we understand if we understand what the word means. The reference, however, is the thing which the word picks out. Hence, as Frege explains, "a proper name (word, sign, combination of signs, expression) *expresses* its sense, [but] *stands for* or *designates* its reference. By employing a sign we express its sense and designate its reference."[3] For example, the sense of 'the longest river in the world' is just what we understand by the words in this phrase. Clearly, having that understanding does not depend on knowing what the reference is (the River Nile, all four thousand miles of it), let alone on having seen the river in question. The last of Frege's three divisions, tone, is the least familiar: it may be defined as that aspect of the meaning of an expression that is irrelevant to the truth value of any sentence in which it may occur. In languages with large vocabularies, like English, it is often possible to restate a phrase using different

---

[3] Gottlob Frege "On *Sinn* and *Bedeutung*" (1892) in Michael Beaney, ed., *The Frege Reader* (London: Blackwell, 1997), p. 156.

words, but preserving both sense and reference. Continuing with the earlier example, consider 'Earth's lengthiest natural watercourse.' The change here is one of tone.

Frege's distinction between sense and reference was not entirely original. Many earlier philosophers, perhaps as early as Aristotle, drew similar distinctions between these aspects of the meaning of a word or expression. In this context the terminology 'intension' and 'extension' is often used instead of sense and reference respectively. With proper nouns, and definite descriptions, like the example in the last paragraph, the terminology coincides exactly. With other sorts of noun, "concept nouns" as Frege calls them, sense and intension have the same meaning, but the reference is to the concept under which the members of the extension fall. The value of distinguishing between the reference and extension of a concept noun is most apparent when talking about short-lived or rapidly propagating things. Expressions such as 'snowflake', 'mayfly', or 'web page' have constantly changing extensions, but more or less fixed references. By concentrating on reference rather than extension, we can disregard superficial changes of this kind. Frege's approach was innovative in several respects, most of which go beyond the scope of this article, and has had a profound influence on subsequent philosophy. A crucial insight of Frege's is that sense cannot be reduced to reference: different terms can have the same reference, but different senses. In his well-known example, 'the evening star' and 'the morning star' both refer to the same object, the planet Venus, although the senses of these phrases are clearly distinct. Indeed, it was a genuine scientific discovery in the ancient world when it was realized that these two familiar sights were one and the same. Without the distinction between sense and reference we would be unable to describe this discovery.

Frege's formalizing project required the suppression of tone: "separating a thought from its trappings" as he puts it.[4] Tone is the part of meaning from which we must abstract before logical analysis can begin. This abstraction is essential to the representation of inference in terms of logical form—that is, formal logic. For example, 'and' and 'but' are formalized in the same way,

---

[4] Gottlob Frege, "Logic" (1897) in *The Frege Reader*, p. 239.

despite their difference in tone. (Consider 'He is a patriot *and* supports the government' *versus* 'He is a patriot *but* supports the government'.) This is entirely appropriate for the logic of mathematics, which was Frege's primary concern, since tone is seldom of significance in mathematical reasoning.

What is nuanced in the master can become dogmatic in the pupils. Many of Frege's successors sought to extend tone-free logical analysis to natural language. Amongst more popular writers this idealism could become extremism. Consider, for example, the psychologist Robert Thouless's claim that "We must look forward to the day when the thinking about political and international affairs will be as unemotional and as scientific as that about the properties of numbers or the atomic weights of elements." Whereas many logicians attempt to treat the terms of natural language as though they were tonally neutral, Thouless hopes to eliminate altogether "Such words as 'progress', 'liberty', 'democratic', 'totalitarian', 'reactionary', 'liberal', 'freedom', ..."[5] This Orwellian scenario exhibits the limitations of Frege's program. Although enormously successful in the formalization of technical language, and an inescapable foundation for any study of natural usage, it has little to say about tonal properties which play a substantial part in ordinary discourse. Thouless's procrustean fantasy of excising from our language what our logic cannot analyze is a desperate remedy diametrically opposed to the real solution: taking tone seriously. Further progress in the study of natural argumentation will require us to rehabilitate this repressed element. We shall see that this project is foreshadowed in the Yale ethicist Charles Stevenson's account of what he called persuasive definition.

Persuasive Definition

As introduced by Stevenson, a persuasive definition (PD) of a term "purport[s] . . . to alter the descriptive meaning of the term . . . but . . . *not* make any substantial change in the term's emotive meaning."[6] Although he coined the terminology, Stevenson was not the first person to spot this phenomenon. Indeed he

[5] Robert Thouless, *Straight and Crooked Thinking* (London: Pan, 1965), p. 15.
[6] Charles Stevenson, *Ethics and Language* (New Haven: Yale University Press, 1944), p. 210.

quotes the memorable attack on PD from Aldous Huxley's *Eyeless in Gaza* with which we began. Stevenson also introduced the converse stratagem, persuasive quasi-definition (PQD), in which the emotive meaning of a term is altered without changing the descriptive meaning. When PD is discussed in logic textbooks it is usually treated as though it were invariably fallacious.[7] However, this betrays the hostility to tone we diagnosed in the last section. As Stevenson recognized, many cases of PD are much less objectionable: the difficulty is in drawing a principled distinction between harmless and malign instances of PD. Stevenson's account of PD is couched in unfamiliar terms: 'descriptive' and 'emotive' meaning. These reflect his understanding of the meaning of an expression as a dispositional property of that expression, representing its potential to cause a psychological response in its hearer or utterer (p. 54). Descriptive and emotive meanings are then distinguished as provoking cognitive or emotive psychological responses respectively. Few if any modern philosophers would find this account even remotely congenial. Detailed criticism would be out of place here, although we can observe that the account is closely related to the emotivist theory of ethics, sometimes called the Boo-Hurrah Theory, on which ethical terms, such as 'good', are merely expressions of an emotional attitude. That Stevenson's ethical and semantic theories have fallen out of fashion may explain the comparative neglect of PD. However, we shall see that this concept is independent of the theoretical context in which Stevenson articulated it.

Specifically, Stevenson's definition of PD may be restated in Fregean terms as changing the sense or reference of a term, while representing the tone as unchanged. Replacing the slippery distinction between emotive and descriptive meaning with that between sense, reference and tone has several advantages, besides the rescue of PD from its theoretically suspect origins. Firstly, tone is not *just* emotive. It can also, for example, be jargon-laden (with any number of different jargons), bureaucratic, politically correct, affectionate, poetic, boorish, metropolitan, circumspect, dated, or many other things. Secondly, a threefold

---

[7] Douglas Walton, "Deceptive Arguments Containing Persuasive Language and Persuasive Definitions" *Argumentation* 19 (2005), p. 173.

Table 1 Options for Change

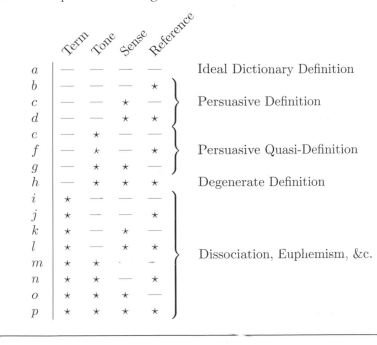

	Term	Tone	Sense	Reference	
a	—	—	—	—	Ideal Dictionary Definition
b	—	—	—	★	
c	—	—	★	—	Persuasive Definition
d	—	—	★	★	
e	—	★	—	—	
f	—	★	—	★	Persuasive Quasi-Definition
g	—	★	★	—	
h	—	★	★	★	Degenerate Definition
i	★	—	—	—	
j	★	—	—	★	
k	★	—	★	—	
l	★	—	★	★	Dissociation, Euphemism, &c.
m	★	★	—	—	
n	★	★	—	★	
o	★	★	★	—	
p	★	★	★	★	

distinction provides for a more fine-grained analysis of dubious definition-like activity than the simple binary of PD and PQD. Table 1 distinguishes the sixteen different possibilities that can arise from changing (★) or keeping fixed (—) the sense, reference and tone of a term, as well as the term itself.

We can also begin to see how the concept of semantic negligence which we derived from Frankfurt's discussion of bullshit may be used to distinguish good from bad PD. The persuasive definer represents the tone of his redefined term as unchanged: this may or may not be negligent of him. He might be justified in believing the tone will not change, making his usage unobjectionable. He might realize that the tone will be dramatically affected by the redefinition, in which case he is unlikely to expect his move to be accepted. Or he may be negligent as to whether the tone is faithfully preserved. This strategy is not overtly deceptive, since the tone could be unchanged. Rather, the speaker's lack of control over the tone, and indifference as to its eventual disposition, makes his utterance semantically negligent. In this respect it is analogous to bullshit, not lying.

In our discussion of semantic negligence we suggested that different degrees of negligence are possible, depending on the risk of deception occurring and how much at fault the speaker is in not foreseeing that deception would result. Aphoristic definitions, such as "By 'work' I mean action done for the divine"[8] and perhaps Huxley's "Conservatism is true socialism," are usually so surprising or paradoxical that they are unlikely to be truly deceptive. Many other definitions are inseparable from the theories which produce them: as Stevenson observes, "To chose a definition is to plead a cause" (p. 210). There's no reason to accept such definitions unless one is convinced by the arguments with which the theory is defended. This situation is common in scientific contexts, where it is typically unproblematic: good practice requires the definer to make the theoretical indebtedness of his definitions explicit. Definers in natural language are likely to be less scrupulous, hence their interlocutors may be misled into endorsing the conclusions of arguments they would not judge sound, were they to be given a fair opportunity to appraise them. The resulting deception may be deliberate, but is just as likely to be inadvertent: it is easy to confuse oneself as well as others with this sort of definition. Such behaviour is less culpable than outright deceit, just as bullshit is less blameworthy than lying, but as with bullshit, it is also peculiarly pernicious since it degrades the standards of discourse.

Broadening the Analysis

In the previous section I introduced and clarified the definition of PD and suggested how it may be related to bullshit. I shall develop this account further below, but first I will explore the relationship between PD and a variety of allied phenomena, all of which may be included within the same analysis, thereby broadening our understanding of semantic negligence.

Low and High Redefinition

As commonly used, these terms describe the redefinition of an expression so as to include extra cases (low redefinition) or

---

[8] The guru Sri Aurobindo, cited in Chaim Perelman and Lucy Olbrechts-Tyteca, *The New Rhetoric: A Treatise on Argumentation* (Notre Dame: University of Notre Dame Press, 1969), p. 444.

exclude existing cases (high redefinition). Hence they are defined solely in terms of what would happen to the reference of the expression if the redefinition were successful. However, the change in reference will typically be effected by a change of sense, since that is the principal means of redefining a term. Moves of this kind partially coincide with PD, although the two should not be confused: PD can occur without a change of reference, as we shall see, and not every change of reference is PD. Strictly speaking, only one of low and high redefinition need be addressed, as each can be defined in terms of the other. A low redefinition of a term is a high redefinition of the complement of that term, and *vice versa*. (The complement of a term is the term under which everything not falling under that term falls.) For example, consider the motorist who, upon conviction for drunk driving, argues that he is not a real drunk driver, but had just been caught out after a miscalculated drink. (One too many double whiskies, perhaps.) His argument could be understood as a high redefinition of 'drunk driver,' or a low redefinition of 'non drunk driver,' so as to include the driver in question. This example could also be understood as PD, since the motorist wishes to avoid the stigma, that is the pejorative tone, of 'drunk driver,' which he hopes will remain fixed as he effects his self-serving redefinition. The motorist may have convinced himself that his redefinition is just, but only by a wilfull blindness to its departure from conventional usage.

The No-True-Scotsman Move

Suppose that some traditionally minded Scot averred that 'No Scotsman takes sugar with his porridge'. When confronted with incontrovertible evidence that one Hamish MacTavish of Inverness does exactly that, he may retreat to the qualified statement 'No true Scotsman takes sugar with his porridge'. A shift of this sort, christened the No-True-Scotsman Move by the British philosopher Antony Flew, is a special case of low or high redefinition.[9] What makes it special is that, since the reference of 'Scotsman' has been redefined specifically to exclude Scotsmen who take sugar with their porridge, the new statement is not

---

[9] Antony Flew, *Thinking about Thinking: Or, Do I Sincerely Want to Be Right?* (London: Fontana, 1975), p. 47.

only true, it is true of necessity. Whereas the original claim said something bold and potentially false about the world, the new claim is equivalent to 'No Scotsman who does not take sugar with his porridge takes sugar with his porridge', which must be true, but says nothing at all. Since the speaker's motivation is presumably to preserve the positive tone he associates with 'Scotsman', his move may be seen as PD. However, the real danger is that the two statements look and sound much alike, and may be confused, giving the impression that the original contentious statement is true, even though it has been clearly falsified. This is as likely to result from carelessness as from outright deceit, making this another instance of semantic negligence, here with respect to either the reference of 'Scotsman' or the truth value of the original statement. Thus, if the speaker continues to behave as though his original statement were true, he is exhibiting classic Frankfurt bullshit.

Monster Barring

The Hungarian philosopher of mathematics Imre Lakatos distinguished several colorfully labeled possible responses that may be made to a counterexample which seems to refute a cherished conjecture. One of the least helpful of these, 'monster barring', consists in the "sometimes deft but always *ad hoc* redefinition" of crucial terms, by which means any counterexample can be eliminated.[10] We can see that this technique, gerrymandering a term to protect a claim from any possible refutation, is comparable to Flew's No-True-Scotsman Move. However, Lakatos's account situates monster barring within a family of related techniques, some of which are more productive. For example, 'exception barring' addresses counterexamples by restricting the scope of the conjecture so that it is no longer falsified. Explicit restatement of this kind, as in 'No Lowland Scotsman takes sugar with his porridge' perhaps avoids the pitfalls of the No-True-Scotsman Move by making explicit the theoretical commitments of the speaker.

---

[10] Imre Lakatos, *Proofs and Refutations: The Logic of Mathematical Discovery* (Cambridge: Cambridge University Press, 1976), p. 23.

Dissociation

This is a very wide-ranging category under which much of the above may be subsumed. It may be defined as the splitting of a concept into two, thereby replacing the term with two qualified terms which divide the reference of the original term between them (*New Rhetoric*, p. 411). Many different pairs of qualifiers can arise, although the most influential is that of 'real' versus 'apparent'. In the 'Scotsman' example the use of 'true Scotsman' may be understood in this way, as may Huxley's explicit dissociation of 'ordinary' from 'true' temperance. Indeed, the Belgian rhetoricians Chaim Perelman and Lucy Olbrechts-Tyteca, in whose work dissociation originates, observe that PD is characteristically a special case of the dissociation of reality from appearance (*New Rhetoric*, p. 447). Dissociation can be explicit and well-motivated, in which case it is not only legitimate but indispensable to complex thought. However, it can also be deployed in pursuit of an unearned advantage in argument. In such cases the dissociating arguer talks as though the tone must remain attached to the part of the concept he has designated as real, but he has no way of ensuring this, making his behaviour semantically negligent.

Courtesy Meaning

This phrase was coined by the classicist and philosopher R.G. Collingwood to describe the use of an expression chosen for its "emotional colouring" rather than its "descriptive function." [11] Collingwood's specific concern was the use of 'art' to describe what might better be called 'entertainment'. He sees this usage as motivated principally by the positive associations, or tone, the word possesses. This may be understood as a special case of PD, since the reference of the term is adjusted while the tone remains fixed, although the usage which Collingwood describes is unlikely to be expressed as a definition. The choice of terms for their courtesy meaning is clearly semantically negligent, since the chooser gives no thought to the sense of the term.

Euphemism

Replacing a word which is perceived as malign in tone with a new expression intended to preserve the sense and reference

---

[11] R.G. Collingwood, *The Principles of Art* (Oxford: Oxford University Press, 1938), p. 9.

while resetting the tone to neutral or benign associations is a tactic of some antiquity. The ancient Greeks thought it politic to refer to the Furies as the 'Eumenides' or 'Kindly Ones', lest the notoriously short tempers of these vengeance demons be provoked. Of course, 'bullshit' itself has had many euphemisms, including 'humbug', 'balderdash', 'poppycock', or 'bunk' (*On Bullshit*, p. 5). In modern times, euphemism is familiar from politically correct usage, such as 'sex workers' or indeed 'persons presenting themselves as commodity allotments within a business doctrine' for 'prostitutes', as well as government or military language, such as 'superprompt critical power excursion' for 'nuclear meltdown'.[12] The proliferation of both these categories of euphemism has been a source of much concern.[13] However, as the feminist critic Germaine Greer observes, "It is the fate of euphemisms to lose their function rapidly by association with the actuality of what they designate, so that they must be regularly replaced with euphemisms for themselves."[14] This phenomenon, which has been termed the "euphemism treadmill"[15] is a common one—consider the sequence of terms which have been used to refer to minorities of race or sexual orientation. The process can only be arrested when underlying attitudes towards the individuals under discussion improve: the comparative stability of 'gay' and 'black' suggest some recent progress. In most PC and nukespeak usage, however, the underlying attitudes are unchanged, and the euphemism tends to backfire just as Greer describes.

Backfire

To see how a definition can backfire, we must first distinguish the various ways in which it may be attempted. We can see from Table 1 that each of PD and PQD now corresponds to three distinct options, and that there are several other possibilities. We shall discuss each of them in turn.

---

[12] Henry Beard and Christopher Cerf, *The Official Politically Correct Dictionary and Handbook* (London: Grafton, 1992), pp. 48, 129.
[13] See, for example, the discussion of 'nukespeak' in Edward Schiappa, *Defining Reality: Definitions and the Politics of Meaning* (Carbondale: Southern Illinois University Press, 2003), p. 131.
[14] Germaine Greer, *The Female Eunuch* (New York: Farrar, Straus, 2002), p. 298.
[15] Steven Pinker, "The Game of the Name," *New York Times* (5th April, 1994), p. A6.

The null case *a*, in which nothing changes, represents the ideal of pure description which dictionary definitions purport to offer. PD corresponds to the cases *b*, *c* and *d*. In most of the examples of PD discussed above a change of sense is used to bring about a change of reference, making such cases instances of *d*. However, in *b* only the reference changes. It might be argued that this cannot happen. When we (re)define a term the aspect of its meaning which we can most easily affect is its sense, so the simplest way of changing the reference of a term is to change its sense. If this were the *only* way of changing the reference, then *b*, as well as *f*, *j* and *n*, would never occur. However, as we saw in the drunk driver example, arguers can attempt to exclude an individual from the scope of the reference of a term while ostensibly preserving the sense. Such attempts may fail, and certainly exhibit semantic negligence, but the intent is to change the reference alone.

Conversely, in *c* only the sense is changed. This may be less typical than *d*, but real world cases exist. One such is the so-called Model Law definition of 'pornography', stated by the radical feminists Catharine MacKinnon and Andrea Dworkin as "the sexually explicit subordination of women, graphically depicted, whether in pictures or in words."[16] The aim of the proposed law was to criminalize existing pornography. So, although the definition changes the conventional sense of 'pornography', it was not intended to alter the reference. Presumably the tone was also intended to remain the same, or perhaps to become even more condemnatory. This definition also provides an insight into the propensity of PD to backfire. Sceptics of MacKinnon and Dworkin's theory of pornography may wonder whether women are ever 'subordinated' by pictures or words, or more generally whether *all* the material conventionally identified as pornography has this effect. The concern is that MacKinnon and Dworkin were negligent in not sufficiently securing the reference of the term they sought to redefine: their definition relies on an argument about the effect of pornography which not everyone finds convincing. This is borne out by the subsequent fortunes of the Model Law. Although ruled unconstitutional in

---

[16] Catharine A. MacKinnon and Andrea Dworkin, *In Harm's Way: The Pornography Civil Rights Hearings* (Cambridge, Massachusetts: Harvard University Press, 1997), pp. 269–270.

the United States, a similar definition has entered Canadian law, where it has led to raids on gay bookshops but has had limited effect on mainstream pornography.[17] Hence the effect of the new definition, although intended as *c*, ended up as *d*: the reference drifted to include materials to which it was not intended to apply, while excluding much of what it was supposed to cover.

Persuasive quasi-definition (PQD) is dual to PD: as we have defined it, it occurs when the tone changes but either the sense or reference remains the same, that is cases *e*, *f* and *g*. As observed above, the easiest aspect of meaning to change directly is the sense. Changing the tone is more difficult. It may be attempted without changing the other components of meaning: an instance of *e*, as in the rehabilitation of abusive terms such as 'queer'. Note that redefinitions of this kind must proceed indirectly, by using the term in contexts liable to encourage an association with the desired tone, or "by gestures, tones of voice, or rhetorical devices such as similes and metaphors" (Stevenson, p. 278), since the tone of a term cannot just be stipulated. It is also possible, as in cases *f* and *g*, to bring about a change in tone through a change in sense or reference. This may be deliberate, but can also happen inadvertently when a would-be persuasive definer loses control of the tone he is hoping to keep fixed. This sort of backfire can also result in case *h*, which we may call 'degenerate definition', since it does not preserve any aspect of the term's meaning.

Even degenerate definition can be deliberately pursued. For example, consider the technical meanings attributed by economists and sociologists to expressions such as 'unproductive labour' or 'conspicuous waste'.[18] In each case the definer not only departs from the standard sense and reference, he also professes to use the terms without their conventional pejorative tone. In practice, that tone swiftly creeps back, even in the works of the definers, making this usage PD, a backfire from *h* to *d*.

An example which shows both how PD can be used legitimately and successfully, and how it can backfire into PQD, or degenerate definition, occurs with the definition of 'rape'. The

[17] Tamsin Wilton, *Finger-Licking Good: The Ins and Outs of Lesbian Sex* (London: Cassell, 1996), p. 154.
[18] Adam Smith, cited by Stevenson, p. 215; Thorstein Veblen, cited in Flew, p. 77.

crime of rape has been recognized for many centuries. Over the course of this history both its sense and its reference have evolved substantially: a process which some modern commentators see as not yet satisfactorily concluded. We cannot hope to recount this narrative in full detail, and will concentrate on three major theories of rape, each of which produces a distinct definition. On the *traditional* theory, rape is a property crime. In societies where women were seen as belonging to men, rape was understood as an injury one man does to another by interfering with the reproductive activity of his women.[19] On the *liberal* theory, rape is sex without consent. This is the definition which is most familiar in the modern world. However the traditional theory cast a long shadow: it lies behind the marital rape exemption clause which was to be found in the rape laws of the United Kingdom and most U.S. states as recently as the 1980s (*Defining Reality*, p. 53). On the *radical* theory, rape is a "terrorist institution" by which the male sex subordinates the female ("Rape and Persuasive Definition," p. 449). The radical feminists who defend this theory seek to "redraw the line between so-called normal (heterosexual) intercourse and rape" by replacing or substantially redefining the criterion of consent (p. 450).

There are two changes of definition here: one historical, from the traditional to the liberal definition, and one hypothetical, from the liberal to the radical. The tone has remained largely intact throughout: always negative, although perhaps increasingly so, as societal attitudes change. The adoption of the liberal definition seems to have begun as case *c*: a change of sense which preserved the traditional reference—at some theoretical cost, since the required marital exemption clause is unjustifiable on the liberal theory. Over time this theoretical tension was resolved with the abolition of that clause, thereby changing the reference of 'rape,' and making the cumulative change an instance of *d*. Each step was stable, and did not backfire, because not only was the new definition backed by a coherent theory, but that theory was argued for successfully by the proponents of the definition.

---

[19] Keith Burgess-Jackson, "Rape and Persuasive Definition," *Canadian Journal of Philosophy* 25 (1995), p. 444.

The proponents of the radical definition are also aiming for *d*, albeit in one step, as they propose not only a new sense, but also a much wider reference. They hope that this can be accomplished without any reduction in the negative force of the tone. However, one recurring criticism of their move is that such reduction is inevitable, and thereby "trivialize[s] legitimate rape, and mocks those women who have been truly brutalized" ("Rape and Persuasive Definition," p. 438). The sometime radical feminist Keith Burgess-Jackson dismisses this concern as question-begging, since it presumes that the new cases falling under the redefined reference of 'rape' are not as bad as the original cases, which he says the radical theory denies. However, this response is itself question-begging: it assumes that the whole theory will be adopted, not just the definition of one word: 'rape'. But, as the rhetorician Edward Schiappa reminds us, "Putting new laws on the books does not ensure that all individuals responsible for enforcing those laws will immediately assimilate the new definitions and categories" (*Defining Reality*, p. 60). The effect on society as a whole is likely to be even more diffuse, especially for a theory as sharply at odds with conventional wisdom as the radical feminists'. Thus it is predictable that, even if a radical feminist definition of 'rape' was enacted into law, the conventional moral weighting of the new cases would persist, thereby diluting the tone. Thus the definition would backfire from *d* to *h*.

The remaining lines in Table 1 correspond to cases where the term itself has changed. There are several ways of bringing this about. Euphemism, if successful, exemplifies case *m*: the new term has a new tone, but preserves sense and reference. The sort of backfire characteristic of the 'euphemism treadmill' is a shift to case *i*: the tone reverts to that of the old term. Euphemism, as conventionally understood, involves a very specific change in tone, from pejorative to neutral or laudatory. However, case *m* covers all shifts of tone, including those that go in the opposite direction ('dysphemisms') and those which are oriented on an entirely different basis. Euphemism (and dysphemism, and other such changes) can be accompanied by other shifts in meaning. For example, 'visually impaired,' although used as a euphemism for 'blind' has a somewhat different sense and reference, taking it in the direction of case *p*.

The results of dissociation, understood as producing two

new terms from one old term, can be found amongst the same cases as euphemism. Characteristically, the two new terms will correspond to a pair of distinct cases, where one of the terms is intended to preserve the original tone, while the other covers circumstances incompatible with that tone. Thus one of the pair will be drawn from lines i through l and the other from lines m through p. For example, 'ordinary temperance' and 'true temperance', understood as a dissociation, would correspond to lines m and l respectively. 'Ordinary temperance' preserves the sense and reference of 'temperance,' but by implication lacks its positive tone; 'true temperance' keeps the tone, but on Huxley's account, nothing else.

Good Definitions

How can backfire be avoided? Can PD ever be used safely, and if so, when? We have seen that a proper account of definition should have regard to the sense, reference and tone of the term at issue. Semantic negligence with respect to any of these components of the meaning of a term can lead to backfire, and the pernicious consequences outlined in the last section. Bad practice is, however, easier to describe than good practice, which we might term 'semantic diligence'. Describing the due diligence required for a satisfactory definition is a topic with a long and inglorious history.[20] The emphasis is often on the pursuit of an 'essence' of the concept being defined: so-called 'real' definitions accurately track the essence, whereas other definitions are merely 'nominal'. This talk of essences made some sense for Plato and Aristotle, in whose works it was first deployed, as it reflects their broader metaphysical commitments. However, for modern thinkers who do not share those commitments, and even for those who do, it is very hard to defend: the most that can be made of essence is that it "is just the human choice of what to mean by a name, misinterpreted as being a metaphysical reality" (*Definition*, p. 155).

Aristotle is also the source of a conventional list of rules for good definitions which has recurred with surprisingly little variation in generation after generation of logic textbooks right

---

[20] Richard Robinson, *Definition* (Oxford: Clarendon, 1950), pp. 2–3.

up to the most recent editions. Although some of these rules, such as 'avoid circularity,' may have a modest but valuable role to play in an account of the semantic diligence necessary for good definition, others are either couched in metaphysically discredited terms: 'state the essential attributes,' or incompatible with proper consideration of tone: 'avoid figurative language'.

The crucial point is that practices such as PD, which seek to stipulate some aspect of the meaning of an expression, are *disguised arguments*. It is common in all branches of knowledge for an initially contentious identification to be transformed into a definition. For example, consider the definition of 'planet' as 'satellite of the sun'. However, this is the hard-won result of protracted consensus building. We saw above how this was essential to the widespread acceptance of the liberal definition of 'rape'. Semantically negligent definitions are parasitical on this process: they foreclose argument about doubtful identities by disguising them as definitions. Hidden arguments are difficult to criticize—but also easy to ignore. Thus the semantically negligent definer may gain short-term rhetorical advantage by disguising his arguments as definitions, but risks the backfire effect, which is a direct consequence of his neglect of the full meaning of his redefined expression. For a definition to be semantically diligent any concealed arguments must be made explicit to all parties. Moreover, if the proposers hope for their definition to prevail, these arguments must be won. Conversely, this explication must be absent for an accusation of malign PD, or similar semantic negligence, to be just.

Is Frankfurt's Definition of 'Bullshit' Itself PD?

Having employed an insight derived from Frankfurt's definition of bullshit to clarify our understanding of definition in general, and PD in particular, we are now in a position to close the circle by asking whether this definition is PD, and if so whether it is malign. 'Bullshit' clearly has a strongly pejorative tone, which Frankfurt intends to preserve. By offering a new, stipulative definition of 'bullshit,' Frankfurt changes the sense of the term. This in turn affects its reference: some cases that qualify as Frankfurt-bullshit would not meet the demotic definition of the term. For example, one might tell a critically injured person that "Help is on its way," despite having no idea whether this was true,

because one was hoping for the best, and did not wish to need-
lessly demoralize someone clinging to life. There are also common uses of 'bullshit' which are outside the scope of reference
of Frankfurt-bullshit, as discussed by Cohen ("Deeper Into
Bullshit," pp. 119–120). So, as an instance of case *d* from Table
1, Frankfurt's definition of 'bullshit' is clearly PD.

For Frankfurt's definition to be semantically diligent it needs
to be defended by an explicit argument, as it clearly is, with particular attention to the points at which it departs from conventional usage. As regards the first of these, the 'Help is on its way'
cases, an argument could be made on the grounds of theoretical simplicity for including them within the scope of reference
of 'bullshit,' but suitably qualified to indicate their good intentions. Something similar already applies to lying: we distinguish
'white lies' as lies to which the generally pejorative tone of 'lie'
should not apply. As Frankfurt observes, bullshit is a "vast and
amorphous" phenomenon upon which "very little work has
been done" (*On Bullshit*, p. 3), so we should not be surprised
that fresh distinctions such as this still need to be drawn. The
omissions identified by Cohen are harder to defend. If Cohen's
dissociation of the "bullshit of ordinary life" from the "bullshit
that appears in academic works" is defensible ("Deeper into
Bullshit," p. 119), then Frankfurt has a hard case to answer.
However, that does not make his definition semantically negligent, but rather indicates that the last word on bullshit will not
be written for some time yet.[21]

---

[21] Precursors to this paper were delivered at St. Catherines, Ontario; St. Andrews,
Scotland; and Oviedo, Asturias. I am grateful for the comments I received, and for conversations with Bruce Russell, Agnès van Rees, Douglas Walton, and the editors of this
volume.

11
Different Kinds and Aspects of Bullshit

HANS MAES and KATRIEN SCHAUBROECK

The publication and subsequent popularity of Harry Frankfurt's *On Bullshit* has inserted a rather conspicuous and somewhat comical point of discontinuity in the philosophy sections of many bookstores. For here we have a small, unassuming book with 'Bullshit' printed on the outside but lacking the quality of bullshit on the inside.

The exact opposite, one cannot fail to notice, is true of so many other books sold under the heading of 'philosophy' today. Books like *Chakra Balancing Kit: A Guide to Healing and Awakening Your Energy Body*, *The Hidden Messages in Water Crystals*, *Numerology Helps You to Master Your Relationship and to Find the Right Career*, or *Astrology: A Cosmic Science* appear in the same bestseller lists and sometimes even on the same bookshelf as *On Bullshit*—almost as if they are put there on purpose to illustrate the unusual topic of Frankfurt's philosophical study and his claim that bullshit is indeed "the most salient feature of our culture."

When Frankfurt's analysis of bullshit was first published as an essay in 1986, no one could have predicted the philosophical sensation (and hilarious situation) it would cause in twenty-first-century bookstores. The original essay was received in much the same way as most academic articles are received, that is, without attention from press or public. The essay did, however, provoke discussion among fellow philosophers; one admiring but critical response is especially worth mentioning since it puts some of Frankfurt's claims in a new perspective.

In "Deeper Into Bullshit" G.A. Cohen gives credit to Frankfurt's "pioneering and brilliant discussion of a widespread but largely unexamined cultural phenomenon," but he also raises some doubts about the scope of Frankfurt's account (Chapter 8 in this volume). Frankfurt's definition, says Cohen, does not cover all types of bullshit. On the contrary, "the *explicandum* that attracted [Frankfurt's] interest is just one flower in the lush garden of bullshit" (p. 120). So, "On Bullshit" is really only about one kind of bullshit. Other flowers in the "lush garden of bullshit" remain unexamined, and Cohen's principal aim in "Deeper into Bullshit" is to identify and define a very specific kind of *stercore tauri*, to be found in academic circles, but altogether ignored by Frankfurt.

Harry Frankfurt on Bullshit

People who produce, package, or sell bullshit, says Frankfurt, are in some way comparable to slovenly craftsmen. They are not really paying attention to the quality of their product. There's some kind of laxity in their work, though this laxity cannot be equated with inattention to detail or carelessness in general. What is lacking in the prime examples of bullshit, to be found in "the realms of advertising and of public relations, and the nowadays closely related realm of politics" (p. 22) is not concern for detail—political spin doctors, for instance, often dedicate themselves tirelessly to keeping every tiny thing under control—but concern for the truth. According to Frankfurt, the essence of bullshit lies in a "lack of connection to a concern with truth—[an] indifference to how things really are" (p. 33). To be sure, advertisements and political speeches may contain true statements but they will nevertheless strike us as bullshit as soon as we realize that the person who produces these statements could not care less whether his statements are true or not, as long as they have the desired effect. As such, it is a feature of the bullshitter's state of mind, namely his indifference to truth, that is crucial to the production of bullshit.

This is not the whole story, however. While an indifference to truth is an essential ingredient of bullshit, it is not the only ingredient, according to Frankfurt. The case of so-called "bull sessions" illustrates this. In a bull session, Frankfurt explains, people try out thoughts and attitudes about various aspects of life (relationships, religion, and so forth) in order to discover how others respond and how it feels to say such things, without it being assumed that they are committed to what they say.[1] These discussions may be very animated and significant, but they are typically not "for real." Thus, bull sessions are "like bullshit by virtue of the fact that they are in some degree unconstrained by a concern with truth" (p. 37). But they are not bullshit. Frankfurt is very explicit about this: "The statements made in a bull session differ from bullshit in that there is no *pretence* that this connection [between what people say and what they believe] is being sustained" (p. 38, italics added). Bullshit, by contrast, always involves a particular form of pretence or deceit. This is the second essential ingredient of bullshit.

Does this mean that the bullshitter is a liar? Not necessarily. Admittedly, both the liar and the bullshitter try to deceive people through misrepresentation but Frankfurt points out that there is a significant difference. The liar essentially misrepresents the state of affairs to which he refers or his beliefs concerning that state of affairs. The bullshitter, on the other hand, may not deceive people, or even intend to do so, about either the facts or what he takes the facts to be. What he says may very well be true. So, unlike lying, bullshit is not a matter of falsity. It's rather a matter of fakery or phoniness.

The bullshitter essentially deceives people about his enterprise. His audience is not to understand that he is utterly disinterested with how things really are and that his intention is not to report the truth. Frankfurt's example of a Fourth of July orator, who bombastically prates about the achievements and divine blessings of his country, serves as a good illustration. "He is not trying to deceive anyone concerning American history. What he cares about is what people think of him. He wants them to think of him as a patriot" (p. 18). So, what the orator misrepresents is not a particular state of affairs but rather his particular state of mind. The truth-value of his statements is of but marginal interest to him; winning votes is his prime concern. However, he cannot and does not admit this openly. Frankfurt calls this tendency to misrepresent what one is up to

---

[1] Think of the little girl, who, being told to be sure of her meaning before she spoke, said: "How can I know what I think till I see what I say?" See Graham Wallas, *The Art of Thought* (London: Watts, 1946).

an "indispensably distinctive characteristic" (p. 54) of the bullshitter, making it as central to the concept of bullshit as the tendency for indifference as to how things really are.

In order to tell a lie, says Frankfurt, one needs to know how
things really are or one must at least think that one knows
what's true. It's clear by now that this does not hold for bullshit.
The bullshitter does not have to keep his eye on the facts,
whereas the liar must do precisely that in order to conceal the
facts. That is why, according to Frankfurt, lying does not render
a person unfit for telling the truth in the same way that bullshitting does. The biggest problem with bullshit, so to speak, is
not that the bullshitter hides the truth, but rather that he does
not even remember where he put it. Hence, Frankfurt's striking
conclusion that "bullshit is a greater enemy of the truth than lies
are" (p. 61) and his appeal to oppose bullshit wherever it may
be found, in defense of a civilization built upon a concern for
truth.

In Frankfurt's analysis, then, the bullshitter is (i) unconcerned
about the truth but also (ii) concerned about hiding this fact and
thus (iii) morally reprehensible. We will now challenge all three
of these claims.

A Different Take on Bullshit

In the first part of his book, Frankfurt describes a rather intrigu-
ing conversation to illustrate his account of bullshit. Fania
Pascal, Wittgenstein's Russian teacher, received a call from
Wittgenstein when her tonsils had just been taken out. Pascal
relates: "I croaked: 'I feel just like a dog that has been run over.'"
He was disgusted: "You don't know what a dog that has been
run over feels like."[2] Frankfurt explains Wittgenstein's strong
reaction to Pascal's innocent remark as follows: "To the
Wittgenstein in Pascal's story, judging from his response, this is
just bullshit." (p. 29)

Given Frankfurt's own account of bullshit, this diagnosis
seems problematic. For one of the essential ingredients of bullshit is clearly missing. Fania Pascal is not hiding something or

---

[2] F. Pascal, "Wittgenstein: A Personal Memoir," in R. Rhees, ed., *Recollections of
Wittgenstein* (Oxford: Oxford University Press, 1984), p. 29.

deceiving someone and there seems to be no fakery or phoniness involved. So why should her statement be interpreted as bullshit?

Frankfurt might reply that it should, in fact, *not* be interpreted as bullshit and that it is only *Wittgenstein* who thinks that Pascal is talking bullshit. Frankfurt seems to take this stance when he says: "It seems extraordinary, almost unbelievable, that anyone could object seriously to what Pascal reports herself as having said" (p. 25) and "Wittgenstein's reaction . . . is absurdly intolerant" (p. 31). So, Frankfurt himself seems unconvinced that Pascal's utterance is bullshit. But Wittgenstein thinks it is—that's the point. Should we assume then that Wittgenstein thinks that Pascal is deceiving people about her enterprise or hiding something? If we hold on to Frankfurt's analysis of bullshit, we should. But this assumption is plainly false. Wittgenstein's objection does not amount to an accusation of either fakery or phoniness. That is not what bothers him. Another explanation is needed.

Fania Pascal is not concerned with how things really are, that much seems certain. She obviously does not know, except in the most vague sense, how a run-over dog feels. Nevertheless, she employs the image to describe her own state of mind. This mindlessness is what bothers Wittgenstein. He finds her indifference to the truth obnoxious and clearly sees this as sufficient ground for discarding her remark as plain bullshit. Wittgenstein, we know from various sources, was extremely demanding when the truth was concerned. In philosophical discussions, but also in daily life, one should never trifle with the facts, he thought. One should always try to get things right. This notorious exactingness probably explains why Wittgenstein almost never engaged in playful "bull sessions" or chitchat, not even when this was part of a language class (Fania Pascal recalls how hard it was to find a suitable subject for a conversation with Wittgenstein: "The conversation lessons were excruciating. We sat in the garden. With the utmost impatience he rejected any topic I would suggest . . . To him they were all absurd, non-topics" (p. 29). It also explains why he was so "disgusted" with Pascal's remark. Pascal was playing fast and loose with the facts and did not even make an attempt to get things right. Wittgenstein found this intolerable.

There is something slightly absurd about this intolerance, as Frankfurt rightly points out. Most of us would not disapprove of, let alone express disgust at a loose remark like Pascal's. It's easy to understand why. Most of us do not share Wittgenstein's exacting standards. We do not always expect people to be as accurate and precise as humanly possible. Sure, Pascal is "cutting corners" like a slovenly craftsman, but who doesn't, once in a while? Besides, the purpose of conversation is not always to give an accurate description of reality. People sometimes say things just to be funny, agreeable or sociable. In many conversations, it's not so important *what* one is saying, but rather *that* one is saying something and talking to someone. It is about making the other feel comfortable, for instance, and not about trying to get things right.

A certain amount of sloppiness in our speech may be tolerated, but this does not mean it goes undetected. Most people, when pressed, would acknowledge that Pascal's comparison of her own feelings to those of a run-over dog, is bullshit. Yet they do not seem to mind as much as Wittgenstein. They do not think this sort of bullshit is unforgivable or unreasonable. Being intolerant in this respect, *that* would be unreasonable.

If this diagnosis is correct, Frankfurt's account has to be revised in at least two ways.

First, pretence is not an essential ingredient of bullshit. Fania Pascal's utterance, for instance, qualifies as such, though there is no element of deceit or fakery involved. A mere indifference to the truth is apparently all that is needed.

Of course, a speaker will often try to conceal his own indifference when he knows that his audience is very concerned about how things really are. A politician, for example, who is primarily interested in getting re-elected instead of getting things right, has to hide this fact. The bullshit he sells will usually be accompanied by pretence and deceit. However, this combination is not inevitable. Just imagine a politician who is fed up with all the fakery and phoniness and starts talking bullshit openly, without hiding his complete indifference to the truth. The audience will probably feel shocked and the outcry, "Bullshit!" will be heard everywhere. Yet, in contrast with the Fourth of July orator mentioned by Frankfurt, this speaker is not hiding what he is up to. Thus, in Frankfurt's view, his speech cannot count as bullshit. This is a very counterintuitive conclusion.

Frankfurt's distinction between bullshit and bull sessions is just as counterintuitive. For suppose one would ask the participants in a playful bull session what they were doing. A natural response would be: "We are just talking bullshit." Likewise, people witnessing a bull session will readily acknowledge that bull sessions consist mainly of bullshit. Frankfurt ignores this and claims there is a fundamental difference between bullshit and bull sessions. This distinction, centered around the presence or absence of pretence, is inevitably artificial. After all, as Frankfurt observes, the term 'bull session' is most likely an abbreviation or sanitized version of 'bullshit session' (p. 38).

Second, bullshit is not always a bad thing. Although the term is typically used to express indignation, irritation or disapproval, bullshit is not always offensive. Frankfurt finds this particularly hard to understand. He is genuinely puzzled by the fact that "our attitude toward bullshit is generally more benign than our attitude toward lying" and leaves it "as an exercise for the reader" to find out why this is so (p. 50). Perhaps the answer is not so difficult. Why is our attitude towards bullshit, resulting from a manifest indifference to the truth, so benign in many circumstances? Because in many circumstances the concern for truth and accuracy is not—and should not be—our primary concern. For instance, it is not our main concern, and rightly so, when someone is in terrible pain and in need of a comforting conversation. Wittgenstein's failure to appreciate this makes him, in Frankfurt's own words, "absurdly intolerant."

A bit of bullshit from time to time might even be a good thing. That is what the old butler Stevens in Kazuo Ishiguro's *The Remains of the Day* comes to realize when he is reflecting on the practice of "bantering," or as contemporary Americans would call it, "bullshitting":

> There is a group of six or seven people gathered just a little way behind me who have aroused my curiosity a little. I naturally assumed at first that they were a group of friends out together for the evening. But as I listened to their exchanges, it became apparent they were strangers who had just happened upon one another here on this spot behind me. . . . It is curious how people can build such warmth among themselves so swiftly. . . . I rather fancy it has [something] to do with this skill of bantering. Listening to them now, I can hear them exchanging one bantering remark after another. It is, I would suppose, the way many people like to proceed. In fact, it is possible my bench companion expected me to banter with him—in which case, I suppose I was something of a

sorry disappointment. Perhaps it is indeed time I began to look at this whole matter of bantering more enthusiastically. After all, when one thinks about it, it is not such a foolish thing to indulge in—particularly if it is the case that in bantering lies the key to human warmth.[3]

Indeed, we should perhaps look at the whole matter of bullshitting more enthusiastically than Frankfurt does. As a means to lay contact with others or keep the conversation going, it can be a source of human warmth and a blessing rather than a curse. Hence, we are not so sure that the world would be a better place without it. Just imagine that every conversation were to be informed by a strong concern for the truth. Conversations would be terribly fatiguing. For as Oscar Wilde once said: "The truth is rarely pure, and never simple." This is probably one of the reasons why Wilde himself was not too concerned about truth and accuracy in conversation. And we may be thankful for that. The world would certainly be a duller place without Wilde's splendid witticisms and epigrams, nearly all of which are brilliant examples of bullshit.[4]

In "Concealment and Exposure," Thomas Nagel discusses another case of "benign bullshit": "If I say, 'How nice to see you', you know perfectly well that this is not meant as a report of my true feelings: Even if it happens to be true, I might very well say it even if you were the last person I wanted to see at just that moment."[5] Despite an obvious lack of concern for the truth, Nagel makes the case for polite formulae like this. "The first and most obvious thing to note . . . is that they are not dishonest, because the conventions that govern them are generally known. If I don't tell you everything I think and feel about you, that is not a case of deception, since you don't expect me to do so" (p. 6). Furthermore, polite formulas are a *sine qua non* of a stable society as they leave a great range of potentially disruptive material unacknowledged and therefore out of play. Nagel certainly seems to have a point. Polite bullshit is often to be pre-

---

[3] K. Ishiguro, *The Remains of the Day* (London: Faber and Faber, 1999), pp. 257–58.
[4] Conversely, Mr. Spock from *Star Trek* always appealed to what is "logical" or "a fact." And what a bore he was, as all the other characters were always rolling their eyes at his humorlessness.
[5] Thomas Nagel, "Concealment and Exposure," in Nagel, *Concealment and Exposure and Other Essays* (Oxford: Oxford University Press, 2002), p. 6.

ferred to truthful expressions of hostility, contempt, derision, sexual desire or aversion.

What about Frankfurt's most central claim, however, that the essence of bullshit is an indifference towards truth?

A Different Kind of Bullshit

According to Frankfurt, the most distinctive feature of bullshit is one situated in the speaker's state of mind. The bullshitter is indifferent and hides this indifference. However, it would appear that an utterance often qualifies as bullshit purely as a result of certain of its objective features independent of the speaker's stance. This suggests that there is another kind of bullshit that should be explained not by reference to the state of mind of the producer but rather by pointing to certain salient features of the "product" itself.

This is the basic idea of G.A. Cohen's response to Frankfurt. In "Deeper into Bullshit," Cohen notes that Frankfurt's definition of the "essence" of bullshit does not sit well with the kind of bullshit that concerns him the most, namely the bullshit abundant in certain academic circles and best exemplified by the French continental tradition. This sort of bullshit cannot be explained by reference to the indifference or insincerity of the producer. After all, some of the most hideous examples appear to be the result of honest academic efforts. What is missing in these cases is an appropriate connection to the truth, not as far as the state of mind of the producer is concerned but with respect to features of the texts themselves. More specifically, it is the "unclarifiable unclarity" of those philosophical or sociological texts, says Cohen, that constitutes their high bullshit content.

An unclarifiable text is not only obscure but is incapable of being rendered unobscure, at least in a text that could be recognized as a version of what was originally said. A helpful trick is this: add or subtract a negation sign from a text and see whether that makes any difference to its plausibility. If not, Cohen says, one may be sure that one is dealing with bullshit (p. 132). Unsurprisingly, he concludes his analysis in the same way as Frankfurt, with a call to oppose and expose bullshit whenever possible. Academic discourse should always aim for the truth, and texts that are so obscure that the question of truth becomes irrelevant are a threat to any serious academic enterprise.

Now that we have a basic distinction between two kinds of bullshit, Frankfurt-bullshit and Cohen-bullshit, we can ask the question: does this distinction enable us to classify all the "flowers in the lush garden of bullshit"? In other words, is every instance of bullshit necessarily an instance of Frankfurt-bullshit or Cohen-bullshit? To answer this question, let us return to books like *Chakra Balancing Kit* or *The Hidden Messages in Water Crystals* or *Numerology Helps You to Master Your Relationship and to Find the Right Career* or *Astrology: A Cosmic Science*. Do we have a convincing account now of the specific kind of bullshit to be found in these pseudoscientific works? It does not appear so.

The plethora of pseudoscientific nonsense, though widely recognized as a paradigm of bullshit (if you Google 'astrology and bullshit', for instance, you get 290,000 hits), remains surprisingly unharmed by the attacks of Frankfurt and Cohen. Neither provides an appropriate explanation for this form of bullshit. Firstly, pseudoscientists typically have a firm and sincere belief in their practice and go to great lengths to prove the truth of the doctrines they endorse. They are not indifferent to the truth, quite the contrary. Thus, Frankfurt's definition of bullshit does not seem to apply. But Cohen's definition falls short as well, for the predictions and statements of pseudoscientists are often very specific and explicit as opposed to unclear or unclarifiable. Just think of astrologers predicting an earthquake or hurricane on a specific date or bogus healers providing a detailed diagnosis and assessment of a patient's condition.

Here's a serious lacuna in the literature on bullshit. Not only is pseudoscientific bullshit very prominent and visible, there is also no doubt that the bullshit of pseudoscientists is at least as damaging and therefore as deserving of strict scrutiny as the bullshit produced by advertisers or academics. After all, how many people are really affected by the philosophical impotence targeted by Cohen? And how many people are nowadays really deceived by advertisers? (In fact, people often seem to expect "good bullshit" from these professionals rather than complete truthfulness . . .) Pseudoscience, though sometimes an innocent pastime, is known to have a large and damaging impact on the lives of many and to pose a threat to the credibility of science, medicine and even politics. These effects certainly warrant further investigation into the what, how, and why of this third kind of bullshit.

But this is not the right place to carry out that kind of investigation. For one thing, it would necessitate a detailed account of the nature of pseudoscience which would go beyond the scope of this chapter. However, we do want to draw attention to a short, pertinent remark made by Cohen. After discussing unclarifiability as the key component of bullshit, he briefly identifies "arguments that are grossly deficient either in logic or in sensitivity to empirical evidence" as another possible source of bullshit (p. 131).

These features, insensitivity to evidence and fallacious reasoning, must be central to any analysis of pseudoscientific bullshit. Admittedly, this characterization remains rather vague. But as a general rule, and in order to avoid bullshit, we believe it is better to be vaguely right than precisely wrong.

III

It's All Around Us

Bullshit in Politics, Science,
Education, and the Law

12

The Republic of Bullshit: On the Dumbing-Up of Democracy

MARK EVANS

Harry Frankfurt claims that "bullshit is unavoidable whenever circumstances require someone to talk without knowing what he is talking about" (*On Bullshit*, p. 63). He then suggests that democracy may be especially prone to the production of bullshit because it fuels "the widespread conviction that it is the responsibility of a citizen in a democracy to have opinions about everything, or at least everything that pertains to the conduct of his country's affairs."

It is the most popularly received wisdom about politics that politicians and others close to the exercise of power—media commentators, lobbyists, and suchlike—are inordinately disposed to pollute the polity with bullshit. It is much more unusual and arresting to contend that the 'ordinary citizens' are also somehow responsible for some of democratic political culture's less edifying elements, particularly with respect to Frankfurt's very specific conception of bullshit as discourse which is essentially indifferent to the truth: bullshitters, for him, don't really even *care* that they don't know what they are talking about.[1]

For many, to claim such a thing would be not only arrogantly and offensively patronising but also a fundamental assault on democracy itself. The ordinary citizens are democracy's heroes: the people who are ultimately sovereign in the land, who graciously bestow the trust of office on those few of their number

---

[1] *On Bullshit*, pp. 33–34. Specifically, Frankfurt would claim that the paradigmatic bullshitter doesn't care that he doesn't know in the sense that he is not interested in whether what he says is true or not.

who have convinced them through the rigors of public debate of their fitness to rule, and who revoke that grant when they judge their representatives to have failed them. Their plain, good common sense is, at the heart of its self-image, democracy's very lifeblood. It's the basis on which citizens are to be honored, equally, as masters of their own political fates. Their elected politicians may be prone to bullshit and other misdemeanours, but democracy survives their failings—so the story runs—because of its genius in its ultimate empowerment of the ordinary citizens.

So to say, with Frankfurt, that democracy itself actually encourages citizens to bullshit looks like a critical blow to one of its justificatory props. If such bullshitting isn't already bad enough in itself, the propensity to bullshit would also indicate a crucial degradation, if not total lack, of the critical acumen required to guard against other, perhaps more devastating forms of deformity in political life which thrive on untruth. And yet . . . there is something very reminiscent of the Emperor's new clothes here. Hasn't Frankfurt simply dared to utter something which is, when we pluck up the courage to query the treasured commonplaces of democratic life, really rather obvious? Hasn't it actually been said from democracy's very inception onwards, by those who share Plato's insight that political understanding is an expertise that we cannot possibly all share?

I shall call this claim "the Frankfurt thesis," and I argue that it should be taken very seriously. But, even setting aside democracy's own rosily optimistic mythology, some might immediately object to the thesis. Suspecting that it is paradoxically manifesting an indifference to the truth all of its own, they might claim that, in contemporary democracy, the fact of the matter is not that citizens don't care about the truth. The real crisis democracy faces is that, nowadays, citizens just don't care about politics. And many who make this observation central to their understanding of democracy would reject the idea that it connotes political incompetence on the citizenry's part. Rather, they would say that apathy or indifference is generally rooted in a well-founded cynicism about a system that so consistently fails to provide good government: why should citizens care much about, and engage with, a process that apparently cannot deliver what they would wish of it?

This alternative view can be called "the cynicism thesis" and I think that, actually, both are partly right. Adopting them thus does not turn one into an anti-democrat; the theses are arguments *about*, not *against*, democracy, and the point of elaborating them is to analyse how we might tackle the problems they identify. In fact, many supporters of the cynicism thesis have urged that what we need is more meaningful opportunities for citizens' participation (what political theorists today often refer to as 'deliberative democracy.') And they would highlight modern information and communications technology as the means by which greater and more informed participation can be realised.

The Frankfurt thesis shows—if it is valid—that matters cannot be as simple as that—and this is good reason for throwing such an uncomfortable argument into the debate about the health of democracy.

Bullshitting and Lying in Politics

The full elaboration of the Frankfurt thesis will require other conceptions of 'bullshit' to supplement Frankfurt's own, but we can begin with his 'indifference-to-truth' definition to see how we might use 'bullshit' both polemically and conceptually in political analysis. It's probably fair to say that when people condemn their politicians as bullshitters, they generally haven't made Frankfurt's distinction between bullshitting and lying.[2] For him, in contrast to bullshitting, the act of lying is premised upon knowledge of, and concern for, the truth: the liar knows what is true and is concerned to conceal it (*On Bullshit*, p. 33).

Most politicians probably do tell lies some of the time, and some perhaps do tell lies a lot of the time. And it is belief in the truth of this claim that often gives rise to support for the cynicism thesis, basing its rejection of political engagement on the assumption that 'all politicians are liars and hypocrites, only in

---

[2] The tendency not properly to distinguish 'bullshitting' and 'lying' is evident in Laura Penny's discussion of politics in *Your Call Is Important to Us: The Truth about Bullshit* (New York: Crown, 2005), Chapter 5. See also p. 1: the fact that "never in the history of mankind have so many people uttered statements that they know to be untrue" is offered as a characterisation of "an era of unprecedented bullshit production." This example is particularly noteworthy as on page 5 Penny seems to embrace Frankfurt's definition.

politics for their own selfish ends no matter what lofty goals and
concerns they pretend to have'. Less subtle articulations of this
view treat politicians almost as if they are a sub-species of
humanity (or a species of sub-humanity) defined by its congen-
ital disposition to lying and incompetence. But it's surely
implausible to think that the *modus operandi* of politicians is to
apprehend the truth and then systematically attempt to conceal
it, *all the time*, as 'Frankfurt-*lying*' would have it.

Many different kinds of people go into politics, and for many
different kinds of reason, at least some of which are sincerely
based on principled commitment; and it is anyway incredible to
believe that everyone in the political process can consistently
muster the peculiar psychological energies necessary literally to
live by lying in the way many seem to assume politicians must.[3]

This isn't to deny, however, that political behavior and discourse is beset with evasion, prevarication, dissembling and
other forms of disconnection to the truth: what Frankfurt has
given us, with his conception of bullshit, is a way of character-
ising this without misleadingly sweeping it into the overly narrow category of 'lying'. To appreciate its utility in this regard, let
us also equip ourselves with G.A. Cohen's distinction between
"aim-bullshitters"—those whose consciously entertained goal it
is to produce bullshit—and "disposition-bullshitters," who are
unintentionally prone, for whatever reason, to produce bullshit.
On Frankfurt's definition, liars are always 'aim-liars', so to speak,
but not all bullshitters aim to bullshit (see Chapter 8 in this volume).

Consider what can retrospectively be seen as a classic state-
ment of political bullshitting provided by George Orwell in
Nineteen Eighty-Four's account of Winston's work in the
Ministry of Truth:

> Day by day and almost minute by minute the past was brought up
> to date. In this way every prediction made by the Party could be
> shown by documentary evidence to have been correct, nor was
> any item of news, or any expression of opinion, which conflicted
> with the needs of the moment, ever allowed to remain on record.

---

[3] The resistance to these facts on the part of some who cling to the cynicism thesis itself
exhibits a bullshitting approach to the 'understanding' of politics in their refusal to contemplate that politicians could be anything other than shameless liars.

All history was a palimpsest, scraped clean and reinscribed exactly as often as was necessary. In no case would it have been possible, once the deed was done, to prove that any falsification had taken place. . . . Even the written instruction which Winston received . . . never stated or implied that an act of forgery was to be committed: always the reference was slips, errors, misprints or misquotations which it was necessary to put right in the interests of accuracy. But actually he thought . . . it was not even forgery. It was merely the substitution of one piece of nonsense for another. Most of the material that you were dealing with had no connexion with anything in the real world, not even the kind of connexion that is contained in a direct lie.[4]

What's of particular interest here is how the routinized production of falsehood converts what might have started out as lying into bullshitting: the truth becomes essentially *forgotten* in the process of telling whatever story is told to serve the regime's purposes. To see this, we should realize that Winston might actually insert a truth in one of his daily corrections to the historical record of *The Times*. But it isn't there because it's true, or believed to be false, and the institutionalized rewriting of history is deliberately undermining the capacity—and, crucially, the willingness—to distinguish between the true and false. (The Party aims to destroy the very distinction, of course.)

As Orwell's satire suggests, totalitarianism provides the most obvious examples of ideologies and regimes attempting to embed themselves not simply in a web of lies—because that implies the truth remains, in its conscious concealment, as a potentially refuting presence in their midst—but in a morass of bullshit, where the premium is on adherence to their tropes and to the tales they tell to legitimate themselves and their actions, removing any notion that there could be a genuine realm of facts underneath by which the veracity of what are forwarded as truth-claims could actually be tested. The 'interests of the working class', the 'manifest destiny of the superior race', the 'wise guidance' of the party, or 'the great leader', when intoned often enough as mantras, become criterial of 'reality', manipulable to explain away anything and insulated from the very conceptual possibility of facts which would expose their bankruptcy. (I

---

[4] George Orwell, *Nineteen Eighty-Four* (London: Penguin, 1954), pp. 39–40.

think it is implausible, for example, to think that racists are typically liars in the Frankfurtian sense. They dogmatically persist in their views, impervious to, and hence essentially uninterested to confront, the facts which could undermine their beliefs.[5]) Hence, when Vàclav Havel famously campaigned, in Communist Czechoslovakia, to "live in truth" he is actually best understood as calling for a political order which did not require one to live in this kind of political bullshit. Such totalitarianism *aims* at bullshit and many of its hapless victims become disposed to reproduce it even as they mistakenly think themselves already to be 'living in truth.'[6]

Without implying any degree of moral equivalence between them and totalitarianism, I claim that an analogous disengagement with the truth is evident in the belief-systems and the practices of liberal democracies and their governments. It is no less pertinent for its tragic obviousness to cite the Bush Administration's notorious "weapons-of-mass-destruction" story told to justify the invasion of Iraq in 2003 as a prime example of such bullshit.

When we consider its demonstrably false elements, we might reasonably conclude that some outright lies were indeed told in the construction of that case. But I doubt that Bush, Rumsfeld, Rice, Powell, and their many vocal lieutenants and supporters were *always* consciously lying. Rather, they manifested a quintessentially bullshitting disconnection to, and disinterest in, the truth, or in the evidence to the contrary of their intentions that pointed to truths about WMDs in Iraq which they wished to resist. And when the facts to the contrary became too visible to ignore, the bullshitting shifted tack to suggest other supposed

---

[5] Some might think it inappropriate to label the abhorrent discourse of totalitarianisms 'bullshit', because it might seem to be too frivolously dismissive, too lightweight in its condemnatory force, to capture its full repulsiveness. Certainly, in this regard to call something 'bullshit' often seems to be an expression of *amused* contempt. But even if that is its rhetorical effect, it is worth noting that some forms of humor can constitute powerful strategies of attack against even the most appalling tyrants: see, for illustrations, some of the political jokes compiled by Steven Lukes and Itzhak Galnoor, eds., *No Laughing Matter* (London: Penguin, 1987). The collection's title gives the clue to the main point, however: such jokes only function as jokes when they, and their tellers and audiences, appreciate how profoundly *non-funny* their subject-matter actually is. Failure to appreciate this in jokes render them in bad taste, not funny—not *jokes*—at all.

[6] See 'The Power of the Powerless', in Vàclav Havel, *Open Letters* (New York: Knopf, 1991), p. 132.

justifications were also in place all along: 'humanitarian inter-vention', 'democratisation' and suggestions, made both directly and indirectly, of Saddam Hussein's complicity in the 9/11 attacks.

These examples of ordure may have issued from aim-bull-shitters who consciously sought to deflect concerns for the truth (for example: the 'humanitarian' justification may not be a lie as such, but the post-war insistence on its strength as a justification may be intended to divert attention away from the fact of the failure of the original official justification: a *post hoc* 'rejustifica-tion'). But there's no reason to think that such tales were not or could not also be spun with the sincerity of those who were merely disposition-bullshitters.

The point is that, just as totalitarian mythologies do, the story took on a life of its own: it had to, insofar as the decision to invade was not something which, for the Bush Administration and its allies, could be allowed to stand or fall on the evidence. What might indeed have *started* as lie-telling gradually slipped free of reality altogether in a way that lying doesn't. What mat-tered was that, from the Administration's perspective, *some* jus-tification for the invasion had to remain in play; what was actually the case on the ground, so to speak, was not essentially germane. (The same refusal to face relevant facts is evident in its claim that the invasion has not been subsequently disastrous for Iraqi society.[7])

The Myth of the 'Well-Informed' Citizen

At this point, a supporter of the liberal-democratic *status quo* might object that the Iraq invasion is just a one-off, and not therefore evidence of a systematic propensity to bullshit as is present in totalitarian regimes. But even if they fall well short of totalitarian proportions it is hardly difficult to come up with other examples of such bullshitting on the part of just about every liberal-democratic government. (The partisan belief that it

---

[7] The claim that bullshitting tactics were deployed in the attempt to justify the Iraq inva-sion, which I believe is incontrovertible, might not itself suffice to yield the conclusion that the invasion was therefore unjustified. Just because no non-bullshit justification was used does not mean none was available. However, though the present analysis rests on no specific view about *that* possibility, it is difficult to resist the conclusion that the resort to bullshit is at least *prima facie* evidence that there was no genuine justification.

is obviously *only* 'the other side' that bullshits is itself bullshit.) This is evidence that can be adduced in support of a claim that liberal democracy as a form of political order functions in a way that disposes those in, and around, power to bullshit—and if we rested content with that claim, we might be tempted to conclude that the cynicism thesis is well on the way to vindication. For on this basis one could perhaps plausibly surmise that the reason for such a prevalent disposition to bullshit is that politicians invariably have a lot that they wish to hide. Their dissimulation becomes so routine that they cease to tell lies as they retreat into a self-justificatory fantasy-land of bullshit whose illusions have to be propped up by ever greater piles of the stuff.

To insist again, Frankfurt-thesis advocates don't deny that politicians produce lots of strikingly malodorous bullshit. But they would warn against the frequent tendency to be so over-come by its pungency as to fail to discern its other sources. Not only do we have their claim (a): that citizens do their own fair share of (Frankfurt-) bullshitting about politics, but we can also extend the thesis as stated thus far with a further claim (b): that democracy exhibits a tendency to produce other, non-Frankfurt forms of bullshit which act to reinforce the Frankfurt-bullshitting of citizens.

Substantiating (a) first: it is obvious that not all citizens are political cynics, or are as cynical as they like to think themselves to be. Many of them buy into the bullshit of their politicians in their own 'understanding' of the political world and doubtless do their own bit to embellish and propagate it. Indeed, it's plausible to suggest a rule of thumb that, insofar as the citizens in question know even less about the facts with respect to which politicians are bullshitting, they are therefore *more* likely to be bullshitting whenever they confidently offer political opinions and evaluations. Now, the key to the Frankfurt thesis is not simply to understand why citizens formulate and voice such opinions but also to grasp why they tend to do so with such *confidence.*

An explanation for this runs as follows. The political world and the choices that have to be made therein are incredibly complex, very difficult to grasp and negotiate. The idea that even its essentials can be properly understood by anyone lacking a high degree of intellectual ability and trained expertise is frankly absurd. But electoral democracy *has* to resist acknowledgment of this truth: in both its theory and practice it assumes a degree of political competence on the part of the citizenry— in the ideal of the 'well-informed' citizen—that it does not (indeed cannot reasonably be expected) to possess. Citizens are effectively encouraged, indeed they often feel themselves obligated *qua* citizens, to formulate what often turn out to be incorrect, over-simplified or otherwise flawed views on a whole range of issues *without a concern for these failings being properly accommodated in either the mindset or the institutional embodiment of democratic deliberation.*

The electoral need to pander to such views surely accounts for a significant amount of the bullshit spewed forth by politicians. For when they campaign for votes they are forced, consciously or not, to present things in terms that citizens can understand (and of course many of them do not in fact possess much more than their voters in the way of such expertise anyway).[8] Candidates for office have to attempt to pull off a very delicate balancing trick. They have to (a) offer a sufficiently compelling critique of their opponents along with (b) an equally compelling account of what they would do in office instead, all the while (c) saying and (d) doing a host of things to try to co-opt typically dissimilar groups of supporters into what they hope to be a winning coalition, and (e) explaining away whatever actions and statements in their past (no matter how recent or distant) might cause them personal and/or political embarrassment.

Sometimes they will deal with such difficulties by *dodging* the crucial issues, for example by pretending that certain concerns are of great importance when in fact, they are not—a strategy which has the effect (intended or otherwise) of deflecting critical attention to those issues which are really important (the 'politics of distraction'). Or they confront the political world with dogged (sometimes 'fundamentalist') adherence to a simplistic set of ideological nostrums and a refusal (again, intended or not) to contemplate the possibility that they might fail to explain that world and orient us satisfactorily in it. And

---

[8] Given this, it is perhaps no surprise to find, as the *Princeton Review* did, that in the 2004 presidential debates, Bush spoke at a sixth-grade level of competence, whilst Kerry just about made it to seventh-grade level. See www.thedartmouth.com/article.php?aid= 2004101502020.

of course the flow of this bullshit is hardly stemmed once election time is over . . .

Anyone who has actually studied politics—beyond the
superficial, more-or-less partisan ephemera reproduced in the
media to the more coolly detached, scrupulous and theoretically
rigorous writings from academia, say—is fully aware of how
simplistic and naive (and, to that degree, deluded) much everyday ('real-world'⁹) political discourse tends to be. And the point
is that it has to be: not, perhaps, in every respect as actually
manifest, but over-simplification is a functional necessity for
democracy. Citizens indulge in the same kind of bullshit as
politicians when they affirm such over-simplified views, and its
metaphorical stench becomes more noxious the more doggedly
such views are affirmed in defiant indifference to the facts which
would reveal the suppressed complexities.¹⁰ As already suggested, even acceptance of the cynicism thesis may sometimes
be based on bullshit: most citizens fail properly to pursue the
question as to *why* politicians always seem incapable of deliv-
ering their campaign promises, often resting content with the
assumption that this must be down to their personal characters
rather than being indicative of far more profound systemic problems in the polity. Depressingly, what keeps this whole system
going in the wake of such a judgment is invariably more of the
same: other campaigners feed on this 'diagnosis', promising to
be a 'different sort of politician', trotting out platitudes on governance designed to accord with the voters' own 'plain common
sense'—which is in fact usually a highly fragmentary, partial and
ill-informed experience of the world, very poorly equipped to
deal with political realities. When this leads to what could be
called the 'Governor Schwarzenegger Syndrome', perhaps this is
not too serious: but dangerous demagogues and fundamen-
talisms also thrive in such circumstances.

Yet all of this can hardly be said to be a fair *criticism* of the
citizens in question, if it is wholly unreasonable to expect them
all to have the time and competence properly to understand pol-

---

⁹ A term which itself often features in bullshitting conceptions of politics.

¹⁰ At its extreme, this fact-indifference parallels how Frankfurt views a lot of advertising:
"My presumption is that advertisers generally decide what they are going to say in their
advertisements without caring what the truth is. Therefore, what they say in their advertisements is bullshit"; Harry Frankfurt, "Reply to G.A. Cohen," in Sarah Buss, Lee
Overton, eds., *Contours of Agency* (Cambridge, Massachusetts: MIT Press, 2002), p. 341.

itics. I certainly don't think that democracy produces a lot of aim-bullshitters amongst the citizenry and I share Cohen's preference to focus critically on the product—the bullshit—rather than its producers. And even if, on these lines, we agree with Winston Churchill that "the best argument against democracy is a five minute conversation with the average voter," we're not committed to rejecting democracy altogether (We have a reason instead to adopt Churchill's belief that "democracy is the worst form of government except for all the others that have been tried from time to time.") But we shouldn't shy away from the observation that some of democracy's problems arise from the bullshitting misapprehensions of political reality that citizens as well as politicians manifest.

'Dumbing-Up': Some Distortions of Democratic Equality

All of this is not to say that we cannot increase current levels of knowledge and critical appreciation of political realities and arguments among the citizenry as a whole (although the present argument would be hoist by its own petard if it thought this partial amelioration was an easy thing to achieve). But now we must confront claim (b)'s deepening of the Frankfurt thesis, for this proposes that there are certain obstacles in democratic culture even to modest proposals for improvement which again are difficult to own up to in a democracy.

Although one of modernity's defining moments was the conversion of 'democracy' from 'bad' to 'good' thing, many defenders of democracy in modern times have nevertheless peddled highly elitist conceptions of who is actually fit substantially to engage in politics: for them, democracy works only if an elite political class is largely left alone to rule, barring the occasional election to keep them in check. But apart from any other reservation we might have about this as an ideal, such 'democratic elitism' is clearly prone to internal tensions: how can any such elitism be reconciled with the principle of equal respect for citizens, on which democracy is founded? The problem that claim (b) draws our attention to, however, is that this tension has in recent times been 'resolved' in ways that are detrimental to the very modest kind of purely intellectual elitism needed in the fight against bullshit.

To explain: elitists have traditionally feared that increasing the voice of the ordinary citizens in politics, and culture more widely, would inevitably lead to a dumbing-down in those spheres, such is the mediocrity of the latter's competence and tastes. There has been a powerful reaction against this view in the name of democratic equality, but one form it has taken has challenged the very idea of the objective standards invoked to distinguish, for example, good and bad, right and wrong, or sophisticated and mediocre, beliefs and judgments. 'Equal respect' leads to the relativist game of 'I'm valid, you're valid: we're all entitled to our opinions', wherein having 'an equal right to express an opinion' becomes conflated with the claim of 'equal validity of whatever opinion is expressed' (where 'validity' means 'equal intellectual merit').[11] And no matter what nonsense this may legitimate, the anti-elitist aim is to *raise* everyone's view to some level of substantive equal worth: it is, in effect, a dumbing-*up*.

Such vulgar relativism is famously easy to dispatch in the fabled Philosophy 101 course and, perhaps more pertinently, those who *think* that they affirm it consistently can very often be shown not to do so absolutely. Few such putative relativists, when pushed on the matter, are happy to play the equal-validity game with the serial murderer's, rapist's, or child-molester's conceptions of the good life. Some will readily embrace the idea that there are clear objective standards of evaluation for performance and achievement in sport and art, say, without thinking that those who objectively achieve less are thereby denied equality of respect as *people*. But many do not apply this idea to the evaluation of specifically political views. In a putatively democratic way—which actually leaves out the crucial *deliberative* element of democratic discourse—it seems to be enough for opinions to be aired and left to stand as they are. From such a perspective, any argument about one's views against those of others—as anything more constructive than mere 'sounding off'—is pointless: nothing is bullshit (or, if something is, then everything is).[12]

---

[11] Frankfurt is keen to stress that relativism yields much bullshit; *On Bullshit*, pp. 64–65.
[12] This uncritical sanctification of personal opinion may well partly explain the heightened prominence of 'personality' issues and the *ad hominem* argument in political life: if you can't attack the argument, then attack the arguer.

Frankfurt-bullshit has a natural bedfellow in relativism and, to remove it from political discourse, we must retrieve the democratic ideal of equal respect from the relativist clutch that has taken such a strong hold on it.

Those who prefer to think of the situation in political culture as a dumbing-down might describe such relativism as an obvious product of ignorance: overwhelmed and embarrassed by the complexities of politics, perhaps jealous of those few who seem more capable of getting to grips with them, the ordinary citizen—encouraged by a distorted reading of what democratic equality implies—reacts by stubbornly refusing the possibility of such qualitative distinctions in political knowledge. But this quasi-Nietzschean story of democratic *ressentiment*, of 'timid little people' dragging us all down to some lowly, facile common cultural denominator, fits rather poorly with the dumbed-up self-images of the age. I agree with Laura Penny's belief that we live in "an era of unprecedented bullshit production" (*Your Call Is Important to Us*, p. 1). And a significant amount of it is, I submit, the result not of a timid but an assertive, indeed aggressive, demand of equal validity in the discourse of multifarious spheres in social life.

Part of the phenomenon I have in mind is exemplified by the peculiarly 'in-your-face' form of 'respect' that many wish to command today (sometimes ironically at the expense of any respect they might show for others). But I wish to highlight another aspect to it, which is much more responsible for bullshit. As societies become ever more complex it is only to be expected that types of knowledge multiply and the division of labor becomes ever deeper. Old hierarchies of knowledge and expertise are bound to be displaced: but there is an underlying but striking resistance to the *idea* that what arises in their place is a new *hierarchy* of expertise, in the following sense. Almost every field of human endeavor, almost every profession, no matter how humdrum, increasingly indulges in its own forms of discourse and 'knowledge', its own professions of 'expertise'. This is exhibited by the pseudo-intellectual jargon so many of them increasingly spout. In other words, expertise has in a sense become 'democratized', and in a way that threatens to hollow out the very notion of 'expertise': everyone is an expert in something. We know that some types of bullshitter pretend to an expertise or experience that they do not in fact possess. But in the democratization of expertise we encounter others who are pretending to be experts in something that is not in fact a matter of 'expertise' at all. To posit any causal link between this and democratic equality of respect is probably to oversimplify quite seriously its provenance. But this phenomenon comports well with the relativizing understanding of such respect and, I suspect, it provides a powerful cultural bolster to the insulation of ordinary citizens' political views from expert critique, and more widely to the toleration of bullshit in politics and, indeed in many other spheres of life.

My example of this phenomenon is the 'management-speak' that the growth of the 'American business model' of economic organisation has fostered; it has particular pertinence here insofar as its paradigms have been used radically to redesign not just direct economic activity but much modern governance and indeed many other social institutions and practices more generally (who, to take just one small example of it, can get away without a 'mission statement' nowadays?) Much of it—as I'm sure readers who are not utterly complicit with it will readily agree—is fatuously pretentious and overblown. But it provides succor for those who *are* complicit with it: they can show off their 'expert' familiarity with a putatively privileged set of discursive terms that masquerade as referents for supposedly complex matters which mimic genuine intellectual complexity and profundity but which are not, in truth, complex at all. Some of it is undoubtedly bullshit in something like Frankfurt's sense. The word 'downsizing', for example, is, I suspect, deliberately chosen to overlook the facts about the human cost of the policies it denotes. But here is an area which requires other conceptions of bullshit to get its full measure as a dissembling discourse.

So, to identify more fully the targets in the struggle against bullshit, we need to expand on the typologies of bullshit provided by Frankfurt and Cohen. For future elaboration and analysis, then, I would suggest the following. In addition to (1) 'Frankfurt-bullshit', *indifference to truth*, and that proposed by Cohen (2): *unclarifiable unclarity*, discourse which is not only unclear, but whose meaning cannot be rendered clear even on analysis, we have:

(3): *clarifiable unclarity*: discourse which over-complicates the expression of claims that can be much more straightforwardly expressed.[13]

Bullshit (4) might be plain, straightforward *rubbish*: discourse that is plainly deficient in logic, coherence or factual grounding.

Bullshit (5) is *irretrievable speculation*: discourse that may be perfectly clear, and *might* not be rubbish but is crucially lacking in any plausible means of verification.

Bullshit (6) is *pretension* or *over-portentousness*: discourse which may or may not be superficially complex but which over-intellectualises the straightforward, the obvious, sometimes even the trivial and banal.

Bullshit (7) includes *evasion, elision, insincerity, procrastination* and other forms of dissembling in discourse that fall short of lying, which is very common in, though hardly exclusive to, politics.[14]

Philosophy versus Bullshit

The various forms of bullshit that have dumbed-up democratic culture and paradoxically drowned out the voice of genuine expertise in political conversation have sources and effects that lie well beyond politics as well, of course. The battle against them will have to be fought on many fronts, and with a variety of weapons. My own small contribution to the struggle includes a call to restore objective standards to our political arguments, and a respect for such standards in evaluating their quality. This has elements of an intellectual elitism in that such respect will incorporate greater acknowledgment of the authority of certain people to lead certain debates, not only with their greater factual knowledge but also their greater acumen in critically analysing the interpretations and arguments made in politics than we find in, say, partisan media commentary.[15] But this

---

[13] Criticising Cohen's castigation of a sentence by Etienne Balibar as unclarifiable unclarity, Frankfurt plausibly clarifies it: Frankfurt, "Reply to G.A. Cohen," p. 342. But if it is clarifiably unclear, then it may still qualify as a different form of bullshit.

[14] Along with Bullshit (2), Bullshits (4) and (5) are identified by Cohen in Chapter 8 of this volume.

[15] I have in mind here something analogous to Peter Singer's conception of the 'moral expert': see "Moral Experts," in Peter Singer, *Writings on an Ethical Life* (London: Fourth Estate, 2002), pp. 3–6.

implies no extra social or political advantages for them. When I say that they are to 'lead' debates, I signify the intention that these should continue to be democratically inclusive; I am not advocating a political discourse in which the elite only talks to itself and hence effectively monopolises input into the political process.

If one suspects that such an arrangement would still be very much 'us-and-them'—the handful of experts versus the mass of distinctly inexpert citizens—then we should consider how such a gap might be narrowed. For even if citizens will never all have high levels of political expertise, that is no reason to rest content with the low levels of critical political understanding many of them currently possess. Certainly, liberal democracies should think about how they 'train' the citizens of tomorrow in their 'citizenship', or 'civics', school education to see how political knowledge might be deepened and critical acumen sharpened. In order to develop thus as citizens, people have to learn more of the Socratic skills of self-examination: to recognise how their own views may be imperfect, and how one may go about refining them.

More generally, I propose that an anti-bullshit discursive culture may develop if there is greater practice of, and respect for, the techniques of a good old-fashioned analytic-philosophical style, which prizes clarity of exposition and rigor of analysis in pursuit of truth and the 'best argument' objectively understood. A tutor of mine at Oxford, one of analytic philosophy's spiritual homes, once told me that analytic philosophy was "a very good bullshit detector."

The expertise I have in mind, then, will exemplify this style and will aspire not only to command respect and acquire intellectual ('opinion-leading') authority in its competent execution of analytic-philosophical critique but also to provide models of, and standards for, analysis and argument that others should want to try to share. It's a small tragedy for democracy when the taste and aptitude for this kind of philosophical discourse is confined to the ivory towers of academia. For such philosophy would seem to be a prime tool in tackling, in its variegated forms, bullshit not just in politics but in all other spheres of life.

It is thus highly regrettable that the analytic-philosophical style has very many critics in philosophy itself, nowadays; many philosophies overtly want to eschew truth, objectivity and clarity. For this reason, as Cohen points out, in the struggle against bullshit it is not enough to have an enthusiastic mass or 'lay' audience for philosophy *per se* in order to increase people's bullshit-spotting capabilities. Too much philosophy nowadays exhibits one or more of the forms of bullshit,[16] and this may be partly due to the desire to produce interesting, arresting, 'fashionable' ideas for an impressionable lay audience to consume: 'being lay, that audience will read philosophy only if it is *interesting*', he suggests, and this does not necessarily mean 'being interested in truth.'[17]

When for whatever reason "truth is not even aimed at, false, or rather, untrue theses abound' and typically 'they are protected against exposure by obscure statement and/or by obscure defense when they are challenged: so bullshit, too abounds" (p. 39). So a philosophical culture has to have the right kind of philosophy in order to be disposed against bullshit.

When we consider just how important truth is in politics (as indeed it is in most other areas of our lives), and how the forms of bullshit degrade our political and social life, it seems simply absurd to embrace styles of philosophy which disparage truth (whether in aim-bullshitting manner or not) and end up contributing to the clogging of our discourse and 'understanding' with bullshit. Apprehension of hard and uncomfortable truths, and clear and rigorously sophisticated thinking about their resolution, are absolutely vital as we confront the huge, and hugely perplexing, problems in the world today.

But the presence of bullshit in our political discourse severely problematizes our efforts to grasp them. Much of this bullshit is the product of the politicians, but the political bullshit of the citizens themselves also significantly obscures accurate perception of these tough challenges. The Frankfurt thesis helps us to focus on its source and hence to ponder its resolution. As such, it deserves much greater attention; for certainly

---

[16] Some of this is identified (in the field of philosophy of science) and criticised in Alan Sokal and Jean Bricmont, *Intellectual Impostures* (London: Profile, 1998).
[17] G.A. Cohen, "Why One Kind of Bullshit Flourishes in France," manuscript, p. 33. I'm very grateful to Jerry Cohen for permission to cite from this unpublished paper.

one thing it would be potentially catastrophic to do is to use the ubiquity of bullshit as an excuse to adopt instead the crippling inertia which can so easily become the natural upshot of the cynicism thesis.[18]

---

[18] These thoughts were first expressed at the political theory workshop in the Department of Politics and International Relations, University of Wales, Swansea. The session marked the visit of my ex-student Christine Stender, and I am grateful to Christine not only for appreciating that there was nothing personal to the choice of theme but also for subsequent discussion. I'm also grateful for comments to James Beard, Heidi Brown, Scott Bruning, Maria Paz Calvo Felton, Alan Finlayson, James Hill, Sarah Moran, Richard Murphy and Richard Van Der Watt. I am deeply indebted to George Reisch for excellent criticism of the penultimate draft of this chapter. As always, Anne Evans's scrupulous reading removed some of the inadvertent bullshit and other errors from the final version; those remaining are my own responsibility.

13
Political Bullshit and the Stoic Story of Self

VANESSA NEUMANN

Bullshit is not, as it is popularly misconstrued, hot air—the remaining exhalation after speech is done. Far from it. Bullshit is a certain kind of speech, intended to distract or obfuscate in a general way, in order to achieve a desired effect—often one that is nonrational and emotional, where emotions become reasons for a course of action.

Bullshit is fertile ground for philosophical investigation because it is intentional and identity-forming. Either of these conditions would suffice to make it a subject of philosophical interest; both together make it an important matter for investigation.

Bullshit is particularly useful and interesting in the arena of political discourse, where it is most often recognized by the general public. Its familiarity and pervasiveness in politics are good reasons to examine bullshit in the political context. However, political bullshit has important consequences that it would be a mistake to overlook.

How to Analyze Bullshit

Two major strategies have emerged in the definition of bullshit, and each has its proponents. Mine is neither of these. The first strategy is to discuss the agent-relative action of bullshitting, addressing the question of what it is to bullshit—or, the related question of how one knows when someone is bullshitting. The second strategy is to identify bullshit by its content: what is bullshit or the related (but not equivalent) question of how one can spot bullshit. Harry Frankfurt is the main proponent of the first strategy and G.A. Cohen of the second.

As Cohen demonstrates ("Deeper into Bullshit"), Frankfurt defines bullshit in reference to the agent producing the bullshit—namely, the bullshitter. Bullshit is defined in reference to the speaker's intent to conceal the fact that the truth-values of his statements are of no central interest to him.[1] As Cohen rightly points out, in Frankfurt's theory the bull wears the trousers. Cohen offers a different definition of bullshit that makes reference solely to its content. In essence, he tries to make the shit wear the trousers.

As Cohen sees it, the main difference between his approach and Frankfurt's is that Frankfurt's bullshit is concerned with utterances in everyday life. This sort of bullshit corresponds to the second definition in the *Oxford English Dictionary* ("trivial or insincere talk or writing") and, for Frankfurt, its primary locus is the activity and its essence indifference to truth. Cohen, in contrast, argues that *his* bullshit is concerned with utterances in the academic setting, and corresponds to the first definition in the *Oxford English Dictionary* ("nonsense, rubbish"). Cohen takes bullshit's primary locus to be *output* and its essence to be unclarifiability. Producers of Cohen bullshit may not be bullshitters, as they may not have the intent Frankfurt's requires—they may not be insincere, though their product is nonsense. Frankfurtian bullshitters, likewise, may or may not produce Cohen bullshit: they may be insincere but succeed only in producing "nonsense, rubbish." Still, their *intent* to deceive makes them bullshitters.

Cohen makes no secret of the fact that there is a reason for these divergent approaches: they are concerned with different contexts. While Cohen is concerned to identify and eradicate bullshit in the academic context, Frankfurt is concerned to identify bullshit and bullshitters in ordinary life. Cohen wants to examine bullshit in the academic setting, and he deems the identification of content a more promising strategy on two counts. First, it is more diplomatic or courteous—and less agent-relative. Second, it is more practical, since content is more easily identified than intention, although, as Cohen grants,

---

[1] *On Bullshit*, p. 33.

identification of content may indeed lead to an identification of strategy. "For reasons of courtesy, strategy and good evidence," he writes, "we should criticize the product, which is visible, and not the process, which is not. We may hope that success in discrediting the product will contribute to extinguishing the process" (p. 135n).

Frankfurt and Cohen do not exhaust the intellectual landscape of bullshit. My concern is a third, largely unnoticed, context: the mechanism of bullshit—how it works and what its effects are, irrespective of whether we are confronted with Cohen bullshit or Frankfurt bullshit. Cohen grants that "the word 'bullshit' characteristically denotes *structurally* different things that correspond to those different interests" (p. 119, italics in original). The setting or context therefore affects the form of bullshit. There is a relation that is critical to this third strategy: the relation between speaker and listener—between bullshitter and bullshittee.

This alternative way of looking at bullshit helps us see how bullshit typically works in political discourse. What makes a speaker or writer (I'll here use 'speaker', for short) initiate or spread bullshit? How does it work on the listener or reader (I'll here use 'listener', for short)? We will see that bullshit plays a significant role in political discourse, and that, as such, it is difficult to extricate.

In politics, bullshit distracts or obfuscates, in order to create an impression that may or may not be true. I follow Frankfurt in the contention that bullshit may or may not be true, and that bullshit's truth-value is irrelevant. It is not by virtue of its falsity that a statement can be considered bullshit. Even a true (or partly-true) statement may be bullshit. Even if true, a statement may be non-germane, irrelevant, or obfuscatory—thereby making it a prime candidate for bullshit. Bullshit therefore differs from lying and resembles bluffing, though it is not bluffing. Often, bullshit is a mix of true and false statements, the mixture determined to suit the purpose of the bullshit in question.

In politics, purpose is crucial for analyzing bullshit. The better it fulfills its purpose, the better the bullshit. There are several possible purposes, but they fall into two broad categories. The first typical purpose of political bullshit is to depict the speaker as someone different ('better,' given the circumstances) than she is. It is usually intended to identify the speaker as someone desirable to the listener. This is familiar from the personal and the political arena: "I'm one of you," or "I am what you need or want." This is familiar from electoral campaigns, but also from political commentary. The second purpose is to identify groups of people, usually to specify a target or justify a political course of action—as in the Orientalist or structuralist approach: "They are different from us, so we should treat them like this." From slavery to the war on terrorism to the racially-underpinned left turn in South American politics, this second purpose is pervasive—and dangerous.

Bullshit is difficult to extricate from political discourse because it is so useful: it serves the interests of so many different groups. Both sides of a debate resort to bullshit, and bullshit gives them power over the parameters of the debate. A prominent example of this is the pervasive use of moral language, without the attendant commitment to moral constraints. Moral language is used to praise and condemn actions, and those who perform them, as just and unjust, virtuous or vicious, or just plain right or wrong. The speaker (a politician especially) seeks to score points with her constituency by putting forth the narrowest judgments without providing the underpinning normative commitments that might constrain her future actions. Such talk, rather than illuminating a framework for morally acceptable behavior, is designed to make the speaker appear superior to some competitor, while giving the speaker wiggle room for the future.

Take the common example of one politician condemning another for accepting a free trip or other favor from a corporate entity. The second politician is condemned as bad or corrupt, without any further explanation of why accepting such a favor is bad, or of what it is that is morally compromising. Avoiding such an analysis or fundamental discussion then allows the speaker to "wiggle out" of future accusations of a similar sort by citing various alleged differences: "Well, my case is different, because the corporation in question is different, the type of favor is different," and so forth. So, the speaker can appear morally concerned and, even, to speak for morality itself (not unlike speaking on behalf of God, espousing what is surely "God's will"), although she does not say anything that would constrain her from accepting a different sort of bribery. Here, moral language is used solely to advance personal or group interests—not to illuminate ethics in politics. Moral language is reduced to a tool in the competitive struggle for political advantage.

The stakes are high. The struggle for political advantage is a winner-take-all game. Surely the power of one agent is constrained by the relative power of other agents, and this in turn is constrained by a system of procedural checks and balances. However, since the rules are themselves subject to revision by those in power, the struggle for political power is a struggle for control over the rules of the game. Bullshit is the main tool for the ultimately *unconstrained* struggle for the flexible and malleable rules of political power.[2]

There's a distinction worth making here. In the context of public political discourse we get both kinds of bullshit: the kind custom-crafted by those deviously intending to obfuscate and the kind innocently repeated by those too uncritical to recognize bullshit, who often seize upon bullshit that strikes a chord with them or fits some self-image or narrative they embrace.

Stories Shape Our Feelings

Bullshit's role in political narratives gives it one of its most interesting features. Bullshit links images and types which are both familiar and fascinating, and so taps into cultural prototypes. It uses familiar expressions to convey mental images, and leaves an impression that achieves the speaker's goal.

A narrative, or story, is not merely an interpretive framework superimposed on otherwise disconnected acts, images, impressions and emotions. As Peter Goldie argues, a person's narrative is that person's life insofar as it is understood as a sequence of meaningful and emotional episodes.[3] The narrative structures of our lives themselves shape and color how we understand and how we feel about particular episodes in the past, and how we will perceive and interpret episodes in the future. Narrative also shapes how we view others, their lives and their attendant worthiness, and how *they* relate to *us* and affect *our* lives. In short, it forms our understanding of our place in the world.

---

[2] I thank Thomas Pogge for this insight.
[3] P. Goldie, *Emotions: A Philosophical Exploration* (New York: Oxford University Press, 2002), p. 5.

The narrative is therefore much more than the mere string-ing together of impressions and emotions into a coherent struc-ture. The narrative structure itself shapes our feelings towards objects and, by extension, to particular episodes. It's largely due to an event's location in the narrative that we feel the way we do about something or someone. When asked why we feel as we do about someone or something, we often say, "Well, there's a story behind it." It's this background story that gives the emo-tion its content—we wouldn't feel anything if there weren't a story. So the relation of an event or emotional episode to a nar-rative is symbiotic; it flows both ways. The episodes shape the narrative of which they are a part and give it meaningful con-tent, and the narrative shapes the content of the emotion we experience. As the narrative and the background story evolves, so do our emotions.

To understand how bullshit functions in this light, we need to look at the nature of emotions themselves. As Goldie shows, emotions relate to values in important ways. First, emotions give epistemic access to values. If I feel love or fear, for example, then there is some*thing* that I love or fear (p. 4). This is a stronger claim than saying merely that emotions have *aboutness* or *ofness*. This is demonstrated by the fact that emotions can be phrased as transitive verbs of the standard form, 'A Fs B', where B is the object picked out by the emotion-verb F experienced by the person A. "An object of an emotion, in this sense, could be a particular thing or person (that pudding, this man), an event or an action (the earthquake, your hitting me), or a state of affairs (my being in an aeroplane)" (p. 17). Emotions thereby reveal the people, objects, events, and states of affairs we value, positively or negatively—the ones we want and the ones we wish to avoid. There is a caveat here, though, that applies to any intentional state.

> First, the object of the emotion has to be identified in a sufficiently fine-grained way to capture why the person feels that emotion about that object: Oedipus might be delighted he married Jocasta, but would not be delighted that he has married his mother. Secondly, the object of an emotion need not exist. Jimmy might be afraid of the Abominable Snowman, when there is no such crea-ture. (p. 18)

Emotions, finally, are not created in a void: there are significant conceptual relations between emotions and the beliefs that ground them. I fear losing the man I love because I believe that my life would be substantially impoverished without him. If I believed I would be better off without him, I probably would not have the same fear. Perhaps this is an assessment rather than a belief? Then consider a different example. I might be angry at seeing another woman with a coat like mine if I believe it's mine and she has stolen it. I wouldn't feel the same anger if I believe she has simply bought it at the same shop, rather than stolen mine; I would find it an amusing coincidence.

Martha Nussbaum believes that the narrative of an emotion is in fact the narrative about judgments.[4] These judgments are about things important to us that we do not fully control—both the lack of control and the importance are implicit in the intense experience of an emotion. This is, in fact, the Greek Stoic view of emotions. Not only are emotions intentional in that they point at their object, but they are deeply intentional in the way they are internal and encompass a set of beliefs about the object. These beliefs pertain to the value of the object. The object is seen (believed, judged) to be important. "So there seem to be type-identities between emotions and judgments; emotions can be defined in terms of judgment alone" (p. 196).

Emotions also shape values. Pride, vanity and resentment are predispositions, but they are also emotions that shape what we value, what is important. If I'm proud, I will value respect or independence or both. If I'm vain I will value praise and attention. If I'm resentful, I will value stories of perceived rivals brought low. These emotions and their attendant value are not disruptive of a life's narrative, but very much part of it. The triumvirate of emotion, judgment and narrative is as old as philosophy itself. The Greek concept of *eudaimonia*, commonly mistranslated as 'happiness', encompasses them. In eudaimonistic theory a well-lived life (mistranslated as a 'happy' life) is one that includes all those things to which the agent ascribes intrinsic value—all that the person deems important in her life,

---

[4] Martha Nussbaum, "Emotions as Judgments of Value and Importance," in Robert C. Solomon, ed., *Thinking about Feeling: Contemporary Philosophers on Emotions* (New York: Oxford University Press, 2004), p. 184.

without which she would not consider her life complete (p. 190).

Imagination, and the dynamic character of judging ourselves, takes place against the background of narrative (p. 51): "what would my life be like with/without/if . . . ?" The evaluation of importance is, as mentioned above, shaped by the narrative and pushes the agent's cognition towards an object, itself assessed within the framework of the narrative. "When we have an emotion," Goldie says, "we are engaged with the world, grasping what is going on in the world, and responding accordingly." That's why "the emotions can be educated" (p. 48). Goldie gives the example of how children are raised to have an appropriate, and proportionate, response to appropriate stimuli: "this warrants sympathy," "this should make you proud," and so on. As we will see, the most dangerous of political bullshit tries to educate our emotions by telling us what should make us proud or patriotic, angry or frightened.

These processes are a part of every life: the ebb and flow of one's life and reason, one's narrative. The power of bullshit is that it can be used to tell us what should be eudaimonistically included among our feelings, wants, and needs. It tries to make us desire and long for things we had not previously considered. In other words, it tells us what *philia* should be important to us. It tells us what we should consider our civic duty, what we should covet and—ultimately—who we are with respect to those around us. The special problem with bullshit, however, is that it gets its power by appealing to and motivating that part of us that is base and non-rational. In that respect, it degrades us. Let's look at some examples from international politics.

Bullshit Around the Globe

The sentence 'we are waging a war on terror' is specifically designed to elicit a strong and specific emotional response—not to give any further facts, elicit a debate, or give ethical justifications for actions. It is useful here to parse out the mechanism of this phrase, one word at a time. First, there is the 'we'. This is a clear identification of a group *vis-à-vis* another group: 'we', not 'they', not 'others'. If the listener is engaged in the activity (here, fighting in the war on terror—more on this in a second), then the listener is included in the group. If she is not, then she is not in the group—and may be, possibly, on the other side of the confrontation (maybe even an 'enemy combatant', to use another popular and vague phrase). Second, this us-versus-them feeling is reinforced by the imagery of waging a war, which conjures visceral reactions of patriotism (possibly jingoism) and a call to violent and unquestioning action. If we are at war, then we must join our compatriots—and fight without questioning our orders. This is very useful for those seeking extra powers and a curb on civil liberties in order to wage this war.

Last, but not least, there is that word 'terror'—not terror*ism* or terror*ists*, as these would be too specific for the bullshit purpose at hand. 'Terror*ists*' would designate individual people who are defined with reference to specific actions. Our attention would then turn to these individuals and perhaps look at them closely to see if they fit that category and are being judged accurately. 'Terror*ism*' would designate a type of action: again, something that can be defined and specified—perhaps as the murder of innocent civilians, who are at least innocent in the sense that they are not the individuals that perpetrated whatever offense has come to be the excuse for violence.

'Terror', on the other hand, is suitably vague. It is an emotion and figures powerfully, even universally, in human narratives. We have all know terror from childhood, when we were terrified of being punished or of the bogeyman. The 'war on terror', then, is a 'war' on an emotion? 'We' will vanquish this extreme form of fear?' Again, 'we are waging a war on terror' is a bullshit phrase not because we are not undertaking a course of action to end terrorism. That would certainly be a laudable cause. It is a bullshit phrase because it is a narrative that evokes emotions, rather than the thought and discussion wise, democratic policy and military decisions require. It teaches us to fear some vague Other, 'terror', and, by tapping into our deep-seated craving for security, urges us to hunt this bogeyman Other.

Whether it is 'the war on terror' or 'Western imperialism', parties in international conflicts or standoffs will use bullshit to persuade their followers to support their actions rather than engage in a lucid debate about the underpinning moral commitments. For instance, the United States government does not explain why such extraordinary resources and curbs on civil liberties are justified to eliminate something that even in 2001 caused only 0.13 percent of all deaths in the US. Likewise, the militant

Muslims calling for *jihad* on all Westerners on the premise that this "jihad is God's will" do not elucidate how they are able to know (and espouse) God's will to murder innocents (a term used even by Osama bin Laden in his *Ummat Daily* interview of September 28th, 2001, where he denied involvement in the 9/11 attacks) especially within a religion that explicitly forbids the murder of women and children even in warfare. Neither the militant Muslim terrorists nor the Bush administration fighting them has addressed how bombing or torturing people who are not the ones that actually inflicted harm (whether to Palestinians or New York City) will bring peace or end fear.

We can see, therefore, precisely how political bullshit degrades us. On the one hand, it seeks to shape our values in a manner that circumvents our treasured human faculty to be moved by ideas. It appeals to our emotions and avoids engaging those faculties of reason and debate that make us human. The call to spread democracy, for example, lulls us into feeling that it is our civic duty to share our freedom, but it says little about whether the people in fact want democracy or how such an intervention is to be justified. To tell one's constituency that the administration's task is to spread democracy, without any discussion of how such a "spread" is to be justified or undertaken, is to insult the intelligence of the constituency.

On the other hand, as this example suggests, bullshit has an almost irresistible pull because it so effectively appeals to our baser impulses. It can give us a strong sense of identity and importance as we become players in the narrative of others— and they in ours. If we're lucky, they will view us as valuable— especially if we are spreading democracy or God's will. In this way, bullshit plays a large role in current claims of nationalism, liberty, and democracy. It is used to unite, to band together, and also persuade.

This is not to say that we do not or should not have a role in the world, for I concur with Richard Haass that given the present global situation the United States has a role and indeed an opportunity to define a moment in history, an opportunity it is missing.[5] This is an opportunity to discuss and define, an oppor-

---

[5] R.N. Haass, *The Opportunity: America's Moment to Alter History's Course* (New York: Public Affairs, 2005).

tunity too precious to be squandered on the bullshit of obfuscation and suppressed debate. Yet as long as we derive a strong sense of identity from bullshit, we will be hard-pressed to eradicate it.

This, of course, presents a challenge for the consumer of bullshit, namely, to ascertain the speaker's intent and to surmise the speaker's state of mind. Does the speaker *intend* to obfuscate? This is no simple task, but one that is certainly facilitated by the Cohen strategy: identifying the content will lead to an eradication of the process, and eradicate it we must, if we are to maintain our human dignity and maintain our capacity to reason and be moved by ideas, especially the ideas of right and wrong that allow us to lead lives we value.

14
Bullshit at the Interface of Science and Policy: Global Warming, Toxic Substances, and Other Pesky Problems

HEATHER DOUGLAS

In recent public discussions about the use of science in policy-making, confusion has bred bullshit. The interface between science and policy is notoriously difficult, requiring technical competence and political savvy. At this difficult boundary, the need for quality science advice remains a pressing concern.

Ever since Plato's parable about the stargazer as expert navigator for the ship of state in *The Republic*, governments have grappled with the problem of how to get accurate and reliable expert advice on technical matters central to policy-making. In recent decades, as the scope of government concern has expanded and the need for technical advice becomes more acute, the debate surrounding the quality of science advice for policy-making has shifted, from excluding pseudoscience, to worries over "junk science," to the most recent concern over "politicized science." These shifts, however, merely rephrase the same question: On whom should we rely for expert advice? The question is not easily answered, and the resulting confusion allows bullshit to proliferate.

Two different kinds of bullshit flourish at the science-policy interface. The first trades on the complexities of evidence and technical detail on which many substantive policy choices rest—complexities that make it easy to confuse the public about the extent of uncertainties and contravening evidence in particular cases. This leads to a pervasive kind of bullshit in which statements are made that are not false, and thus not lies, but are deeply misleading. Operators on the interface can propagate these true but misleading statements, thus building support for desired policy choices.

The second kind of bullshit is more pervasive. It occurs when critics of scientific claims suggest that the evidence on which a decision is based is insufficient to support the decision. What makes this argument bullshit in most cases is that it often presupposes that we have a universal standard of evidential support which all claims must meet in order to be "scientific." Yet there is no such standard—particularly in cases where one must take into account evidence from multiple sources—and thus any appeal to such a standard is pure bullshit. Usually, what the critic really thinks is that the evidence is insufficient in this case to overcome their concerns about the implications of the claims, particularly if the claim is wrong and is accepted (or correct and is rejected). The consequences of error, of making an inaccurate empirical claim with political implications, is what is of concern to the critic, but rather than discuss these concerns openly, the critic simply declares that the evidence available does not meet the standards of "sound science" or is an example of "politicized science." This move confuses genuine cases of junk or politicized science from cases where burdens of proof are disputed, helping only to obscure the issues at stake.

Both of these kinds of bullshit are prevalent in discussions of science and policy-making, and they will be difficult to eliminate. The technical and esoteric nature of much of the evidence on which policy is based will make the first kind of bullshit attractive to anyone seeking to score political points in a science-based dispute. Constant vigilance is the only remedy. The second kind of bullshit is more amenable to cure, but only if we adjust our ideas about scientific reasoning to emphasize the weighing of evidence, uncertainty, and the consequences of error. Unfortunately, this will make science-based policy debates more complicated, and the temptation to oversimplify things and assume the existence of a universal standard of proof will always have an allure, especially in our sound bite age. Bullshit is more compact, portable, and convenient than full and open discussion.

Bullshit of the Isolated Fact

In many policy disputes that depend on technical or scientific backgrounds, a welter of facts are relevant to the issue at hand.

Even in the relatively simple cases of regulating toxic substances, for example, one needs to know the details of animal toxicology studies, whether there have been any accidental human exposures studied, what is known about the biochemistry of the substance, and how humans are currently exposed and to what levels. This welter of facts must then be considered in total to figure out whether and how to regulate a substance. Missing just one crucial piece of the puzzle can throw the whole picture off. For example, if a chemical causes liver cancer in rats, and is consumed by many people (although no studies of human effects have been conducted), it would seem prudent to regulate the chemical. But if one also knows that the rats have a substance in their livers that interacts with the chemical of concern to produce their cancers, a substance that is absent in humans, one will likely be much less alarmed. One must have as much of the available picture as possible.[1] But having that takes a lot of work to develop, takes time to present to others, and even worse, may undermine the political outcome you desire. It's much easier in these inherently complex cases to pick and choose one's facts rather than grapple with all of the available evidence.

Cherry-picking one's facts, thus producing bullshit of the isolated fact, is particularly problematic in the case of the climate change debate. If the case of toxic substances seems complex, the case of global climate change magnifies this complexity many times over. Here we need to reflect upon past climate and its variability, current climate measurements, and future climate projections, which need to take into account as much of the earth's energy dynamics as possible. At the same time, we need accurate descriptions of atmospheric chemistry and physics, including the particulars on the many greenhouse gases that have been identified.[2] All this complexity is in place before one

---

[1] And having a more complete mechanistic account may not reduce all the concern. For a real case with such complexity (regarding saccharin and bladder cancers in rats) see D. Guston, "Principal-Agent Theory and the Structure of Science Policy Revisited: 'Science in Policy' and the US Report on Carcinogens," *Science and Public Policy* 30:5 (2003), pp. 347–357.

[2] Although carbon dioxide gets most of the attention, we should also remember chlorofluorocarbons, nitrous oxide, methane, and of course, water. Each has a different capacity to trap heat, and a different average lifespan in the atmosphere, ranging from a few years to centuries.

even begins to address the possible effects of climate change on human and natural systems. It is little wonder that with such a complicated issue and such high stakes, the lure of selecting particular facts, even true ones, that in isolation prove totally misleading, is so tempting.

One example of this selectivity, and the bullshit that results, can be found in the use of recent climate records in the debate over climate change. Modestly reliable global temperature readings became available in the late nineteenth century, as climate data collection locations spread across the globe and regular sea surface temperature data began to be taken. The temperature records based on this data indicate a climate *warming* from 1890 to 1940, and then a climate *cooling* from 1940 to 1975. In the mid-1970s, the earth began to *warm* again according to these records, and has continued to do so. At first glance, this recent climate record does little to support the idea that humans, in producing greenhouse gases, are warming the climate. The early warming period corresponds to a modest increase of greenhouse gas production, but greenhouse gas production really went up after 1940, when the cooling began. This means that the world warmed during the smaller increase in greenhouse gases, and then cooled during the larger increase in greenhouse gases. If humans were influencing the climate between 1940 and 1975, why were global temperatures dropping?

This was a legitimate scientific question during the 1980s. Although global temperatures had begun to rise again by the mid-1970s, why temperatures had dropped during one of the most intensive periods of industrial expansion—and the accompanying increase of greenhouse gas productions—was unclear. In the early 1990s, however, as more research was completed on the functioning of the global climate, scientists discovered the importance of *aerosols* for the climate. Aerosols are particulates, including dust and sulfates, that cool the atmosphere. They tend to be short-lived in the atmosphere, washing out after a few days (or a few years at most), but their impact on global climate can be dramatic. Research on aerosols allowed climate modelers to successfully predict the amount of global cooling that would follow from the eruption of Mt. Pinatubo in June 1991, an eruption that spewed significant quantities of aerosols into the atmosphere.[3]

---

[3] R.A. Kerr, (1993), "Pinatubo Global Cooling on Target," *Science* 259 (1993), p. 594.

Volcanoes are not the only important source for aerosols however. The burning of fossil fuels also produces aerosols, aerosols that not only cool climate, but can cause acid rain. When we became concerned about acid rain in the 1970s and began to reduce the release of sulfates into the atmosphere (using "scrubbers" on smokestacks), we reduced the amount of aerosols that could cool the climate. The excess aerosols left in the atmosphere washed out in a few years, and when combined with the continued build-up of greenhouse gases, the warming trend reappeared. Thus, the increased industrial output from 1940 to 1975 produced both more greenhouse gases and more aerosols. The cooling effect of the aerosols likely masked the warming effect of the greenhouse gases during this period, and with the reduction of aerosol releases by industry, the warming trend re-emerged. The longer-lasting greenhouse gases were finally having their impact.

Including the fact of aerosols in one's understanding of climate records could be inconvenient, but ignoring aerosols produces bullshit. The research on aerosols was widely available by 1993. Several prominent articles and essays had appeared in *Science*, the foremost journal for scientific research in the United States.[4] The research was summarized for a more popular audience in *Scientific American* in 1994.[5] While questions remained about the precise impact of aerosols on the climate, aerosols had become an important part of understanding the climate and a likely explanation for the decrease in global temperatures between 1940 and 1975. Anyone who honestly participated in the climate change debate was aware of this crucial scientific development.

Yet skeptics of global warming continued to point to the 1940–1975 decline in temperature as being out of sync with what one would expect were humans really changing the climate. For example, in his essay from *The True State of the Planet*, published in 1995, Robert Balling Jr. reinforces his skepticism over human-caused global warming by pointing to the lack of warming between 1940 and 1975.[6] As he complains

---

[4] See, for example, Volumes 255, 256, 258, 259, and 260.
[5] R.J. Charlson and T.M.L. Wigley, "Sulfate Aerosol and Climate Change," *Scientific American* (February 1994), pp. 48–57.
[6] Robert C. Balling Jr. (1995), "Global Warming: Messy Models, Decent Data, Pointless Policy," in R. Bailey, ed., *The True State of the Planet* (New York: Free Press), p. 91.

about how pre-1990 models predict more warming (based on greenhouse gas increases) than was actually measured, he fails to mention the research on aerosols and their masking effect. This slight omission was probably unnoticed by the casual reader, but it allowed Balling to suggest that the entire global warming scenario was poppycock. Such is the effectiveness of isolated fact bullshit.

Fred Singer is probably the most egregious spreader of this brand of bullshit for the global climate change debate. In a series of essays published in newspapers and other public sources, Singer repeatedly casts doubt on the reliability of climate models because of this warming, then cooling trend in the temperature record.[7] He never mentions the possibility that human-produced aerosols might account for this record, nor that research was continuing on the topic. And the bullshit spread beyond Singer and Balling. In his report in Toronto's *Globe and Mail* newspaper in 1997, Guy Crittenden cited Singer and Balling as two of the "four horsemen of the nonapocalypse," giving heavy credence to Singer and Balling's claims, emphasizing the pre-1940 warming trend.[8] So much the worse for public debate about climate change.

This is not to say that there were no problems with global climate models and the theory of climate change in the 1990s, or that they are all settled today. One concern was the discrepancy between land-based and satellite temperature readings of the planet. Satellites launched in the late 1970s had been collecting temperature data for over a decade, but the results did not square with ground-level temperature readings. The satellite data showed almost no warming where the ground level readings showed significant warming for the period 1980–1995.

Skeptics *legitimately* made much of this discrepancy, which was quite baffling to climate scientists. Indeed, the satellite data,

---

[7] "A More Sensible Approach to the Environment," *Wall Street Journal Europe* (28th January, 1994), p. 10; "Climate Claims Wither Under Luminous Lights of Science," *Washington Times* (29th November, 1994), p. A18; "Is Man-Made Global Warming a Proven Environmental Threat? No: Doomsayers Are Just Trying to Scare Money out of Government," *Insight* 11 (1995), p. 19; "The Global Warming Debate: . . . Not Scientific Consensus," *Wall Street Journal* (25th July, 1997), p. A14; and "Global Warming Is Not Happening," *Natural Science* (29th January, 1998).

[8] Guy Crittenden, "The Day the Earth Warmed Up," *The Globe and Mail* (22nd November, 1997), p. D1.

coming from the purity of space, uncontaminated by human error or local land-use changes, seemed to have a *prima facie* claim to greater reliability. Eventually, however, closer examinations of the data revealed that the satellite data *agreed* with the ground-level readings after all.[9] The absolute reliability of satellite data, both in terms of instrumental purity and ability to capture global temperature accurately, could not be sustained. When the systemic errors of satellite readings were accounted for, and the raw data properly processed, there was a steady and significant warming trend. Although this re-examination of satellite readings has been widely publicized among scientists (with articles and news stories in *Science* and a National Academy report on the issue, cited in footnote 9), we can expect some skeptics to once again ignore this development as they claim that the earth is not *really* warming.

This bullshit of the isolated fact, the selected emphasis on particular data, is seductive. Science is a continually changing body of knowledge, and few can claim to be fully up-to date on any given issue. Even scientists working in the field have difficulty in maintaining a cutting-edge awareness of every new piece of evidence, of every new interpretation. By bringing forth an isolated fact, and ignoring the complexities that undermine the desired significance of that fact, bullshitters play upon our intellectual limitations. They may succeed in some cases, but repeated emphasis on the isolated fact—especially after new evidence and its significance have been placed in prominent scientific outlets (such as *Science*, *Nature*, or a National Academy report)—is to show oneself to be playing a disingenuous intellectual game. As Harry Frankfurt suggests, it is to reveal oneself to be unconcerned with the truth. It is to show that one is willing to spread bullshit to win.

Bullshit of Universal Standards

While isolated-fact bullshit trades on the impossibility of staying well-informed about every technical issue central to modern governance, universal standards bullshit has a more philosoph-

---

[9] R.A. Kerr, "Getting Warmer, However You Measure It," *Science* 304 (2004), pp. 805–07; see also B.D. Santer *et al.*, "Influence of Satellite Data Uncertainties on the Detection of Externally Forced Climate Change," *Science* 300 (2003), pp. 1280–84; and National

ical source. Rather than showing a lack of concern for available evidence as with the isolated fact bullshit, universal standards bullshit appeals to a nonexistent standard of proof for science. It assumes that there is one standard met by all scientific claims worthy of the name, and that we can tell what is sound science or good science from what is junk science or bad science (or non-science or pseudoscience) by simply checking with this standard. Lately, the universal standards bullshit has found new employ in bolstering arguments about the politicization of science. This is a disturbing trend, increasing not only the spreading of this bullshit, but also obfuscating crucial issues in the use and misuse of science in political life.

Where does a sense of universal standards in science come from? Most likely, it comes from the way most of us were taught science in school—from a textbook. The textbook lays out the complexities of science, both theory and fact, and then uses exercises at the end of each chapter to test our comprehension. How to apply the newly learned science to the specific case in the problem can be a challenge, but we were all reassured that there is a right answer, if not in the back of the book, then in the back of the *teacher's* book. This leads us to think of science as a black-and-white affair of facts, organized by theories into concrete knowledge. Occasionally, textbooks may hint at the frontiers of science, where the theories and facts are not so well nailed down. But they generally make science look like a done deal, ready to be applied to any problem situation. And the answers are all there, in the back of the book.

Any honest look at science in action, however, shows that things are far messier. For many problems, even the experts disagree over which theory to apply, and how to apply it. And, frustratingly, most of our science policy issues sit in areas like this where science is developing and textbooks have yet to be written. While some facts are undisputed—indeed that something is undisputed among scientists is the only reliable marker that it is a scientific fact—there is much that remains controversial. Universal-standards bullshit assumes that there is some threshold that any body of evidence must meet before it is "sci-

---

Research Council, *Reconciling Observations of Global Temperature Change* (Washington, D.C.: National Academy Press, 2000).

entific" and "proven" and only then can we act on it. It assumes there is a universal standard of proof that allows some ideas into the vaulted halls of science, and keeps the rest out. What I want to suggest here is that not only is there no such standard, but that we don't want one. Thus appealing to this standard as if it both existed and could solve all of our problems at the science-policy interface perpetuates a pernicious form of bullshit.

Appeals to the universal standard of proof appear in criticisms of politicized science from all sides. The Union of Concerned Scientists, in their report on *Scientific Integrity in Policy-Making*, rightly points to suppression of evidence and the refusal to release studies as examples of politicizing science.[10] If the evidence cannot be made public and discussed, then science's open forum of debate is severely compromised. But the report also considers *the weighing of uncertainty* by the Bush administration to be a politicization of science. It says that "Bush administration spokespersons continue to contend that the uncertainties in climate projection and fossil fuel emissions are too great to warrant mandatory action to slow emissions" (p. 5). If this is politicizing science, however, then there must be some objective universal threshold that once passed make the uncertainties irrelevant.

But there is honest debate about both the level of uncertainty in climate projections (although that uncertainty is generally decreasing each year) and about what level of certainty we would need to have to warrant mandatory fossil fuel use reductions. The latter choice is clearly a political decision, and depends on how protective one wants to be of the fossil fuel industry versus the global climate's stability. We might lambaste the Bush administration for valuing the former too much over the latter, but any appeal to some universal standard of proof, a nonexistent ideal, to address this issue would be bullshit.

A similar example can be found in the introductory chapter of the volume *Politicizing Science*,[11] in which Michael Gough, in providing an overview of the book, writes that:

---

[10] Union of Concerned Scientists, *Scientific Integrity in Policymaking: An Investigation into the Bush Administration's Misuse of Science* (2004). Available at www.ucsusa.org.
[11] M. Gough, "Science, Risks, and Politics," in M. Gough, ed., *Politicizing Science: The Alchemy of Policymaking* (Washington, D.C.: Marshall Institute, 2003), pp. 1–25.

The authors of the chapters . . . describe scientists masking policy decisions as 'scientific', and politicians labeling politically driven decisions as scientific, attempting thereby to place them outside the realm of political discussion, debate, and compromise. But this is an illusion. All policy matters involving human health and the environment are political. The more that political considerations dominate scientific considerations, the greater the potential for policy driven by ideology and less based on strong scientific underpinnings. (p. 3)

This sounds like a useful unmasking of politicized science, but only until one asks what those strong scientific underpinnings are supposed to be. When is a body of evidence enough to be considered "strong"? Surely we want evidence to serve as one basis for our decisions, but is evidence alone sufficient? Even Gough admits it is not. He writes a few pages later that Karl Popper has informed us science requires two things: hypothesis formation and hypothesis testing[12] (Gough p. 12). He then claims that neither models underlying predictions of human cancer rates nor climate change models can be tested. (The ability to predict the cooling following the eruption of Mt. Pinatubo mentioned earlier can be considered a fair short-term test of climate models.)

Yet hypothesis formation and testing are not sufficient for something to be an acceptably strong scientific underpinning for a policy decision. The crucial issue is usually *how much* evidence and testing there has been, *what kinds* of testing have been done, and whether the available evidence is enough. Deciding that it is enough is in part a political decision, as it requires the weighing of the acceptability of uncertainty. Gough is implicitly relying upon a non-existent universal standard of proof for science, one that he never articulates or defends. Thus is it easy to claim that those who attempt to martial evidence in favor of increased regulation have failed to provide sufficiently strong evidence. Unnamed universal standards can always be adjusted higher when desired.

---

[12] Ironically, Gough lampoons philosophers at the end of his chapter, quoting Feynman: "Philosophers say a great deal about what is absolutely necessary for science, and it is always, so far as one can see, rather naive, and probably wrong." Gough seems completely unaware that he has undermined a key point made earlier in his chapter when he was relying upon *philosopher* Karl Popper.

Why is there not one standard of proof, one hurdle for evidence before a claim becomes credible and scientific? In part, it is because the evidence that supports claims about the world comes in so many different forms. The evidence that would support a claim of causation about a chemical substance causing cancer in a mammal (evidence from animal toxicology and perhaps biochemistry) looks quite different from evidence that would support a claim about a geological causal process that leads to certain mountain formations. Even statistical significance claims, arguably a "gold standard" in science (commonly thought to be $p < 0.05$ or a less than a one-in-twenty chance that the results are spurious) are not universally applicable. Not all evidence is statistical, and some studies require more stringent or less stringent standards for the results to be "statistically significant." Among different disciplines and fields, what it takes to convince the scientists in those fields will vary, depending on what they already take to be accepted knowledge and accepted techniques. As the adage goes, extraordinary claims require extraordinary evidence. But what an extraordinary claim *is* can vary with disciplinary background and personal experience.

Perhaps we could standardize all this complexity, and require that scientists keep to a single standard for sufficient evidence. One could argue that drug testing has developed such standards—that a statistically significant result from a double-blind control study with placebos is the standard that must be met. But does this standard make sense for climate studies, for example, where there is no alternate earth on which to experiment? These studies involve predictions about how perturbations will affect the climate, and such predictions provide useful checks on climate models. But a simple model for controlled experiments when applied to environmental sciences is neither accurate nor helpful. Also, consider whether the universal standard employed by the Food and Drug Administration (FDA) is really so simple. Even with this standardization of study type, the FDA must still decide whether the study was conducted with an appropriate sample of people, and whether the study ran for long enough, to support the claims made for the drug. And it must decide whether the apparent risks of a new drug are outweighed by their benefits, a judgment made in the context of other medications available. So even with the apparently standardized approach to evidence, judgment in weighing the risks and benefits of error is needed. The question will still remain, is the evidence enough?

No universal answer to this question is available because the contexts in which these judgments must be made vary so widely. Whether the evidence available is sufficient depends in large measure on what the risks are of getting it wrong. These risks arise because of the uncertainty inherent in the enterprise of science, uncertainty that is endemic and unavoidable (although reducible). Even if uncertainty is similar in two cases, the risks of error vary with the claim being examined and the context of the claim. Consider a few everyday examples. Suppose I told you I thought it likely that your gas tank gauge was off, and that you would run out of gas on the way home. The risk of error in rejecting my claim is not terribly huge. It would be inconvenient for you to run out of gas, but probably not life-threatening. You would want to know exactly why I thought this about your as gauge, on the basis of what evidence, and decide whether it really was enough to get you to take the car directly to a mechanic rather than wait and see for yourself. On the other hand, if I told you I thought there was a bomb in your car, the slightest amount of evidence would suffice to get you to think twice about driving it, just as the mere presence of an unattended package at a major airport can cause terminals to be evacuated.

Decisions at the interface of science and policy are no different. If you care deeply about climate stability and not much about the economic health of oil companies, less evidence will be needed to convince you that we have sufficient reason to act to curtail climate change—that the scientific underpinnings are strong enough. If, on the other hand, you care deeply about the health of oil companies and not much about climate stability, far more evidence will be needed to convince you that the we have sufficient evidence to act. Decisions about uncertainties are political (and ethical), and thus the decision that evidence is sufficient *is* a political decision.

This is not to say that science can't be politicized. It can. One can suppress evidence, by either refusing to record it because one doesn't like it, or by refusing to allow it to be published. One can refuse to allow politically unpopular views to be pursued. One can ignore studies one doesn't like, or fire people who produce the "wrong" results. One can surround oneself with pseudo-experts who only say what one wants to hear. Science can be detrimentally and catastrophically politicized. Yet, there is no standard for how much evidence is enough to settle a scientific dispute. The only standard we have is that we should consider all the available evidence. How much evidence we need before a claim is sufficiently well-supported to be scientific, to enter the canons of science, changes with the context. To appeal to a non-existent universal standard of proof in science is bullshit.

Combatting the Two Kinds of Bullshit

With the ever-increasing importance of scientific or technical expertise as a basis for policy-making, it's not surprising that we are increasingly confronted with the problem of how to ensure quality in that advice. How do we make sure we are hearing all the available evidence? How do we ensure that the debates occurring among experts are not being distorted by political pressure to not say some things, or to say others, because it pleases certain powers? How do we know whom to trust?

Isolated-fact bullshit plays upon our inherent intellectual limitations that keep us from being fully informed and up-to-date on all the important issues of our time. As long as political operators want to win debates no matter the cost, this kind of bullshit will occur. Those who refuse to acknowledge fair criticism of their claims, that they are ignoring key work, should be rejected as intellectually dishonest. While we can exclude dishonest operators from the academic forum, the public forum must remain open to all. Fred Singer can continue to write commentaries resting on the isolated fact, and some newspapers will publish them, spreading the bullshit. Only those who follow the particular issue closely are likely to notice the spreading of bullshit in these cases, bullshit that is borne of selective omission and emphasis. Even those who spread such bullshit may not realize the nature of their claims, as the claims often wear an apparent obviousness.

But universal standards bullshit can be permanently undermined once we recognize that there are no such things. We should be asking about the strength of evidence and the risks of error for science-based policy, rather than waiting for something to become "scientific" or text-book science. With a more robust discussion on these terms, perhaps isolated-fact bullshit will lose some of its appeal as well. When we get used to expert disagreement, and understand better its causes, settling a debate on the basis of one expert raising one isolated fact might be recognized for the naive approach it is. We can only hope this would reduce the bullshit in the end.

15

Rhetoric Is Not Bullshit

DAVID J. TIETGE

I begin my discussion of the role of rhetoric in modern society with an aphorism: Rhetoric isn't devious and untrustworthy; those are features reserved for language itself. This is a distinction, however, that is lost on the public at large, whose perception of the word 'rhetoric' renders it synonymous with 'bullshit'.

Several years ago, I conducted an admittedly unscientific, journalistic experiment for a course in rhetorical theory I was teaching at the time. Over the course of three-and-one-half months (the length of a typical university semester), I encountered some 156 occasions via print, radio, and television where the term 'rhetoric' occurred. Of these, only once did the user of the word seem to understand what rhetoric really was. In all other instances, the person employing the word used it only in the most unfavorable sense, for example, "John Kerry is attempting to use rhetoric to disguise his true agenda," or "The rhetoric in the Senate was thick regarding the proposal of the new bill."

The one case in which the user understood the meaning of 'rhetoric' was an interview of the comedian, George Carlin, conducted by Jon Stewart. Stewart had asked Carlin why his comedy routines so often centered on language (a very good interview question, in my opinion), to which Carlin responded that he was, in essence, a rhetorician; it was his job to unpack the meaning behind words, and this process often had comic results. He said he was a performer, and as such, a focus on language was imperative to his success or failure. By reflecting on this practice, he had also demonstrated that he was equally cognizant of the theoretical process that drove his craft.

The decline of rhetoric as a central humanistic discipline in both public and academic circles has been one of the great intellectual tragedies of the last couple of centuries. The common perception of rhetoric as a mode of discourse lacking substance, of being the epitome of empty embellishment, is prevalent in popular and political representations of it, as evidenced in its frequent appearance in phrases like "once one gets past the rhetoric" or "all rhetoric aside."[1] In the twentieth century, the privileged status of rhetoric in the Trivium of the Seven Liberal Arts came to be regarded as ancient history, to be supplanted by "purer," more material intellectual pursuits in the sciences. Rhetoric, like its close disciplinary cousin, philosophy, has been relegated in the public mind to the ever-growing realm of "bullshit," reflecting an error in understanding of what scholars do when they practice rhetoric, and even more profoundly, what they do when they use rhetoric as a tool for critically decoding discourse. At the same time, members within academe regularly challenge modern rhetorical studies as too broad and interdisciplinary—lacking the prestige of specialization. Academicians outside of rhetoric usually see rhetoric only as an archaic study of how to persuade through the instructional lenses of Aristotle or Cicero. Taken together, it is surprising that the popular and the academic perceptions of rhetoric have not managed to bury it altogether.

In fact, the opposite seems to be the case. Rather than fading quietly into the past as some academic anachronism like philology, rhetoric is fast becoming one of the more popular humanistic studies in many major American universities today. How can it be that, while the public at large claims to distrust rhetoric, and academics outside of fields like English or Communication see it only in reductionistic or archaic terms, rhetoric is thriving as a field of study, especially at the graduate level?[2] One answer may be that initiating students into the schol-

---

[1] A salient example of this attitude is a review of Frankfurt's *On Bullshit* on Amazon.com that complains it "is filled with obvious rhetoric that makes the book sound scientific, when it is actually drivel."

[2] Rhetoric and writing topped the list of programs experiencing growth during the late 1980s, besting programs in creative writing, technical writing, and literature and interdisciplinary studies. See Bettina J. Huber, "Recent and Anticipated Growth in English Doctoral Programs: Findings from the MLA's 1990 Survey," *ADE Bulletin 106* (Winter, 1993), pp. 45–60.

arly and professional activities that rhetoric enhances—just as they are exposed to its breadth of scope—reveals to them how unfair and inaccurate these popular impressions are. Many come to realize that rhetoric enables a command of language, and that if one controls language, one has power—that is, they come to realize that "bullshit" is a marketable talent, and an understanding of rhetoric allows one to more carefully cultivate one's skills in this timeless human ability.

We live, it would appear, in something like a societal paradox. Rhetoric—taken to be expertise in "bullshit"—is ethically suspect, yet we value it in practice. Judging from the salaries and prestige of lawyers, politicians, university presidents, and advertising executives, we value it quite highly. One must wonder, then, why rhetoric has inherited such a poor reputation. I will attempt to sort this out by explaining the value of and use of rhetoric in popular culture and society; and show that our own intellectual history and rhetorical activity supports a place for rhetoric in education, the professional world, and our daily lives. This two-pronged approach will help dispel a popular "truth-falsity" dichotomy, according to which we think of statements or beliefs as either true or false, regardless of the complexity and gray areas that rhetoric shows us are always involved.

The Problem (and Politics) of Rhetoric

This may seem to fall outside the purview of rhetoric as it is traditionally understood by most academics, what is known as *rhetorica utens*. But the contemporary study of rhetoric is more than what most academics understand as the Aristotelian "art of persuasion"; it is *rhetorica docens*, the theoretical treatment of words used to discover how language means among different agents, motives, cultural and social idiosyncrasies, and external events. While some might argue that Aristotle was as philosophically interested in the nature of language as he was in instructing how it could best be used, his most influential work on the subject, *On Rhetoric*, is ultimately a "how-to" primer on the use of rhetoric as a civic tool. He identifies many principles and constructs many definitions, but there is no real effort to view rhetoric as anything but a practical mechanism for effective speaking. Aristotle himself coined the distinction between *utens* and *docens*, but he was far more concerned with the former.

Aristotle's prejudice has survived him. We are mostly ignorant of rhetoric as a tool for communication, and entirely ignorant of it as a set of methods for textual analysis. The most likely explanation for this cites the mass media and the political pundits who carelessly toss around the word in only its most uncomplimentary form. The pundits who display their contempt for rhetoric may in fact be using the word 'rhetoric' in a rhetorical way. That is, they may well understand that the public's erroneous understanding of the word is occasion to use it to reinforce the associations the public already has for it. Rather than correct this error, it is easier to perpetuate it, taking advantage of the fashionable preference for "plain" language. In this regard politicians are among the most adroit insofar as they criticize rhetoric while relying upon it heavily for their own advancement. Everyone else uses "mere rhetoric," the pundit of the moment tells us, as if effective use and understanding of language were something to "get beyond" or "overcome."

For a good example of how one can both disdain rhetoric and utilize it for political gain, consider a statement by George W. Bush regarding Supreme Court nominee Samuel Alito: "My hope of course is that the Senate bring dignity to the process and give this man a fair hearing and an up-or-down vote on the Senate floor."[3] Bush, long a proponent of what he considers "plain speech," would perhaps not recognize the rhetorical layers of this statement, but they exist. The first is his "hope" that the Senate will "bring dignity to the process," the suggestion being that any attempt to extend debate (by filibuster, for instance) would be *undignified.* The statement is odd for it implies that democracy itself, which relies on open discussion of important decisions, is undignified. Such an unpatriotic sentiment cannot be what Bush intended his listeners to hear, so we have to consider more layers to figure out what's going on.

Bush also appeals to the notion of a "fair hearing." But this is a subjective term, depending upon individual beliefs and tolerances. Edward Kennedy's and Samuel Alito's definitions of

---

[3] Jesse Holland, "Senate to Open Alito Nomination Hearings." Associated Press. Online 9th January, 2006.

fair, for instance, surely differ considerably depending on who may be getting the criticism at the moment. What about this "up-or-down vote"? It's an interesting requirement and is no doubt related to the issue of "fairness" as well as to the public image that helped bring Bush two presidential elections. Bush is widely seen, that is, as a man of few words—a man of action who does not wish to waste time sallying the pros and cons back and forth all day. Either vote with the confirmation or against it, the statement suggests, but do not, above all, be indecisive or contemplative about it. For careful, thorough debate, after all, would effectively delay and possibly derail his nomination. The real thrust of Bush's statement, then, is something more like the reading of it suggested by the *faux* newspaper, *The Onion*, which headlined "Bush Urges Senate to Give Alito Fair, Quick, Unanimous Confirmation," as if any outcome besides the one Bush hoped for would be unfortunate and undignified.[4]

In this way, rhetorical scrutiny of language allows us to see past the glittering generalities in language and get to an authentic meaning, both in regard to what is being analyzed and to the analyst in question. It should be clear, for example, that I do not like Bush and do not agree with his politics. I assure you that I deliberately made no attempt to obscure this (much less with "mere rhetoric"), because I want to emphasize that subjectivity need not compromise the integrity of the reading. Subjectivity is part of language, especially language that reflects beliefs and strongly guarded convictions. All language reflects both personal and collective orientations—some are just more obvious than others. In the case of science, the ethos of scientific objectivity can, in fact, aid the rhetor in achieving the necessary persuasion or identification, since people are less likely to question the integrity of a system of knowledge with a reputation for objectivity. Yet even science, like every discursive instrument, relies on words that are imprecise and ambiguous.

The Truth about Postmodernism

One issue that helps obscure the universality of rhetoric, and thus promotes the pejorative use of 'rhetoric', is the popular

---

[4] "Bush Urges Senate to Give Alito Fair, Quick, Unanimous Confirmation," *The Onion* (17th January, 2006). ⟨http://www.theonion.com/content/node/44467⟩

tendency to oversimplify the "truth-lie" dichotomy. In *The Liar's Tale: A History of Falsehood*, Jeremy Campbell reminds us that the reductionistic binary that separates truth from falsity is not only in error, but also that the thoroughly unclear and inconsistent distinction between the true and the false has a long, rich cultural history.[5] Those doing much of the speaking in our own era, however, assume that the dividing line between truth and untruth is clear and, more significantly, internalized by the average human. Truth, however, is an elusive concept. While we can cite many examples of truths (that the sky is blue today, that the spoon will fall if dropped, and so forth), these depend on definitions of the words used. The sky is blue because 'blue' is the word we use to describe the hue that we have collectively agreed is bluish. We may, however, disagree about what shade of blue the sky is. Is it powder blue? Blue-green? Royal Blue? Interpretive responses to external realities that rely on definition (and language generally) always complicate the true-false binary, especially when we begin to discuss the nature of abstractions involved in, say, religion or metaphysics. The truth of 'God is good' depends very heavily upon the speaker's understanding of God and the nature of goodness, both of which depend upon the speaker's conceptualization, which may be unique to him, his group, or his cultural environment, and thus neither clear nor truthful to other parties.

Is this rampant relativism? Some might think so, but it is perhaps more useful to suggest that the Absolute Truths that we usually embrace are unattainable because of these complexities of language. Some cultures have seen the linguistic limitations of specifying the Truth. Hinduism has long recognized that language is incapable of revealing Truth; to utter the Truth, it holds, is simultaneously to make it no longer the Truth.

Note here the distinction between capital 'T' truth and lower-case 't' truth. Lower-case truths are situational, even personal. They often reflect more the state of mind of the agent making the utterance than the immutable nature of the truth. They are also temporally situated; what may be true now may not be in the future. Truth in this sense is predicated on both perception and stability, and, pragmatically speaking, such truths are tran-

---

[5] Jeremy Campbell, *The Liar's Tale: A History of Falsehood* (New York: Norton, 2001).

sitional and, often, relative. Capital 'T' Truths can be traced back at least as far as Plato, and are immutable, pure, and incorruptible. They do not exist in our worldly realm, at least so far as Plato was concerned. This is why Plato was so scornful of rhetoric: he felt that rhetoricians (in particular, the Sophists) were opportunists who taught people how to disguise the Truth with language and persuasion. Whereas Plato imagined a realm in which the worldly flaws and corruption of a physical existence were supplanted by perfect forms, the corporeal domain of human activity was saturated with language, and therefore, could not be trusted to reveal Truth with any certainty.

Contemporary, postmodern interest in truth and meaning turns the tables on Plato and studies meaning and truth in this shifting, less certain domain of human activity. Campbell cites many thinkers from our philosophical past who helped inaugurate this development, but none is more important than Friedrich Nietzsche. For Nietzsche, humans have no "organ" for discerning Truth, but we do have a natural instinct for falsehood. "Truth," as an abstraction taken from the subjectivity of normal human activities, was a manufactured fiction that we are not equipped to actually find. On the other hand, a natural aptitude for falsehood is an important survival mechanism for many species. Human beings have simply cultivated it in innovative, sophisticated, ways. As the rhetorician George A. Kennedy has noted, "in daily life, many human speech acts are not consciously intentional; they are automatic reactions to situations, culturally (rather than genetically) imprinted in the brain or rising from the subconscious."[6] Our propensity for appropriate (if not truthful) responses to situations is something nourished by an instinct to survive, interact, protect, and socialize. Civilization gives us as many new ways to do this as there are situations that require response.

This is why Nietzsche carefully distinguished Truth from a belief system that only professed to contain the Truth. Ken Gemes notes that Nietzsche co-ordinated the question of Truth around the pragmatics of survival,[7] an observation echoed by

---

[6] George A. Kennedy, *Comparative Rhetoric: An Historical and Cross-Cultural Introduction* (New York: Oxford University Press, 1998), p. 25.
[7] Ken Gemes, "Nietzsche's Critique of Truth," *Philosophy and Phenomenological Research* 52, pp. 47–65.

E METHOD, THAT WHICH BACON WOULD USHER IN, IS COMPARABLE TO THE

Kennedy, who provides examples of animals that deceive for self-preservation. Camouflage, for example, can be seen in plants and animals. Many birds imitate the calls of rival species to fool them to distraction and away from their nests or food sources. Deception, it seems, is common in nature. But Nietzsche took doctrinal Truth (note the "T") to be one of the most insidious deceptions to occur in human culture, especially as it is articulated in religions. It is not a basic lie that is being promulgated, but rather a lie masquerading as the Truth and, according to Nietzsche, performing certain functions. Truth, that is, is a ritualized fiction, a condition manufactured for institutions and the individuals who control them to maintain their power.

Rhetoric and Bullshit

Truth, deception, control over others. This survey of rhetoric thus brings us close to the territory that Harry Frankfurt explores in *On Bullshit*. For Frankfurt, however, bullshit has little to do with these complexities about truth and Truth that rhetoric helps us identify. Indeed bullshit, for Frankfurt, has little do with truth at all, insofar as it requires an indifference to truth. Does this mean, then, that language that is *not* bullshit has settled the matter of truth and has access to truth (or Truth)? Does this lead us to a dichotomy between truth and bullshit that is similar to the dichotomy between truth and falsity that postmodernism criticizes? It may seem that postmodernism has little place in Frankfurt's view, insofar as he rejects "various forms of skepticism which deny that we have any reliable access to objective reality, and which therefore reject the possibility of knowing how things truly are" (p. 64). Indeed, postmodernism is often vilified as the poster child of relativism and skepticism.

Yet postmodernism is far subtler than a mere denial of "objective reality." Postmodernism claims, rather, that reality is as much a construct of language as it is objective and unchanging. Postmodernism is less about rejecting beliefs about objective reality than about the *intersection* between material reality and the human interpretations of it that change, mutate, and shift that reality to our own purposes—the kind of small-t truths that Nietzsche addressed. The common complaint about postmodernism, for example, that it denies "natural laws," forgets that humans noticed and formulated those laws. Postmodernism attempts to supply a vocabulary to describe this kind of process. It is not just "jargon," as is so often charged; it is an effort to construct a metalinguistic lexicon for dealing with some very difficult and important epistemological questions.

And, not surprisingly, so is rhetoric. Constructing language that deals with the nature of language is a unique human problem. It is meta-cognition at its most complicated because it requires us to use the same apparatus to decode human texts that is contained in the texts themselves—that is, using words to talk about words, what Kenneth Burke referred to in *The Rhetoric of Religion* as "logology."[8] In no other area of human thinking is this really the case. Most forms of intellectual exploration involve an extraneous phenomenon, event, agent, or object that requires us to bring language to bear upon it in order to observe, describe, classify, and draw conclusions about its nature, its behavior, or its effect. For example, scientific inquiry usually involves an event or a process in the material world that is separate from the instruments we use to describe it. Historical analysis deals with texts as a matter of disciplinary course, yet most historians rarely question the efficacy or the reliability of the language used to convey an event of the remote (or, for that matter, recent) past. Even linguistics, which uses a scientific model to describe language structure, deals little with meaning or textual analysis.

Law is one of the closest cousins of rhetoric. Words are very much a part of the ebb and flow of legal wrangling, and the attention given to meaning and interpretation is central. Yet, even here, there is little *theoretical* discussion about *how* words have meaning or how, based on such theory, that meaning can be variously interpreted. Law is more concerned with the fact that words can be interpreted differently and how different agents might interpret language in different ways. This is why legal documents are often so unreadable; in an attempt to control ambiguity, more words (and more words with specific, technical meanings) must be used so that multiple interpretations can be avoided. If theoretical discussions about how language

---

[8] Kenneth Burke, *The Rhetoric of Religion: Studies in Logology* (Berkeley: University of California Press, 1961).

generates meaning were entered into the equation, the law would be impossible to apply in any practical way. Yet, to understand legal intricacies, every law student should be exposed to rhetoric—not so they can better learn how to manipulate a jury or falsify an important document, but so they understand how tenuous and limited language actually is for dealing with ordinary situations. Moreover, nearly every disciplinary area of inquiry uses language, but only rhetoric (and its associated disciplines, especially philosophy of language and literary/cultural criticism, which have influenced the development of modern rhetoric considerably) analyzes language using a hermeneutical instrument designed to penetrate the words to examine their effects—desired or not—on the people who use them.

What, then, qualifies as "bullshit"? Certainly, as I hope I have shown, rhetoric and bullshit are hardly the same thing. They are not even distant cousins. When a student begins a paper with the sentence, "In today's society, there are many things that people have different and similar opinions about," it's a pretty good guess that there is little of rhetorical value there. About the only conclusion a reader can draw is that the student is neither inspired nor able to hide this fact. This is the extent of the subtext, and it could conceivably qualify as bullshit. In this sense, Frankfurt's characterization of bullshit as "unavoidable whenever circumstances require someone to talk without knowing what he is talking about" (p. 63) is a useful differentiation.

But aside from these rather artificial instances, if bullshit does occur at the rate Frankfurt suggests, we have an arduous task in separating the bullshit from more interesting and worthy rhetorical situations. We have all met people whom we know, almost from the moment of acquaintance, are full of bullshit. It is the salesman syndrome that some people just (naturally, it seems) possess. In one sense, then, poor rhetoric—a rhetoric of transparency or obviousness—can be construed as bullshit. For the person with salesman syndrome is certainly attempting to achieve identification with his audience; he may even be attempting to persuade others that he is upright or trustworthy. But he fails because his bullshit is apparent. He is a bad rhetorician in the sense that he fails to convince others that he should be taken seriously, that his words are worthy of attention and, possibly, action.

Bullshit is something we can all recognize. Rhetoric is not. My remedy for this situation is simple: learn rhetoric. While students are required to take first-year composition at most colleges and universities, the extent of their training in rhetoric is usually limited to the rhetorical "modes"—yet another curricular misnomer which forces students to write preordained themes that reflect "skills" like definition, comparison and contrast, process analysis, and narrative.[9] This is a far cry from teaching the extent of rhetorical analysis. At best, this method creates an artificial environment in which to generate predetermined papers and ideas. At worst, it perpetuates the illusion that this is how real writers really write. A better approach is to offer hypothetical situations that require a rhetorical response (for example, ask students to imagine that they are the principal of a high school with low test scores and are required to explain the problem to the parents). Having students read model essays and deconstruct, edit, critique, or imitate these essays is also good. Yet another approach is to have students watch for occurrences of interesting rhetorical situations—to produce a "commonplace book" of rhetoric. No matter how students learn to think about the language they use and the language that dominates their lives, as long as they are thinking about language, they have a better chance of not falling victim to bullshit. In this age of the Internet, this is an important skill. However, since not everyone is a teacher or a student, the common citizen must be diligent on her own.

If the trend in graduate humanities programs favoring rhetoric is any indication, interest in a theoretical knowledge of language is on the rise. Likewise, since Frankfurt has opened the door for considering an issue that we can only conclude by its sheer popularity has some cultural currency in American society, we can also conclude that people have some genuine interest in the topic of language. His is not the last word on the subject, however. Nor is it the first. Thinkers have been discussing and writing about bullshit for millennia, and the service

---

[9] There are some important exceptions. At both the University of Iowa and the University of Minnesota, for example, students are required to take Rhetoric (offered by a Rhetoric, not English, department) in *lieu* of the usual required Composition courses. It would be interesting to document the contribution to an education through a comparison of these different models.

that Frankfurt has supplied is an opportunity for the general public to think about bullshit on more than just a casual, colloquial level. However, it is equally important to bring rhetoric to the table, if only because there is a remarkably vast gray area between what passes for Truth, truth, and what can be dismissed as bullshit, and this is the domain in which rhetoric thrives. Without some ability to navigate this area, without some understanding of how language works, we can only hope to avoid the pitfalls of bullshit by sheer chance.

16
Just Bullshit

STEVE FULLER

On Bullshit is the latest contribution to a long, distinguished, yet deeply problematic line of Western thought that has attempted to redeem the idea of intellectual integrity from the cynic's suspicion that it is nothing but high-minded, self-serving prejudice.[1] To their credit, some of history's great bullshit detectors—though not Harry Frankfurt nor his role model Ludwig Wittgenstein—have pled guilty as charged without hesitation. Friedrich Nietzsche and his great American admirer, the journalist H.L. Mencken, who coined the euphemism "bunk," come to mind. It helped that they were also cynics. They never held back from passing moral judgment on those they debunked. Moreover, both even tried to explain the adaptive advantage of specific forms of bullshit: Bullshitters may be craven but they are not stupid. Jews, Christians, and Muslims—or, more precisely, their clerics—may lack any definitive proof of a transcendent deity, but the sheer possibility of its existence does wonders to focus the mind and discipline the body in often politically effective ways.

Nietzsche's and Mencken's multifarious pronouncements invited others to judge them: Does either the mentally unstable Nietzsche or the hard-drinking Mencken inspire confidence in our ability to live in a bullshit-free world? More generally, does

---

[1] Plato's unflattering portrayal of poets and Sophists mark the opening salvo in the philosophical war against bullshit, even though Plato availed himself of bullshit in promoting the "myth of the metals" as a principle of social stratification in his *Republic*. This doublethink has not been lost on today's neo-conservative followers of Leo Strauss.

241

the dogged pursuit of bullshit refine or coarsen one's sense of humanity or, for that matter, raise or lower one's likelihood of recognizing the truth if confronted with it? For everyone who saw Nietzsche and Mencken as exposing false prophets, there were others who viewed them as the ultimate Doubting Thomases. If bullshit is too easily found, and found to run too deep, the bullshit detector's own judgment is reasonably called into question. Henrik Ibsen's classic dramas, *The Wild Duck* and *Hedda Gabler*, explored this prospect in terms of the need for a "life lie." For their part, both Nietzsche and Mencken have been dubbed "nihilists" by their detractors, who reverse the harsh light of truth to reveal the bullshit detector as a self-appointed absolutist who happens to take an unhealthy interest in people whose minds he is incapable of either respecting or changing. Scratch a nihilist, and you get a dogmatist in exile.

The bullshit detector aims to convert an epistemic attitude into a moral virtue: Reality can be known only by the right sort of person. This idea, while meeting with widespread approval by philosophers strongly tied to the classical tradition of Plato and Aristotle, is not lacking in dissenters. The line of dissent is best seen in the history of "rhetoric," a word Plato coined to demonize Socrates's dialectical opponents, the Sophists. The Sophists were prepared to teach anyone the art of winning arguments, provided you could pay the going rate. As a series of sophistic interlocutors tried to make clear to Socrates, possession of the skills required to secure the belief of your audience is the only knowledge you really need to have. Socrates famously attacked this claim on several fronts, which the subsequent history of philosophy has often conflated. In particular, Socrates's doubts about the reliability of the Sophists' techniques have been run together with a more fundamental criticism: Even granting the Sophists their skills, they are based on a knowledge of human gullibility, not of reality itself.

Bullshit is sophistry under this charitable reading, which acknowledges that the truth may not be strong enough by itself to counteract an artfully presented claim that is not so much outright false as, in the British idiom, "economical with the truth." In stressing the difference between bullshit and lies, Frankfurt clearly has this conception in mind, though he does sophistry a disservice by casting the bullshitter's attitude toward the truth as "indifference." On the contrary, the accomplished bullshitter must be a keen student of what people tend to regard as true, if only to cater to those tendencies so as to serve her own ends. What likely offends Frankfurt and other philosophers here is the idea that the truth is just one more tool to be manipulated for personal advantage. Conceptual frameworks are simply entertained and then discarded as their utility passes. The nature of the offense, I suspect, is the divine eye-view implicated in such an attitude—the very idea that one could treat in a detached fashion the terms in which people normally negotiate their relationship to reality. A bullshitter revealed becomes a god unmade.

The theological overtones are deliberate. In the hierarchy of Christian sins, bullshit's closest kin is *hypocrisy*, the official target of Nietzsche's and Mencken's ire. However, as Max Weber famously observed with regard to the rise of capitalism, Christians were not uniform in their condemnation of hypocrisy. Some treated it more as an unfortunate by-product in the efficient pursuit of ends. Benjamin Franklin's *Autobiography* developed this position with striking explicitness.[2] Indeed, Franklin modeled his understanding of "economical with the truth" on the economy one might exercise in the use of any valuable resource. A lesson he claimed to have learned in life is that one's truthfulness should always be proportional to the demands of the speech situation. It's always possible to say either too much or too little, speaking truthfully in each case, yet end up appearing as incompetent or dishonest. Such verbal misfirings benefit no one, though it may have served to represent some abstract sense of "truth."

Franklin's advice is often read as a counsel of cynicism, but it marked a crucial transition in the conception of the human mind from a passive receptacle to a creative agency. Like many of the US founding fathers, Franklin's Christianity veered toward Unitarianism, according to which the person of Jesus signifies that the human and the divine intellects differ in degree not kind. Just as the Biblical God communicated with humans on a "need-to-know" basis without total revelation, in part to stimulate our own God-like powers as free agents, so too should be

---

[2] An updated defense of Franklin's position ("the civilizing force of hypocrisy") is Jon Elster, "Deliberation and Constitution Making," in Jon Elster, ed., *Deliberative Democracy* (Cambridge: Cambridge University Press, 1998), pp. 97–122.

the ethic that governs secular human communication. The result is that we elicit from each other our own creative potential. The success of this injunction can be measured by advertising's colonization of corporate budgets in modern times: What sells is ultimately not intrinsic to the product but one's idea of the product, which advertising invites the consumer to form for herself.

Whatever one makes of Franklin's theology, it's clear that bullshitters *qua* hypocrites are rough cognitive equals of liars and truth-tellers, not people who lack a specific competence that, were they to possess it, would inhibit their propensity to bullshit. I stress this point because bullshit detectors gain considerable rhetorical mileage by blurring the epistemic and ethical dimensions of the phenomenon they wish to root out. Often this involves postulating a psychologically elusive state of *integrity*. To be sure, in these democratic times, bullshit detectors are rarely so overt as to declare that bullshitters lack "good character," which might suggest something objectionable, let alone unprovable, about the bullshitters' upbringing or even genetic makeup.[3]

But the same impression can be conjured by other means. For example, ten years ago, Alan Sokal notoriously argued that French literary philosophers and their American admirers would not have so easily inferred postmodern conclusions from cutting-edge mathematical physics had they been scientifically literate: If you knew more, or were better trained, you would behave better.[4] But notice what "behave better" means: It is not that the Francophile philosophers should have derived *anti*-postmodern conclusions from cutting-edge science. Rather, according to Sokal, they should have refrained from drawing any conclusions whatsoever, since the science does not speak directly to the wider cultural issues that interest the Francophile philosophers. (This position is harder to maintain with a straight face when such great scientists as Bohr and Heisenberg seem to have crossed the line themselves.)

---

[3] Nevertheless, the emerging literature in "virtue epistemology" courts just such uninhibited judgments. See Linda Zagzebski and Abrol Fairweather, eds., *Virtue Epistemology: Essays on Epistemic Virtue and Responsibility* (Oxford: Oxford University Press, 2001).

[4] Alan Sokal and Jean Bricmont, *Fashionable Nonsense: Postmodern Philosophers' Abuse of Science* (London: Profile, 1998).

Thus, while it is convenient to focus on the lightly veiled incompetence of bullshitters, bullshit detectors are ultimately disturbed by what they take to be the lack of self-discipline revealed by the bullshitter's verbal camouflage. When venturing into terrain yet to be colonized by a recognized expertise, where "true" and "false" are not clearly signposted, bullshitters assert authoritatively rather than remain silent. What accounts for this difference in attitude? A distinction borrowed from Kant and conventionally used to understand the history of early modern philosophy comes to mind: Bullshitters and bullshit detectors examine the same uncertain knowledge situation from, respectively, a *rationalist* and an *empiricist* perspective. Bullshitters see the resolution of uncertainty in terms of selecting one from a number of already imaginable alternatives, whereas bullshit detectors seek some externally caused experience—a.k.a. evidence—to determine where lies the truth. I shall argue that the scientific method is largely a "dialectical synthesis" of these two attitudes, by which I mean that each cancels out the excesses of the other to produce a more powerful form of knowledge than either could provide alone.

Bullshit as a Call to Open-Mindedness

Bullshit detectors take comfort in the fact that the time required to master a body of knowledge virtually guarantees the initiate's loyalty to its corresponding practices and central dogmas. Moreover, the overarching discipline may have been crafted over the years to render as difficult as possible the contrary "truth" a bullshitter might wish to advance. In Thomas Kuhn's hands, this tendency was enshrined as "normal science." According to Kuhn, a radical alternative to the scientific orthodoxy must await the self-destruction of the dominant paradigm, which may take a very long time, as ill-defined conceptual objections (a.k.a. bullshit) struggle against the paradigm's made-to-order empirical successes. Equally, the self-transformation from potential critic to compliant subject is a matter of reducing what social psychologists call "cognitive dissonance": How could all that scientific training effort have been in vain, especially once it has resulted in a secure social identity and (perhaps less secure) means of employment? The mathematician Blaise Pascal's famous wager is a very general version of this line of thought: We should bet our lives on God's existence by adopting a Christian lifestyle that would then make us receptive to any signs of divine presence, should they ever appear. As in science, so too in religion: Discovery favors the prepared mind.

But what if it were made easier to assert and challenge knowledge claims without having to undergo the personal transformation required of, say, doctoral training? In the absence of such institutionalized immunity to bullshit, the result would be a Sophist's paradise. Truth would be decided on the day by whoever happens to have the stronger argument or survives some mutually agreed test. Never mind prior track records or prima facie plausibility: Show me here and now. The scientific method was developed largely in this frame of mind, one deeply distrustful of all forms of authority, be it based on a canonical text or some canonical representation of collective experience. This distrust fed on the frequently observed failure of authoritative statements to accord with what one's spontaneously thinks, feels, or experiences.

The signature moment in the Western tradition for this sentiment, which made the hearer's conscience—and not the speaker's sincerity—the final court of appeal, was the guilt that Martin Luther continued to feel even after having been exonerated of sin in the Catholic sacrament of Penance. This provoked a more wide-ranging questioning of Catholicism's royal road of ritual to divine salvation. The result was Protestantism's greater tolerance for bullshit, with the understanding that everyone skates on thin ice in this life. The phrase "playing it by ear" captures well the inevitably improvisational character of attending to conscience as a guide to truth. In the end, there is only one bullshit detector: God. Accept no substitutes.

The bullshit detector believes not only that there is a truth but also that her own access to it is sufficiently reliable and general to serve as a standard by which others may be held accountable. Protestants appeared prepared to accept the former but not the latter condition, which is why dissenters were encouraged—or perhaps ostracized—to establish their own ministries. The Sophists appeared to deny the former and possibly the latter condition as well. Both Protestants and Sophists are prime candidates for the spread of bullshit because they concede that we may normally address reality in terms it does not recognize—or at least does not require it to yield straight "yes-or-no," "true-or-false" answers. In that case, we must make up the difference between the obliqueness of our inquiries and the obtuseness of reality's responses. That "difference" is fairly seen as bullshit. When crystallized as a philosophy of mind or philosophy of language, this attitude is known as *antirealism*. Its opposite number, the background philosophy of bullshit detectors, is *realism*.

The difference in the spirit of the two philosophies is captured as follows: Do you believe that everything you say and hear is bullshit unless you have some way of showing whether it is true or false; or rather, that everything said and heard is simply true or false, unless it is revealed to be bullshit? The former is the antirealist, the latter the realist, response. Seen in those terms, we might say that the antirealist regards reality as inherently risky and always under construction (*Caveat credor!*[5]), whereas the realist treats reality as, on the whole, stable and orderly—except for the reprobates who try to circumvent the system by producing bullshit. In this respect, *On Bullshit* may be usefully read as an *ad hominem* attack on antirealists. Frankfurt himself makes passing reference to this interpretation near the end of the essay (pp. 64–65). Yet, he appears happy to promote the vulgar image of antirealism as intellectually, and perhaps morally, slipshod, instead of treating it as the philosophically honorable position that it is.

A case in point is Frankfurt's presentation of Wittgenstein as one of history's great bullshit detectors (pp. 24–34). He offers a telling anecdote in which the Viennese philosopher objects to Fania Pascal's self-description as feeling like a dog that has been run over. Wittgenstein reportedly told Pascal that she misused language by capitalizing on the hearer's easy conflation of a literal falsehood with a genuine condition, which is made possible by the hearer's default anthropocentric bias. Wittgenstein's objection boils down to claiming that, outside clearly marked poetic contexts, our intellectual end never suffices alone to justify our linguistic means. Frankfurt treats this point as a timeless truth about how language structures reality. Yet, it would be quite easy, especially recalling that this "truth" was uttered seventy years ago, to conclude that Wittgenstein's

[5] "Let the believer beware!"

irritation betrays a spectacular lack of imagination in the guise of scrupulousness.

Wittgenstein's harsh judgment presupposes that humans lack any real access to canine psychology, which renders any appeal to dogs purely fanciful. For him, this lack of access is an established fact inscribed in a literal use of language, not an open question answers to which a figurative use of language might offer clues for further investigation. Nevertheless, scientists informed by the Neo-Darwinian synthesis—which was being forged just at the time of Wittgenstein's pronouncement—have quite arguably narrowed the gap between the mental lives of humans and animals in research associated with "evolutionary psychology." As this research makes more headway, what Wittgenstein confidently declared to be bullshit in his day may tomorrow appear as having been a prescient truth. But anyone holding such a fluid view of verifiability would derive scant comfort from either Wittgenstein or Frankfurt, who act as if English linguistic intuitions, circa 1935, should count indefinitely as demonstrable truths.

Wittgenstein: Ultimate Bullshit Detector— or Bullshitter?

Some philosophers given to bullshit detection are so used to treating any Wittgensteinian utterance as a profundity that it never occurs to them that Wittgenstein may have been himself a grandmaster of bullshit. The great bullshit detectors whom I originally invoked, Nietzsche and Mencken, made themselves vulnerable to critics by speaking from their own self-authorizing standpoint, which supposedly afforded a clear vista for distinguishing bullshit from its opposite. In contrast, Wittgenstein adopts the classic bullshitter's technique of *ventriloquism*, speaking through the authority of someone or something else in order to be spared the full brunt of criticism.

I use "adopts" advisedly, since the deliberateness of Wittgenstein's rhetoric remains unclear. What was he trying to do: To speak modestly without ever having quite controlled his spontaneously haughty manner, or to exercise his self-regarding superiority as gently as possible so as not to frighten the benighted? Either way, Wittgenstein became—for a certain kind of philosopher—the standard-bearer of linguistic rectitude, where "language" is treated as a proxy for reality itself.

To the bullshitter, this description also fits someone whose strong personality cowed the impressionable into distrusting their own thought processes. As with most successful bullshit, the trick is revealed only after it has had the desired effect and the frame of reference has changed. Thus, Wittgenstein's precious concern about Pascal's account of her state of health should strike, at least some readers today, as akin to a priest's fretting over a parishioner's confession of impure thoughts. In each case, the latter is struck by something that lies outside the box in which the former continues to think.

If Wittgenstein was a bullshitter, how did he manage to take in professed enemies of bullshit like Frankfurt? One clue is that most bullshit is forward-looking, and Wittgenstein's wasn't. The bullshitter normally refers to things whose *prima facie* plausibility immunizes the hearer against checking their actual validity. The implication is that proof is simply "out there" waiting be found. But is there really such proof? Here the bullshitter is in a race against time. A sufficient delay in checking sources has salvaged the competence and even promoted the prescience of many bullshitters. Such was the spirit of Paul Feyerabend's notorious account of Galileo's "discoveries," which concluded that his Papal Inquisitors were originally justified in their skepticism, even though Galileo's followers subsequently redeemed his epistemic promissory notes.[6]

In contrast, Wittgenstein's unique brand of bullshit was backward-looking, always reminding hearers and readers of something they should already know but have perhaps temporarily forgotten. Since Wittgenstein usually confronted his interlocutors with mundane examples, it was relatively easy to convey this impression. The trick lay in immediately shifting context from the case at hand to what Oxford philosophers in the 1950s called a "paradigm case" that was presented as a self-evident standard of usage against which to judge the case at hand. That Wittgenstein, a non-native speaker of English, impressed one or two generations of Britain's philosophical elite with just this

---

[6] On this reading of Galileo, see Paul Feyerabend, *Against Method* (London: Verso, 1975).

mode of argumentation remains the envy of the aspiring bull-shitter. Ernest Gellner, another émigré from the old Austro-Hungarian Empire, ended up ostracized from the British philosophical establishment for offering a cutting diagnosis of this phenomenon as it was unfolding. He suggested that Wittgenstein's success testified to his ability to feed off British class anxiety, which was most clearly marked in language use.[7]

Yet, after nearly a half-century, Gellner's diagnosis is resisted, despite the palpable weakening of Wittgenstein's posthumous grip on the philosophical imagination. One reason is that so many living philosophers still ride on Wittgenstein's authority—if not his mannerisms—that to declare him a bull-shitter would amount to career suicide. But a second reason is also operative, one that functions as an insurance policy against future debunkers. Wittgenstein is often portrayed, by himself and others, as mentally unbalanced. You might think that this would render his philosophical deliverances unreliable. On the contrary, Wittgenstein's erratic disposition is offered as evidence for his spontaneously guileless nature—quite unlike the controlled and calculated character of bullshitters. Bullshit fails to stick to Wittgenstein because he is regarded as an *idiot savant*. In contrast, bullshit detectors aim their fire at those capable of making a strategic distinction in their own minds between the current state of evidence and the state of belief in which they would like to leave their interlocutors. We have seen this mentality before. It is best called by its classical name: "hypocrisy," a word that derives from the masks actors wore in Greek dramas.

Bullshit as Deferred Epistemic Gratification

The bullshitter is the consummate hypocrite. This sounds damning if you imagine that on the masked side of the hypocrite's mental divide is a clear sense of where the weight of evidence lies. But if you imagine instead that behind the hypocrite's mask

---

[7] Ernest Gellner, *Words and Things: A Critical Account of Linguistic Philosophy and a Study in Ideology* (London: Gollancz, 1959). An academically sublimated form of such language-driven class anxiety remains in the discipline of sociolinguistics, whose seminal researcher was Basil Bernstein. His work is compiled in *Class, Codes, and Control: Theoretical Studies towards a Sociology of Language*, three volumes (London: Routledge, 1971–77).

lurks deep uncertainty about the truth, then the outward image is a defiant, though possibly doomed, gesture to inject some order into an otherwise chaotic world. At this point, some readers might query the wisdom of portraying bullshitters as heroic Existentialists, bluffing their way out of the abyss. After all, on most matters, don't we usually have a reasonably clear sense of which way the evidence points? If so, the only relevant decision is whether to admit, deny, or spin what one believes. However, as might be expected, the bullshitter's take on evidence is not so straightforward. It is influenced by the sophistic principle that to control the moment of decision is to control its outcome. The first line of sophistry, then, is to call the question when the balance of arguments is to one's advantage. But provided sufficient time, resources, and wit, the truth of *any* proposition could be demonstrated—or so the sophists presumed. The problem is that we are rarely afforded these luxuries, and so there is a strong temptation simply to declare for what strikes us now as most evident.

Bullshitters stress the impressionistic character of this decision, since contrary to promiscuous appeals to "reliability" in both philosophical and public discourse, we are usually in no position to assess the actual track records of those who would lay claim to our beliefs. We might be able to access a partial record or, more likely, recall our personal experience, as colored by the vagaries of memory. Perhaps this is why epistemologists have increasingly leaned on the quasi-moral concept of "trust," and affiliated theological notions of "witness" and "testimony," to make up the difference between our genuine strength of feeling toward a proposition and the actual paucity of our evidence in its favor.[8] Under the benign interpretation of the Scottish cleric Thomas Reid, the spark of the divine in the human (a.k.a. common sense) ensures that, in the main, humans are reliable sources of information. But under the more malign reading of those touched by the more heretical Kierkegaard, the prevalence of such concepts simply betrays our cowardice, as we delegate to others responsibility for beliefs we should take personally, admitting error when shown wrong but otherwise

---

[8] A good collection of recent work on the epistemology of testimony is the following special issue: Martin Kusch and Peter Lipton, eds., *Studies in History and Philosophy of Science* 33: 2 (June 2002), Part A, pp. 209–423.

accepting modest credit for having expressed them.[9] In either case, by papering over the gap between evidence and belief, reliability would appear to be a bullshit concept—a problem, of course, only for those like Frankfurt keen on eliminating bullshit.

It is possible to detect the bullshit in the bullshit detectors by setting up an analogy between the *epistemic economy of evidence* and the *moral economy of sensation.* Evidence for what is true and false is typically described in the same terms of "compelling experience" as sensations of pleasure and pain. But why should we be so easily moved by evidence in spheres of knowing, when most philosophers would not have us automatically succumb to sensation in spheres of acting? For example, Utilitarianism, the modern ethical theory most closely tied to a moral economy of sensations, explains welfare in terms of the deferment of immediate gratification in favor of a more substantial good projected in the long term. Thus, the redistribution of income afforded by taxation insures against our tendency to discount the value of our future selves or, for that matter, future generations. Similarly, the bullshitter's imperviousness to the current weighting of the evidence may be understood as an attempt to forgo the opportunity costs associated with discounting what might turn out to be, in the fullness of time, a more promising line of inquiry. Analogous to taxation here would be an "affirmative action" strategy that would handicap better evidenced positions so as to give weaker ones a chance to develop. As Franklin might put it, the virtue exemplified in both the moral and the epistemic economies is *prudence*: the one saves for the future, whereas the other plays for time.[10]

The Scientific Method as a Search for the Justice in Bullshit

The natural conclusion to draw from these considerations so far is that bullshit abounds, not least among those keen on detect-

---

[9] Among those touched by Kierkegaard were not only the Existentialists but also the young Karl Popper. See Malachi Hacohen, *Karl Popper: The Formative Years, 1902–1945* (Cambridge: Cambridge University Press, 2000), pp. 83–84. I read Popper sympathetically as a "scientific existentialist" in Steve Fuller, *Kuhn versus Popper: The Struggle for the Soul of Science* (Cambridge: Icon, 2003), pp. 100–110.
[10] One way to look at the inter-temporal comparison of the evidentiary basis of

ing and removing it. But must this be such a bad thing? The success of Francis Bacon's invention of the scientific method suggests that it might not be so bad, as long as everyone admits upfront they are producing bullshit, and decisions about what is and is not bullshit are left to a third party. Bacon wrote as the top lawyer to England's King James I in the early seventeenth century, a period we now describe as having been in great scientific and religious ferment, though the difference between these two sources of unrest was not so clear at the time. Bacon realized as much. Radical religious thinkers often proposed and occasionally proved knowledge claims of general scientific merit. Yet, they typically insisted that only those sharing their religious commitments were fit to test and appreciate the validity of those claims. Bacon saw that the public interest was best served by devising a way to test the validity of knowledge claims without having to accept whatever controversial metaphysical assumptions might have motivated the claimants. This procedure—the scientific method—was modeled on a trial, indeed, of the sort conducted in the inquisitorial legal systems of Continental Europe, which Bacon admired.[11]

What distinguishes the inquisitorial from the accusatorial system traditionally favored in England is that the judge, as opposed to the plaintiff, frames the terms of the trial. This typically means that before a verdict is reached, the judge will have conducted his own investigation of, say, what counts as normal conduct in the relevant sphere of life, in order to determine whether the defendant is being held to an unreasonably high standard—or, equally, a reasonable standard that few people actually meet. Thus, it is not sufficient for the plaintiff to prove her case on its merits. In addition, it must be clear that the defendant is not being unfairly singled out for something that, for better or worse, is routinely tolerated. After all, the defendant may be guilty as charged but others are potentially guilty of much worse, in which case the judge must consider how—and

---

knowledge claims in the present and the imagined future is in terms of sacrificing a short-term adherence to "only the truth" in favor of "the whole truth" in the long term. I discuss this as a trade-off between correspondence and coherence theories of truth in Steve Fuller, *The Intellectual* (Cambridge: Icon, 2005), pp. 51–60.

[11] On the influence of inquisitorial legal systems on Bacon, see James Franklin, *The Science of Conjecture: Evidence and Probability before Pascal* (Baltimore: Johns Hopkins University Press, 2001), pp. 217–18.

whether—justice is served by making an example out of the defendant.

A notorious recent example of how a shift from an accusatorial to an inquisitorial perspective can significantly affect the disposition of a case is that of the political scientist Bjørn Lomborg, whose international best seller, *The Skeptical Environmentalist*, was brought before the Danish Research Council's Committee on Scientific Dishonesty by an entrepreneur in alternative energy sources who held that Lomborg systematically distorted research findings in ways that undermined his business. (Lomborg's basic message was that the future of the global environment is not nearly as desperate as most ecologists make it out to be.) The plaintiff received major foreign support from, among others, *Scientific American* magazine and E.O. Wilson, founder of sociobiology and latter-day champion of biodiversity. Lomborg was initially found guilty, but the verdict was overturned on appeal—indeed, the very purpose of the Committee on Scientific Dishonesty was called into question—because it appeared that Lomborg was unfairly targeted, given that in the field of environmental studies, the politicization of research is the norm not the exception. Lomborg was guilty of little more than having extrapolated from the relevant statistical data a much more optimistic ecological forecast than usual. But all such extrapolations are ultimately speculative and motivated to raise consciousness among research funders, policy makers, and the general public. In other words, no special legal action is necessary because these matters are already fairly aired and debated, leaving audiences to draw their own conclusions.[12]

The history of the Lomborg case beautifully illustrates how a legal proceeding can foster both the manufacture and removal of bullshit. The plaintiff held the defendant uniquely responsible for an event backed by the testimony of impressive experts, while the defendant professed his own purity of motive and questioned the politics of his accusers. Bullshit abounds here on both sides. In his inquisitorial role, the judge (in this case, a panel) was expected to devise a test that would conclusively decide between the two parties by virtue of incorporating their

---

[12] For an account of the Lomborg Affair, focusing on the legal issues, see Steve Fuller, "The Future of Scientific Justice: The Case of the Skeptical Environmentalist." *Futures* 36 (2004), pp. 631–36.

shared assumptions and eliminating the ones they contest. Transferred to the scientific realm, this is what Bacon called a "crucial experiment." The great virtue of the crucial experiment, as extolled by the various intellectual movements that have traveled under the banner of "positivism," is that it forces a clear distinction to be drawn between theory and method: A scientific society may be divided by theories but it is united in method. But there is also a political point about *free expression* close to the heart of democracy, what Karl Popper called the "open society": Everyone can bullshit to their heart's content, as long as there is agreement on how to clean up after it.

I stress "free expression" because, as Franklin would have been the first to observe, the relevant freedom includes freedom to say what one believes needs to be said, even if one does not quite believe it oneself. Some signature moments of public intellectual life have been defined in these terms. For example, when Émile Zola publicly accused the French War Office of framing Captain Dreyfus (*J'Accuse!*), he had no more evidence than the court that convicted Dreyfus of treason. He simply read between the lines and took a chance that there was more than met the eye. Zola turned out to be right, but it was only after the confession of the perpetrators that he discovered why. However, his pre-emptive declaration served to stimulate others to re-open the case, resulting in evidence that corroborated Zola's claims, all the while he was exiled in London. Zola's fate was not so different from Galileo's, whose house arrest after the Inquisition prompted natural philosophers across Europe to take up his hypotheses, which were finally vindicated in Newton's *Principia Mathematica.*

However, Bacon's vision has been realized only imperfectly. In particular, his idea that theory and method should always be distinguished in each case has metamorphosed into the idea they should be distinguished the same way in all cases. Thus, in the positivist imagination, the inquiring judge whose discretion determines how the distinction is anchored in each case came to be replaced by a mechanical procedure that could be applied to all cases. To a large extent, this transition is traceable to the political failure of Bacon's project. After all, Bacon envisaged a royally sanctioned science court, whereas the best a weakened English monarchy could manage after the Civil War was to charter a self-policing private body, the Royal Society of London, whose loyalty to the Crown was demonstrated by its appeal to "method" to exclude potentially controversial matters from the outset.[13]

One feature of the original Baconian model that remains today has often proved a thorn in the side of the legal system: a liberal policy toward the admission of expert witness testimony, much of which would be discounted as hearsay, if it came from the mouth of an ordinary witness.[14] This pro-bullshit policy, derided by some as producing "junk science," is in principle desirable, if only because even orthodox claims to reliable knowledge can rarely, if ever, be evidenced first hand. Such a policy positions the judge as an inquisitor empowered to set up an independent standard by which to detect bullshit in the case at hand. However, if the judge sees herself as no more than a referee between two adversaries, the typical position in Anglo-Saxon law, then the balance of arguments as defined in the terms raised by the plaintiff is likely to prevail. Of course, this does not mean that the plaintiff automatically wins her case, but if she happens to represent the dominant viewpoint on the contested issue, that certainly increases her chances. Thus, Bacon's intention may be undermined in practice.

In conclusion, consider a case in point: the string of US court cases concerning the disposition of evolution and creation—and, more recently, Intelligent Design—in the high-school curriculum. A landmark ruling occurred in 1982, *McLean v. Arkansas*, in which the presiding judge appealed to a philosophical definition of science, as provided by Michael Ruse, to justify the exclusion of creationism from the science curriculum. This was the first time a judge did not simply defer to the weight of scientific experts but, realizing that the nature of science itself was at issue in the case, tried to arrive at a standard that was genuinely neutral to the contesting parties. What matters here is neither that the judge appealed to an oversimplified definition of science, nor that his reasoning reinforced the general pattern of court rulings against creationism. Rather, it is that he turned

---

[13] On the early problematic institutionalization of Baconian ideal, see William Lynch, *Solomon's Child: Baconian Method in the Early Royal Society of London* (Palo Alto: Stanford University Press, 2001).

[14] See Tal Golan, *Laws of Men and Laws of Nature: The History of Scientific Expert Testimony in England and America* (Cambridge: Harvard University Press, 2004).

to a standard that even the creationists had to agree was reasonable. The judge managed to cut through the bullshit on both sides.

Unfortunately, his precedent has not stuck. In the recent case, *Kitzmiller v. Dover Area School District,* where I served as an expert witness, the judge's ruling was based largely on a philosophically customized definition of science supplied by the plaintiffs with the blessing of the US National Academy of Sciences. The definition was "customized" in that the operative doctrine, "methodological naturalism," while lacking a clear meaning within philosophy, was crafted specifically so as to exclude Intelligent Design theory and scientific creationism.[15] While it is to be expected—and even encouraged—that adversaries make arguments that put their case in the best possible light, justice is served by acknowledging the bullshit on *both* sides and cutting through it in an equitable fashion. This aspect of the Baconian legacy, where science and law meet, is all too rarely realized in cases where the truth is deemed to rest witth the side whose bullshit is piled higher and deeper.

---

[15] "Naturalism" is normally regarded as a metaphysical doctrine, a species of monism opposed to supernaturalism. The doctrine has been historically hostile to monotheistic world-views for their postulation of a transcendent deity, resulting in an unforgivable dualism. This point joins, say, Spinoza and Dewey in common cause as naturalists, regardless of their many other differences. However, the prefix "methodological" softens the blow by suggesting that only the conduct of science—not all aspects of human existence—presupposes naturalism. Even this is false, as any honest appraisal of the metaphysical realist (a.k.a. supernaturalist) strand in the history of science should make apparent. I participated in *Kitzmiller* as a "rebuttal witness," specifically to this bit of bullshit that the judge ended up accepting without question. Philosophers have questioned both why adherence to scientific methodology requires naturalism and why adherence to naturalism must remain merely methodological. These two points are made, respectively, in Theodore Schick, "Methodological Naturalism versus Methodological Realism," *Philosophy* 3: 2 (2000), pp. 30–37; Massimo Pigliucci, "Methodological versus Philosophical Naturalism," *Free Inquiry* 23 (2003), pp. 53–55.

Our Distinguished Panel of Incomparable Geniuses

ANDREW ABERDEIN grew up in Liverpool, England, and earned a Ph.D. from the University of St. Andrews in Logic and Metaphysics. He has served as Lecturer in Philosophy at Edinburgh and is currently Assistant Professor of Logic and Humanities at Florida Institute of Technology. His experience with bullshit dates to the day when, as a gullible child of about age five, he was taught in separate classes about both dinosaurs and the Garden of Eden. The cognitive dissonance propelled him into philosophy, and into this volume.

SARA BERNAL is from Ithaca, New York. She has a B.A. from the University of Chicago and, by the time you read this, a Ph.D. in Philosophy from Rutgers, the State University of New Jersey. She lives in St. Louis with her husband, son, and cat, and teaches at St. Louis University. In her spare time she performs regularly as a modern dancer. Her most memorable early exposures to bullshit coincided with early and frequent exposure to the work of Mel Brooks, whose stand-up philosopher Comicus (from *History of the World, Part I*) inspired her. More recently she finds herself fascinated by the way in which the exposure of some painful truth provokes people to spew extraordinary bullshit.

G.A. COHEN was educated at McGill and Oxford Universities where he obtained, respectively, the degrees of B.A. in Philosophy and Politics and B. Phil. in Philosophy in 1963. For twenty-two years he was a Lecturer and then a Reader in Philosophy at University College, London. In 1985 he became Chichele Professor of Social and Political Theory and a Fellow of All Souls, Oxford. Professor Cohen is the author of *Karl Marx's Theory of History: A Defence* (1978; expanded edition, 2000), *History, Labour, and Freedom* (1988), *Self-Ownership, Freedom, and Equality* (1995), and *If You're an Egalitarian, How come You're So Rich?* (2000). Cohen has given lectures all over the world, including the Tanner Lectures at Stanford University in 1991 and the Gifford Lectures at Edinburgh University in 1996. He was made a

Fellow of the British Academy in 1985. The bullshit that for a short while engulfed him, but from which he escaped, was French bullshit, and in particular, the bullshit of Althusser and the Althusserians.

HEATHER DOUGLAS earned her Ph.D. in the History and Philosophy of Science from the University of Pittsburgh in 1998. She has since lived in Tacoma, as the Phibbs Professor of Science and Ethics at the University of Puget Sound, and in Knoxville, as Assistant Professor in the Department of Philosophy at the University of Tennessee. Her experience with bullshit began with intense discussions around the Douglas family dinner table. This early training in competitive discourse laid the foundations for an interest in both philosophy and bullshit. Being a "professional" philosopher these days, she keeps her sanity by discussing issues with her husband, Ted Richards, who is a great bullshit detector, and by hanging out with her large dogs, who are terrible bullshitters, being stunningly honest and forthright creatures. She also likes to grow plants, which do very well with large amounts of fertilizer.

MARK EVANS is currently Senior Lecturer in Politics, Department of Politics and International Relations, University of Wales, Swansea. He received his first degree (in Philosophy, Politics and Economics) from Mansfield College, Oxford, and his doctorate—which was on what he still maintains to be a non-bullshitty concept of self-realization in political theory—from St. Antony's College, Oxford. His ire against bullshit was first aroused in the mid-1980s when some of his student contemporaries, looking forward to the wads of cash to be earned in business, started spouting management-bullshit speak. His decision to stay in academia was bolstered by the hope that he wouldn't have to put up with such stuff in his working life. He is therefore mightily pissed off that it has now well and truly infected the running of universities, without it even being tinged with the kind of ironic tone that would show that the poor souls at the academic coal-face can't possibly take it seriously.

STEVE FULLER is Professor of Sociology at the University of Warwick, England. He was first exposed to bullshit when he took courses in analytic philosophy as an undergraduate at Columbia University. There he ran across people who bluffly promoted the virtues of content-free forms of reasoning. Over the years, he has come to appreciate the subtle virtues of this most rigorous form of rhetoric, the bullshit that dares not speak its name: to wit, logic. He received his Ph.D. in the philosophy of science from the University of Pittsburgh, and through a career that has extended over a dozen books on issues relating to social epistemology, he is nowadays associated with science and technology studies, a field largely dedicated to demonstrating, if not celebrating, the bullshit behind what passes for authoritative knowledge in society these days.

GARY L. HARDCASTLE is Assistant Professor of philosophy at Bloomsburg University in central Pennsylvania, where he teaches philosophy of science, logic, and, if he is asked nicely, introduction to philosophy. His research interests include the philosophy of science, epistemology, and the history of American philosophy in the twentieth century. He is the author of several articles in philosophy of science and the co-editor, with Alan Richardson, of *Logical Empiricism in North America* (2003) and, with George Reisch, of *Monty Python and Philosophy* (2005). Although he inhaled deeply the bullshit-rich culture and ethos of 1970s America, his most memorable encounter with bullshit is his father's presentation of the teleological argument for God's existence as they drove together through the utter wasteland of Youngstown, Ohio, in 1978.

SCOTT KIMBROUGH, Associate Professor of philosophy at Jacksonville University, holds a Ph.D. in philosophy from the University of Pennsylvania and a B.A. in philosophy from Southwestern University. His experience growing up in Texas, among Texans who truly believe that their state is superior and greet the presentation of contrary evidence with an astonished blend of incredulity and contempt, convinced him that Frankfurt is wrong to deny that bullshit can be produced unintentionally. His wife Tonia, a professional editor who frequently informs him of how bad most philosophical writing is, has kept him sensitive to what Frankfurt calls "pretentious bullshit."

HANS MAES received his PhD at the Katholieke Universiteit Leuven, Belgium, and is now affiliated with the University of Kent, England, where he writes on issues in moral theory and aesthetics. He is happily married to Katrien Schaubroeck—no bullshit.

Born in Caracas, Venezuela to an American mother and a Czech father with a Venezuelan passport, **VANESSA NEUMANN** received her B.A. from Columbia University in Economics and Philosophy. After stints in corporate finance and diplomacy, she returned to Columbia University for her M.A., M.Phil., and Ph.D. in moral political philosophy under the tutelage of the John Rawls protégé, Thomas Pogge. Dr. Neumann is currently Adjunct Assistant Professor of political philosophy at Hunter College, City University of New York and sits on the advisory board of the Institute of Latin American Studies (ILAS) at Columbia University.

She also works with political think tanks, including the International Institute for Strategic Studies (IISS). Preferring to spend her days mired in horseshit rather than bullshit, Dr. Neumann finds galloping across a field on horseback a highly effective strategy for dealing with the stresses of daily life.

CONSUELO PRETI earned a PhD in philosophy from the Graduate Center at the City University of New York and is now an Associate Professor of Philosophy at the College of New Jersey. Her interests run to the philosophy of language and the philosophy of mind; she is the author of *On Kripke* and the co-author of *On Fodor*, both in the Wadsworth Philosophers Series. She enjoys surfing, yoga, and English bull terriers, and when asked about her most formative bullshit experiences she is too polite to mention her first department meeting (and many subsequent ones).

GEORGE A. REISCH holds the title (for eight years now) in the All-Chicagoland Summarize Otto Neurath Competition. He received a Ph.D. from the Chicago School of Communist Dance, where he created, produced, and performed in "Fregenstein: *Begriffsschrift* and the Music of ABBA," to wide accolades. He is also the author of many things concerned with philosophy of science and its history, such as the book *How the Cold War Transformed Philosophy of Science* (2005). At parties, he impersonates Gary Hardcastle impersonating Ludwig Wittgenstein (call 800GoValidity for bookings). As for bullshit in popular culture, he thinks it all began with The Monkees.

ALAN RICHARDSON likes candlelit dinners, reading Reichenbach to children at the public library, and long walks on the beach in Vancouver, where he is Professor of Philosophy and Distinguished University Scholar in the Department of Philosophy at the University of British Columbia. He has a Ph.D. from the University of Illinois, Chicago Circle, and is the author, editor, and reader of many things with 'logical empiricism' in the title. He wrote *Carnap's Construction of the World* (1997). This biographical blurb is his most recent encounter with bullshit, although his earliest political memory is that of going to a Nixon rally in Clifton Heights, Pennsylvania, in 1968, escorted by his father, who is, like his mother, a life-long Republican.

KATRIEN SCHAUBROECK is assistant at the Center for Logic, Philosophy of Science and Philosophy of Language at the Katholieke Universiteit Leuven where she is writing a dissertation on Harry Frankfurt and the debate on practical reason. Her interests are in moral psychology, meta-ethics, and theories of practical reason.

STATEMENTS THE FACTUAL COMPONENT SHOULD BE NULL; AND THESE AR

KENNETH A. TAYLOR is Professor of Philosophy and Chair of the Department of Philosophy at Stanford University, where he thinks about questions at the intersection of the philosophy of language and the philosophy of mind (with an occasional foray into the history of philosophy). He is the author of many papers in the philosophy of language and philosophy of mind, as well as *Meaning and Truth: An Introduction to the Philosophy of Language* (1998) and *Reference and the Rational Mind* (2003). With his colleague John Perry he hosts *Philosophy Talk* (www.philosophytalk.org), a weekly, one-hour radio series that brings the richness of philosophic thought to everyday subjects.

DAVID J. TIETGE is Assistant Professor in English and Associate Director of Writing at Monmouth University in West Long Branch, New Jersey. He has a Ph.D. in Rhetoric from Southern Illinois University at Carbondale and an M.A. in English Literature from Indiana State University. His scholarly interests include rhetoric theory, literary theory and criticism, rhetoric of science, and history and cultural studies, and he is the author of *Flash Effect: Science and the Rhetorical Origins of Cold War America* (2002). His seminal experience with bullshit occurred before his first memory.

CORNELIS DE WAAL studied Economics and Philosophy at Erasmus University Rotterdam, The Netherlands. He learned to detect bullshit in the trenches while working as an editor and journalist for a glossy engineering magazine in Amsterdam. In 1992 he emigrated to the U.S. to begin a Ph.D. in philosophy at the University of Miami in Coral Gables. Currently he is Associate Professor at Indiana University Purdue University Indianapolis, where he also directs the philosophy graduate program. He is one of the editors of the *Writings of Charles S. Peirce,* a thirty-volume scholarly edition that is being published by Indiana University Press. He is the author of books on Peirce and pragmatism, which he happily typed with two fingers (K is his favorite letter), and he is a culinary adventurer who likes to eat raw fish and red ants.

Our Index, Exquisitely Crafted for Your Illumination

265

ERY *LITERARY* DÉCADENCE? THAT LIFE NO LONGER DWELLS IN THE WHOLE.